ASPECTS OF POETRY.

JOHN CAMPBELL SHAIRP.

ASPECTS OF POETRY

BEING

Lectures delivered at Oxford

BY

JOHN CAMPBELL SHAIRP

Essay Index Reprint Series

BOOKS FOR LIBRARIES PRESS
FREEPORT, NEW YORK

First Published 1882
Reprinted 1972

Library of Congress Cataloging in Publication Data

Shairp, John Campbell, 1819-1885.
   Aspects of poetry.

   (Essay index reprint series)
   "First published 1882."
   1. Poetry. I. Title.
PN1031.S53 1972   808.1   72-4606
ISBN 0-8369-2976-4

PRINTED IN THE UNITED STATES OF AMERICA

PREFACE.

THE following pages contain twelves Lectures se-
lected from those which I have delivered from the Chair
of Poetry in Oxford during the last four years, some
of which have already been published separately. To
these have been added three Chapters (XI., XII.,
XIII.), which were not delivered as Lectures in Ox-
ford, but which are, by the kind permission of the Pro-
prietor, reprinted from *Good Words*.

Some might, perhaps, expect to find in this book a
systematic theory of poetry, and a consecutive course
of Lectures. But the conditions of the Professorship,
which require one Lecture to be delivered during each
Academic term, render it difficult, even if it were on
other grounds desirable, to preserve such continuity.
The audiences which listen to these Lectures change
from term to term; so that a course begun before one
set of hearers would have to be continued before an-
other, and completed before a third. This renders it
almost a necessity that each Lecture should be, as far as
possible, complete in itself.

As to the mode of treatment pursued, I have tried to
adapt it, as well as I could, to the varied character of
my hearers. These consisted of Undergraduates, of

Graduates, and of some who were of neither of these. Among these last were not a few of those resident Gentlewomen, who now form a new and not unpleasing element in some Oxford Lecture-rooms. As my predecessor in the Poetry Chair said in the Preface to his published Lectures, I felt it to be my duty, having found a large number of persons willing to listen, to do what I could to retain them. This seemed most likely to be done by treating the several subjects under review in a broad way, and by presenting their larger outlines, rather than by dwelling on refined subtleties or minute details. On verbal criticism and scholastic erudition sufficient attention is bestowed in the various Lecture-rooms of the Colleges and of the University. It would seem to be a desirable variety, if, in one Lecture-room filled by a general audience, a different treatment were adopted.

For the rest, the Lectures, both as to the views they advance, and the way in which these views are expressed, must speak for themselves. No formal canons of criticisms have been here laid down, but the principles which underlie and the sentiments which animate the Lectures are, I trust, sufficiently apparent.

When I have been aware that I have derived a thought from another writer, I have tried to acknowledge it in the text. But it is a pleasure to record here, in a more explicit way, many obligations to the kindness of personal friends.

For information on the difficult Ossianic question, which I have tried to condense into a few plain para-

graphs, I have to thank Mr. W. F. Skene, D. C. L.,
author of *Celtic Scotland,* — that work of difficult and
original research, with which he has crowned the labor
of his life. To Dr. Clerk of Kilmallie also, author of
the new translation of Ossian, I am indebted for ever-
ready help on the same subject, as well as for kind aid
afforded, when I was translating the Gaelic of Duncan
MacIntyre's poems.

In the Lecture on Virgil I have to acknowledge the
free use I have made of the scholarly and suggestive
work on Virgil by Professor Sellar; to whom too I owe
my introduction to M. Gaston Boissier's work entitled
La Religion Romaine, from which I derived valuable
assistance.

The Lecture on Cardinal Newman is, in my thoughts,
specially associated with another college friend. Several
of the passages I have cited in the course of this Lect-
ure recall to me walks around Oxford, and evening talks
in college rooms, during which I first heard them from
the lips of the present Lord Coleridge. From him too
I have quite recently received some suggestions, which
I have gladly embodied in the text.

Lastly, the late Dean Stanley, with his never-failing
friendliness, took lively interest in these Lectures, and
frequently talked with me over the subjects of them,
before they were composed.

One occasion, the last on which I enjoyed his delight-
ful society, will long live in my remembrance. I had
paid a two days' visit to him in his hospitable home in
the Deanery, in the early days of last March. I was

then meditating the Lecture on Carlyle; and on the second day of my visit we spoke a good deal about the subject, which interested him and me alike. He suggested several passages, in which Carlyle's poetic power seemed to him conspicuous. On the last day of my visit, Saturday the 5th of March, while I was engaged in a hurried breakfast, before starting for the Scotch Express, he opened a book, Mr. Justice Stephen's *Liberty, Equality, and Fraternity*, and, in the dim light of the early morning, read aloud in his clear, impressive tones the passage I have quoted from Carlyle, which thus ends: —

. . . "through mystery to mystery, from God and to God."

These words were hardly uttered, when I had to rise and go. It was our last parting.

J. C. SHAIRP.

HOUSTOUN, *September*, 1881.

CONTENTS.

CHAPTER VIII.

CHAPTER IX.

CHAPTER X.

CHAPTER XI.

CHAPTER XII.

CHAPTER XIII.

CHAPTER XIV.

CHAPTER XV.

ASPECTS OF POETRY.

CHAPTER I.

THE PROVINCE OF POETRY.

WERE I to begin my first Lecture from this Chair, in which the kindness of the University has placed me, by following an approved and time-honored usage, I might ask at the outset, What is Poetry? and try to answer the question either by falling back on some one of the old definitions, or by proposing a new one, or perhaps by even venturing on a theory of Poetry. But, as you are all, no doubt, more or less acquainted with the definitions and theories of the past, and probably have not found much profit in them, you will, I believe, readily absolve me from any attempt to add one more to their number. For definitions do not really help us better to understand or appreciate subjects with which we have been long familiar, especially when they are, as poetry is, all life and spirit. As my friend the author of *Rab and his Friends* has well expressed it, " It is with Poetry as with flowers and fruits. We would all rather have them and taste them than talk about them. It is a good thing to know about a lily, its scientific ins and outs, its botany, its archæology, even its anatomy and organic radicals ; but it is a better thing to look at

1

the flowers themselves, and to consider how they grow."
So one would rather enjoy poetry than criticise it and
discuss its nature.   But, as there is a time for studying
the botany of flowers, as well as for enjoying their
beauty, there is a time also for dwelling on the nature
and offices of poetry, and that time seems to have come
to-day.

I think I shall be able best to bring before you what
I wish to say at present, if, approaching the subject in a
concrete rather than in an abstract way, I endeavor at
the outset to note some of the more prominent character-
istics of the poetic nature, when that nature appears in
its largest and most healthful manifestation.

In doing so I shall have to tread some well-worn
ways, and to say things which have often been said be-
fore.   But I shall willingly incur this risk.   For my
aim is not so much to say things that are new as things
that are true.   You will therefore bear with me, I hope,
if I try to recall to your thoughts a few plain but
primal truths regarding that which is most essential in
the poetic nature, — truths which are apt to be forgot-
ten amid the fashions of the hour, and to lie buried be-
neath heaps of superfine criticism.

One of the first characteristics of the genuine and
healthy poetic nature is this, — it is rooted rather in the
heart than in the head.   Human-heartedness is the soil
from which all its other gifts originally grow and are
continually fed.   The true poet is not an eccentric crea-
ture, not a mere artist living only for art, not a dreamer
or a dilettante, sipping the nectar of existence, while he
keeps aloof from its deeper interests.   He is, above all
things, a man among his fellow-men, with a heart that
beats in sympathy with theirs, a heart not different from

theirs, only larger, more open, more sensitive, more intense. It is the peculiar depth, intensity, and fineness of his emotional nature which kindles his intellect and inspires it with energy. He does not feel differently from other men, but he feels more. There is a larger field of things over which his feelings range, and in which he takes vivid interest. If, as we have been often told, sympathy is the secret of all insight, this holds especially true of poetic insight, which more than any other derives its power of seeing from sympathy with the object seen. There is a kinship between the poetic eye and the thing it looks on, in virtue of which it penetrates. As the German poet says : —

> "If the eye had not been sunny,
> How could it look upon the sun ?"

And herein lies one great distinction between the poetic and the scientific treatment of things. The scientific man must keep his feelings under stern control, lest they intrude into his researches and color the dry light, in which alone Science desires to see its objects. The poet, on the other hand, — it is because his feelings inform and kindle his intellect that he sees into the life of things.

Some, perhaps, may recall the names of great poets, though not the greatest, who have fled habitually from human neighborhood, and dwelt apart in proud isolation. But this does not, I think, disprove the view that human-heartedness is the great background of the poet's strength, for to the poets I speak of, their solitariness has been their misfortune, if not their fault. By some untowardness in their lot, or some malady of their time, they have been compelled to retire into themselves, and to become lonely thinkers. If their isolation has added some intensity to their thoughts, it has, at the same time, narrowed the range of their vision, and diminished the breadth and permanence of their influence.

But this vivid human sympathy, though an essential condition or background of all great poetry, by no means belongs exclusively to the poet. Taking other forms, it is characteristic of all men who have deeply moved or greatly benefited their kind, — of St. Augustine, Luther, Howard, Clarkson, and Wilberforce, not less than of Homer, Shakespeare, and Walter Scott.

I must therefore pass on to points more distinctive of the poet, and consider —

What is the object or material with which the poet deals.

What is the special power which he brings to bear on that object.

What is his true aim ; what the function which he fulfils in human society.

The poet's peculiar domain has generally been said to be Beauty ; and there is so much truth in this that, if the thing must be condensed into a single word, probably none better could be found. For it is one large part of the poet's vocation to be a witness for the Beauty which is in the world around him and in human life. But this one word is too narrow to cover all the domain over which the poetic spirit ranges. It fits well that which attracts the poet in the face of nature, and is applicable to many forms of mental and moral excellence. But there are other things which rightly win his regard, to which it cannot be applied without stretching it till it becomes meaningless. Therefore I should rather say that the whole range of existence, or any part of it, when imaginatively apprehended, seized on

the side of its human interest, may be transfigured into
poetry. There is nothing that exists, except things ig-
noble and mean, in which the true poet may not find
himself at home, — in the open sights of nature, in the
occult secrets of science, in the "quicquid agunt homi-
nes," in men's character and fortunes, in their actions
and sufferings, their joys and sorrows, their past history,
their present experience, their future destiny. All these
lie open to him who has power to enter in, and, by
might of imaginative insight, to possess them. And
such is the kinship between man and all that exists
that, as I have elsewhere said, "whenever the soul
comes vividly in contact with any fact, truth, or exist-
ence, whenever it realizes and takes them home to itself
with more than common intensity, out of that meeting
of the soul and its object there arises a thrill of joy, a
glow of emotion ; and the expression of that *glow*, that
thrill, is poetry." But as each age modifies in some
measure men's conceptions of existence, and brings to
light new aspects of life before undreamt of, so Poetry,
which is the expression of these aspects, is ever chang-
ing, in sympathy with the changing consciousness of the
race. A growth old as thought, but ever young, it
alters its form, but renews its vitality, with each suc-
ceeding age.

As to the specific organ or mental gift through which
poets work, every one knows that it is Imagination.
But if asked what Imagination is, who can tell ? If we
turn to the psychologists, — the men who busy them-
selves with labelling and ticketing the mental faculties,
— they do not much help us. Scattered through the
poets here and there, and in some writers on æsthetic
subjects, notably in the works of Mr. Ruskin, we find

thoughts which are more suggestive. Perhaps it is a thing to rejoice in that this marvellous faculty has hitherto baffled the analysts. For it would seem that when you have analyzed any vital entity down to its last elements, you have done your best to destroy it.

I may, however, observe in passing that the following seem to be some of the most prominent notes of the way in which Imagination works : —

To a man's ordinary conceptions of things Imagination adds force, clearness, distinctness of outline, vividness of coloring.

Again, it seems to be a power intermediate between intellect and emotion, looking towards both, and partaking of the nature of both. In its highest form, it would seem to be based on " moral intensity." The emotional and the intellectual in it act and react on each other, deep emotion kindling imagination, and expressing itself in imaginative form, while imaginative insight kindles and deepens emotion.

Closely connected with this is what some have called the penetrative, others the interpretative, power of Imagination. It is that subtle and mysterious gift, that intense intuition, which, piercing beneath all surface appearance, goes straight to the core of an object, enters where reasoning and peddling analysis are at fault, lays hold of the inner heart, the essential life, of a scene, a character, or a situation, and expresses it in a few immortal words. What is the secret of this penetrative glance, who shall say ? It defies analysis. Neither the poet himself who puts it forth, nor the critic who examines the result, can explain how it works, can lay his finger on the vital source of it. A line, a word, has flashed the scene upon us, has made the character live before us; how, we know not, only the thing is done. And others, when they see it, exclaim, How true to nature this is! So like what I have often felt myself, only I could never express it! But the poet has expressed it, and this is what makes him an interpreter to men of their own unuttered experience. All great poets are full of this power. It is that by which Shakespeare read the inmost heart of man, Wordsworth of nature.

A further note of Imagination is that combining and harmonizing power, in virtue of which the poetic mind, guided by the eternal forms of beauty which inhabit it, out of a mass of incongruous materials drops those which are accidental and irrelevant, and selects those which suit its purpose, — those which bring out a given scene or character, — and combines them into a harmonious whole.

The last note I shall mention is what may be called the shaping or embodying power of Imagination, — I mean the power of clothing intellectual and spiritual conceptions in appropriate forms. This is that which Shakespeare speaks of : —

> "Imagination bodies forth
> The forms of things unknown."

And conversely there is in Imagination a power which spiritualizes what is visible and corporeal, and fills it with a higher meaning than mere understanding dreams of. These two processes are seen at work in all great poets, the one or the other being stronger, according to the bent of each poet's nature.

While Imagination, working in these and other ways, is the poet's peculiar endowment, it is clear that for its beneficent operation there must be present an ample range, a large store of material on which to work.

This it cannot create for itself. From other regions it
must be gathered; from a wealth of mind in the poet
himself, from large experience of life and intimate
knowledge of nature, from the exercise of his heart, his
judgment, his reflection, indeed of his whole being, on
all he has seen and felt. In fact, a great poet must be
a man made wise by large experience, much feeling, and
deep reflection : above all, he must have a hold of the
great central truth of things. When these many con-
ditions are present, then and then only can his imagina-
tion work widely, benignly, and for all time ; then only
can the poet become a

"Serene creator of immortal things."

Imagination is not, as has sometimes been conceived,
a faculty of falsehood or deception, calling up merely
fictitious and fantastic views. It is preeminently a
truthful and truth-seeing faculty, perceiving subtle as-
pects of truth, hidden relations, far-reaching analogies,
which find no entrance to us by any other inlet. It is
the power which vitalizes all knowledge ; which makes
the dead abstract and the dead concrete meet, and by
their meeting live ; which suffers not truth to dwell by
itself in one compartment of the mind, but carries it
home through our whole being, — understanding, affec-
tions, will.

This vivid insight, this quick, imaginative intuition,
is accompanied by a delight in the object or truth be
held, — a glow of heart, "a white heat of emotion,"
which is the proper condition of creation. The joy of
imagination in its own vision, the thrill of delight, is
one of the most exquisite moods man ever experiences.

Emotion, then, from first to last inseparably attends
the exercise of Imagination, preëminently in him who

creates, in a lesser degree in those who enjoy his crea-
tions.

In this aspect of poetry, as in some sense the imme-
diate product of emotion, some have seen its necessary
weakness and its limitation. Emotion, they say, be-
longs to youth, and must needs disappear before mature
reason and ripe reflection. Time must dull feelings,
however vivid, cool down passions, however fervid.
How many poets have reiterated Byron's lament, that

" The early glow of thought declines in feeling's dull decay " !

How much of the poetry of all ages is filled with pas-
sionate regrets for objects

" Too early lost, too hopelessly deplored " !

No wonder, therefore, that strong men, who despise sen-
timentality, and will not spend their lives in bemoan-
ing the inevitable, are wont, as they grow older, to
drop poetry of this kind, along with other youthful
illusions. The truth of this cannot be gainsaid. The
poetry of regret may please youth, which has buoy-
ancy enough in itself to bear the weight of sadness not
its own. But those who have learnt by experience
what real sorrow is have no strength to waste on im-
aginary sorrows. And if all poetry were of this char-
acter, it would be true enough that it contained no re-
freshment for toiling, suffering men.

But, not to speak of purely objective poets, there is
in great meditative poets a higher wisdom, a serener
region, than that of imaginative regret. There are
poets who, after having experienced and depicted the
tumults of the soul, after having felt and sung the pain
of unsatisfied desires, or uttered their yearning regret

" That things depart which never may return,"

have been able to retire within themselves, thence to contemplate the fever of excitement from a higher, more permanent region, and to illuminate, as has been said, transitory emotion "with the light of a calm, infinite world." Such poets do not ignore the heartless things that are done in the world, but they forgive them; the dark problems of existence they do not try to explain, but they make you feel that there is light behind, if we could but see it; the discords and dissonances of life are still there, but over them all they seem to shed a reconciling spirit. This serene wisdom, this large and luminous contemplation, absorbs into itself all conflict, passion, and regret, as the all-embracing blue of heaven holds the storms and clouds that momentarily sweep over it. It is seen in the "august repose" of Sophocles, when he prepares the calm close for the troubled day of the blind and exiled Theban king. It is seen in the spirit that pervades the *Tempest*, one of Shakespeare's latest dramas, in which, to use his own words, he "takes part with his nobler reason against his fury," and rises out of conflict and passion into a region of self-control and serenity. It is seen in Milton, when, amid the deep solitariness of his own blindness and forced inactivity, he is enabled to console himself with the thought,

"They also serve who only stand and wait."

It is seen in Wordsworth, he who, while feeling, as few have done, regret for a brightness gone which nothing could restore, was able to let all these experiences melt into his being, and enrich it, till his soul became humanized by distress, and by the thoughts that spring out of human suffering. Poetry such as this stands the wear of life, and breathes a benediction even over its decline.

As to the aim which the poet sets before him, the end which poetry is meant to fulfil, what shall be said? Here the critics, ancient and modern, answer, almost with one voice, that the end is to give pleasure. Aristotle tells us that "it is the business of the tragic poet to give that pleasure which arises from pity and terror, through imitation." Horace gives an alternative end in his

"Aut prodesse volunt, aut delectare Poetae,"

and he awards the palm to those poems which combine both ends, and at once elevate and please. To take one sample from the moderns: Coleridge, in his definition of poetry, tells us that "a poem is a species of composition, opposed to science as having intellectual pleasure for its object or end," and that its perfection is "to communicate the greatest immediate pleasure from the parts compatible with the largest sum of pleasure on the whole."

May I venture to differ from these great authorities, and to say that they seem to have mistaken that which is an inseparable accompaniment for that which is the main aim, the proper end of poetry? The impulse to poetic composition is, I believe, in the first instance, spontaneous, almost unconscious; and where the inspiration, as we call it, is most strong and deep, there a conscious purpose is least present. When a poet is in the true creative mood, he is for the time possessed with love of the object, the truth, the vision which he sees, for its own sake, — is wholly absorbed in it; the desire fitly to express what he sees and feels is his one sufficient motive, and to attain to this expression is itself his end and his reward. While the inspiration is at its strongest, the thought of giving pleasure to others or of

winning praise for himself is weakest.   The intrinsic
delight in his own vision, and in the act of expressing it,
keeps all extrinsic aims, for a time at least, aloof.   This
might perhaps be a sufficient account of the poet's aim
in short lyrics and brief arrow-flights of song.   But even
in the richest poetic natures the inspiring heat cannot
always or long be maintained at its height,

> "And tasks in hours of insight willed
> In hours of gloom must be fulfilled."

Effort long sustained implies the presence of conscious
purpose.   Great poets cannot be conceived to have
girded themselves to their longest, most deliberate ef-
forts — Shakespeare to *Hamlet*, Milton to *Paradise Lost*
— without reflecting what was to be the effect of their
work on their fellow-men.   It would hardly have satisfied
them at such a time to have been told that their poems
would add to men's intellectual pleasures.   They would
not have been content with any result short of this, — the
assurance that their work would live to awaken those
high sympathies in men, in the exercise of which they
themselves found their best satisfaction, and which, they
well knew, ennoble every one who partakes of them.
To appeal to the higher side of human nature, and to
strengthen it, to come to its rescue, when it is overborne
by worldliness and material interests, to support it by
great truths, set forth in their most attractive form, —
this is the only worthy aim, the adequate end, of all poetic
endeavor.   And this it does by expressing in beautiful
form and melodious language the best thoughts and the
noblest feelings which the spectacle of life awakens in
the finest souls.   This is the true office of poetry, which
is the bloom of high thought, the efflorescence of noble
emotion.   No doubt these sympathies, once awakened,

yield a delight among the purest and noblest man can know; but to minister this pleasure is not the main end which the poet sets before himself, but is at most a subordinate object. The true end is to awaken men to the divine side of things, to bear witness to the beauty that clothes the outer world, the nobility that lies hid, often obscured, in human souls, to call forth sympathy for neglected truths, for noble but oppressed persons, for downtrodden causes, and to make men feel that, through all outward beauty and all pure inward affection, God Himself is addressing them.

In this endeavor poetry makes common cause with all high things, — with right reason and true philosophy, with man's moral intuitions and his religious aspirations. It combines its influence with all those benign tendencies which are working in the world for the melioration of man and the manifestation of the kingdom of God. It is adding from age to age its own current to those great

> "tides that are flowing
> Right onward to the eternal shore."

But, if it has great allies, it has also powerful adversaries. The worship of wealth and of all it gives, a materialistic philosophy which disbelieves in all knowledge unverifiable by the senses, luxury, empty display, worldliness, and cynicism, with these true poetry cannot dwell. In periods and in circles where these are paramount, the poet is discredited, his function as a witness to high truth is denied. If tolerated at all, he is degraded into a merely ornamental personage, a sayer of pretty things, a hanger-on of society and the great. Such is the only function which degenerate ages allow to him, and this is a function which only poets of baser

metal will accept. The truly great poets in every age
have felt the nobility of their calling, have perceived
that their true function is not to amuse, or merely to
give delight, but to be witnesses for the ideal and spirit-
ual side of things, to come to the help of the generous,
the noble, and the true, against the mighty.

And, though some exceptions there have been, yet it
is true that the great majority of poets in all times
have, according to their gifts, recognized this to be their
proper aim, and fulfilled it. Therefore we say once
more, in the words of one of the foremost of the brother-
hood —

> "Blessings be on them and eternal praise!
> Who gave us nobler loves and nobler cares,
> The poets, who on earth have made us heirs
> Of truth, and pure delight by heavenly lays."

If these general views are true, there follow from
them some practical corollaries as to our poetic judg-
ments, which, while true for all times, are yet specially
applicable to this time, perhaps to this place.

The first of these is the need we have to cultivate an
open and catholic judgment, ready to appreciate excel-
lence in poetry and in literature under whatever forms
it comes. It might seem that there was little need to
urge this here, for is not one main end of all academic
teaching to form in the mind right standards of judg-
ment? Of course it is. But the process as carried on
here is not free from hindrances. We too readily, by
the very nature of our studies, become slaves to the
past. Those who have spent their days in studying
the master minds of former ages naturally take from
their works canons of criticism by which they try all
new productions. Hence it is that, when there appears
some fresh and original creation, which is unlike any-

thing the past has recognized, it is apt to fare ill before a learned tribunal. The learned and the literary are so trained to judge by precedents, that they often deal harder measure and narrower judgment to young aspirants than those do who, having no rules of criticism, judge merely by their own natural instincts. Literary circles think to bind by their formal codes young and vigorous genius, whose very nature it is to defy the conventional, and to achieve the unexpected. Many a time has this been seen in the history of poetry, notably at the opening of the present century. Those who then seated themselves on the high places of criticism, and affected to dispense judgment, brought their critical apparatus, derived from the age of Pope, to bear on the vigorous race of young poets who in this country appeared after the French Revolution. Jeffrey and his band of critics tried the new poetic brotherhood, one by one, found them wanting, and consigned them to oblivion. Hardly more generous were the critics of the *Quarterly Review*. There was not one of the great original spirits of that time whom the then schools of critics did not attempt to crush. The poets sang on, each in his own way, heedless of the anathemas. The world has long since recognized them, and crowned them with honor. The critics, and the canons by which they condemned them, — where is their authority now?

Even more to be deprecated than critics, judging by the past, are coteries which test all things by some dominant sentiment or short-lived fashion of the hour. Those who have lived some time have seen school after school of this sort arise, air its little nostrums for a season, and disappear. But such coteries, while they last, do their best, by narrowness and intolerance, to vitiate

literature, and are unfair alike to past eminence and
to rising genius. I can myself remember a time when
the subjective school of poetry was so dominant in Ox-
ford, that some of its ablest disciples voted Walter
Scott to be no poet ; perhaps there may be some who
think so still.

To guard us against all such narrowness, it is well to
remember that the world of poetry is wide, as wide as
existence, that no experience of the past can lay down
rules for future originality, or limit the materials which
fresh minds may vivify, or predict the moulds in which
they may cast their creations. Let those who would
preserve catholicity of judgment purge their minds of
all formulas and fashions, and look with open eye and
ingenuous heart, alike on the boundless range of past
excellence, and on the hardly less boundless field of
future possibility. If we must have canons of judgment,
it is well to have them few, simple, and elastic, founded
only on what is permanent in nature and in man.

Again, in a place like this, men's thoughts are turned,
and rightly, to the great world-poets of all time, — to
Homer, Æschylus, Sophocles, Virgil, perhaps to Dante,
Shakespeare, Milton. For the whole host of lesser,
though still genuine poets, much more for the sources
whence all poetry comes, we are apt to have but scanty
regard. It is well perhaps that for a short time, as stu-
dents, we should so concentrate our gaze ; for we thus
get a standard of what is noblest in thought and most
perfect in expression. But this exclusiveness should
continue but a little while, and for a special purpose.
If it be prolonged into life, if we continue only to ad-
mire and enjoy a few poets of the greatest name, we
become, while fancying ourselves to be large-minded,

narrow and artificial. If our eyes were always fixed on the highest mountain-peaks, what should we know of the broad earth around us ? What should we think of the geographer who should acquaint himself with the rivers only where they broaden seaward, and bear navies on their bosom, and know nothing of the small affluents and brooks that run among the hills and feed the rivers, and of the mountain-wells that feed the brooks, and of the clouds and vapors that supply the wells ? You admire Homer, Æschylus, Shakespeare, perhaps Scott and Wordsworth and Shelley, but where did these get their inspiration and the materials which they wrought into beauty ? Not mainly by study of books, not by placing before themselves literary models, but by going straight to the true sources of all poetry, by knowing and loving nature, by acquaintance with their own hearts, and by knowledge of their fellow-men.

From the poetry of the people has been drawn most of what is truest, most human-hearted, in the greatest poems. Would the *Iliad* have been possible if there had not existed before it a nameless crowd of rhapsodists, who wrought out a poetic language, and shaped the deeds of the heroes into rough popular songs ? Would Shakespeare's work have been possible, if he had not wrought on ground overstrewn with the wreck of mediæval mysteries, of moralities, tales, ballads, and of England's chronicles and traditions, as well as enriched by the regular plays of his predecessors ? When Shakespeare's "study of imagination " was filled with kings and heroes and statesmen such as he had never met with, how was it that he so painted them to the life ? Did not his insight into their characters, his read-

2

ing of their feelings, spring from the power in him of imagination and memory, working on scenes he had witnessed, and on impressions he had gathered, first in the hamlets and the oak woods about his own Stratford, and afterwards in the city and in city life ? It was his own experience, not of books, but of men, idealized and projected into the strange and distant, till that became alive and near.

No doubt, a day comes with advancing civilization, when the poets of the past must exercise more power over younger poets than they did in earlier times. But this at least remains true, that, if the poetry of any, even the most advanced, age is to retain that eternal freshness which is its finest grace, it must draw both its materials and its impulses more from sympathy with the people than from past poets, more from the heart of man than from books. If poetry is to portray true emotion, this must come from poets who themselves have felt it, and seen others feel.

Those who are familiar with the poor know how much of that feeling language, which is the essence of poetry, may be heard at times under cottage roofs. At the fall of autumn I have visited and said farewell to two old Highland women, sisters, sitting in their smoky hut beside their scanty peat-fire. With return of summer I have revisited that hut, and found one sitting there alone, and have heard that sole survivor, as she sat on her stool, rocking her body to and fro, pour forth in Gaelic speech the story, how her sister pined away, and left her in the dead days of winter, all alone. And no threnody or lament poet ever penned could match the pathos of that simple narrative.

In cases like this, not the feeling only is poetic, the

words which utter it are so too. And the poet, instead of adopting the approved diction of poets, or coining tropes and images of his own, cannot do better than adopt the language of genuine emotion, as it comes warm from the lips of suffering men and women. And not the language only, but the incidents of actual life are worth more, as a storehouse of fresh poetry, than all the written poems of all the literatures. Here, more than elsewhere, the saying holds, that the literary language is a stagnant pool. The words which men use under pressure of real emotion, these are the running stream, the living spring.

But it is not nature and human life only as they exist now, but also as we know them to have been in the past, that furnish ever fresh poetic materials. It has often been a marvel to me that English poets, with their own grand national history behind them, have made so little use of it. Since Shakespeare wrote his historical dramas, how few poetic blocks have been dug from that quarry! What I now say applies to England, rather than to Scotland. Our picturesque historians of recent years, while they have done the work of partisans very effectually, have also been in some sort poets of the past. But how seldom have our regular singers set foot on that field! The Laureate, no doubt, after having done his work in England's mythic region, has, late in his career, descended from those shadowy heights to the more solid ground and more substantial figures of her recorded history. Let us hail the omen, and hope that the coming generation of poets may follow him, and enter into the rich world of England's history and possess it. Surely England, if any land, supplies rich poetic material in her long, unbroken story, in her heroic

names, in her battlefields scattered all the island over,
where railways and factories have not obliterated them,

> "in the halls in which is hung
> Armory of the invincible knights of old,"

where hang, too, the portraits of her famous men, and
in the homes in which they were reared, either still in-
habited or mouldering

> "In all the imploring beauty of decay."

These things remain to add life and color to that which
chronicle and tradition and family histories have pre-
served. How is it that our English poets have so
turned their back on all this? I confess it has often
pained me to see fine poetic faculty expended on a poem,
long as *Paradise Lost*, upon some demigod or hero of
Greece, in whom the Teutonic mind can never find more
than a passing interest; or in discussing hard problems
of psychology, better left to the philosophers; or in cut-
ting the inner man to shreds in morbid self-analysis,
while the great fresh fields of our own history lie all
unvisited.

One word as to the relation which substance bears to
form, thought to expression, in poetry. "Lively feel-
ing for a situation and power to express it constitute the
poet," said Goethe. "The power of clear and eloquent
expression is a talent distinct from poetry, though often
mistaken for it," says Dr. Newman. Into this large
question, whether he can be called a poet who lacks the
power of expressing the poetic thought that is in him, I
shall not enter. On the one hand you have Goethe and
Coleridge, maintaining that poetic conception and ex-
pression are inseparable, — powers born in one birth.
On the other hand, Wordsworth and Dr. Newman agree
in holding that

" many are the poets sown by nature,
Yet wanting the accomplishment of verse.'

As, however, the " vision," even if it exist, cannot reveal itself to others without the " accomplishment" of expression, there is little practical need to discuss the question. But while both of these powers are indispensable, they seem to exist in various proportions in different poets. One poet is strong in thought and substance, less effective in form and expression. In another the case is exactly reversed. It is only in the greatest poets, and in those, when in their happiest mood, that the two powers seem to meet in perfect equipoise, — and that the highest thoughts are found wedded to the most perfect words. Among well-known poets, Cowper and Scott have been noted as stronger in substance than in form; Pope and Gray, as poets in whom finish of style exceeds power of thought ; Moore, as hiding commonplace sentiment under elaborate ornament. On the whole, it may be said that the early poets of any nation are for the most part stronger in substance than in style ; whereas, with advancing time, power of expression grows, style gets cultivated for its own sake, so that in later poets expression very often outruns thought.

As an illustration of the wide limits within which two styles of expression, each perfect after its kind, may range, take two poems, well known to every one : Wordsworth's *Resolution and Independence*, and Mr. Tennyson's *Palace of Art*. Each poem well represents the manner of its author. In one thing only they agree, that each contains a moral truth, though to teach this is not probably the main object of either. In all other respects, in their manner of conveying the truth, in form, coloring, and style of diction, no two poems could well be more unlike.

Wordsworth's poem sets forth that alternation of two opposite moods to which imaginative natures are exposed, — the highest exaltation, rejoicing in sympathy with the joy of Nature, quickly succeeded by the deepest despondency. After these two moods have been powerfully depicted, admonition and restoration come from the sight of a hard lot patiently, even cheerfully, borne by a poor leech-gatherer, who wanders about the moors plying his trade. This sight acts as a tonic on the poet's spirit, bracing him to fortitude and content.

The early poem of the Laureate begins by personifying the Spirit of Art, who speaks forth her own aims and desires, her one purpose to enjoy Beauty always and only by herself, for her own selfish enjoyment — the artistic temptation to worship Beauty, apart from truth and goodness. You will remember how she describes the Palace, so royal, rich, and wide, with which she surrounded herself, — the life she led there; how, after a time, smitten to the core with a sense of her own inward poverty and misery, she loathes herself in despair.

Wordsworth's " plain imagination and severe " moves rapidly from the most literal, every-day commonplace, into the remotest distance of brooding phantasy, before which the old man and the visible scene entirely disappear, or are transfigured. And the diction moves with the thought, passing from the barest prose to the most elevated poetic style. Thus, if on the one hand you have such lines as

" To me that morning did it happen so,"
and
" How is it that you live ? and what is it you do ? "
you have on the other —

" I thought of Chatterton, the marvellous Boy,
   The sleepless soul that perished in his pride;
   Of him who walked in glory and in joy,
   Following his plough along the mountain side:
   We Poets in our youth begin in gladness,
   But thereof comes in the end despondency and madness."

You have also the strong lines likening the sudden apparition of the old man on the moor to a huge boulder-stone.

   "Couched on the bald top of an eminence;"

then to a sea-beast that has crawled forth on a sand-bank or rock-ledge to sun itself. Then rising into —

   "Upon the margin of that moorish flood,
   Motionless as a cloud, the old man stood;
   That heareth not the loud winds when they call,
   And moveth all together, if it move at all."

Many may object to the appearance of the plain lines in the poem as blemishes. To me, while they give great reality to the whole, they enhance, I know not how much, the power of the grander lines. I would not, if I could, have them otherwise.

Mr. Tennyson again, from end to end of his poem, pitches the style at a high artistic level, from which he never once descends. Image comes on image, picture succeeds picture, each perfect, rich in color, clear in outline. When you first read the poem, every stanza startles you with a new and brilliant surprise. There is not a line which the most fastidious could wish away.

In another thing the two poems are strikingly contrasted. Wordsworth's is almost colorless; there is only a word or two in it that can suggest color. Mr. Tennyson's is inlaid throughout with the richest hues, yet so deftly as not to satiate, but only to bring out more fully the purpose of the poem. In reading the one you feel as though you were in the midst of a plain bare

moor, out of which the precipiced crags and blue mount-
ain-peaks soar aloof, not inharmoniously, but all the
more impressively, from the dead level that surrounds
them.   In the other you are, as it were, walking along
some high mountain level, which, without marked eleva-
tion or depression anywhere, yields on either side wide
outlooks over land and sea.

I have alluded to these two poems, not by any
means to estimate their comparative excellence, but as
instances in which two great poets give expression to
high thoughts, each in his own characteristic style, and
that style perfect according to its kind and aim.

In these two instances the idea and the expression are
well balanced, in just equipoise.

But it is otherwise with much of the poetry, or at-
tempts at poetry, of the present time.   A tincture of
letters is now so common, that the number of those who
can versify is greatly increased, and the power of expres-
sion often lamentably outruns the thought.   There is
one marked exception to this, which will occur to every
one, in the case of one of the most prominent living
poets, in whom the power of lucid utterance halts,
breathlessly and painfully, behind the jerks and jolts of
his subtle and eccentric thought.   But this is not a
common fault.   Rather, I should say, we are overdone
with superabundant imagery and luscious melody.   We
are so cloyed with the perfume of flowers, that we long
for the bare bracing heights, where only stern north
winds blow.   Or to put it otherwise: in many modern
poems you are presented with a richly-chased casket;
you open it, and find only a common pebble within.
This is a malady incident to periods of late civilization
and of much criticism.   Poetry gets narrowed into an

art, — an art which many can practise, but which, when practised, is not worth much. How many are there in the present day, of more or less poetical faculty, who can express admirably whatever they have to say, but that amounts to little or nothing! At best it is but a collection of poetic prettinesses, sometimes of hysteric exaggerations and extravagances. Had these men, with their fine faculty of expression, only made themselves seriously at home in any one field of thought, had they ever learned to love any subject for its own sake, and not merely for its artistic capabilities, had they ever laid a strong heart-hold of any side of human interest, no one can say what they might not have achieved; but for want of this grasp of substance the result is in so many cases what we see. Not till some stirring of the stagnant waters be vouchsafed, some new awakening to the higher side of things, not till some mighty wind blows over the souls of men, will another epoch of great and creative poetry arise.

The views which I have set forth in this Lecture will, if they are true, determine what value we ought to place on that modern theory which maintains "the moral indifference of true art." The great poet, we are sometimes told nowadays, must be free from all moral prepossessions; his one business is " to see life steadily and see it whole," and to represent it faithfully as it is. The highest office of the poet is " to aim at a purely artistic effect." To him goodness and vice are alike, — his work is to delineate each impartially, and let no shade of preference intrude.

It is to Dramatic Poetry, I suppose, that this theory is mainly intended to apply, and from the Drama it is supposed to receive most confirmation. Be it so.

It is then the aim of the dramatist truly to delineate character of every hue, the base equally with the noble, to represent life, in all its variety, just as it is. But is not life itself full of morality? Is not the substance and texture of it moral to the core? Must not the contemplation of human characters, as they are, awaken liking or dislike, moral admiration or moral aversion, in every healthy mind? And must not the poetry which represents truly that substance be moral too? Must not the spectacle of the characters depicted stir natural feelings of love or dislike, as well in the poet who draws, as in the reader who contemplates them? Did not Sophocles have more delight in Antigone than in Ismene? Did not Shakespeare admire and love Desdemona and Cordelia ; hate and despise Iago and Edmund?

This theory of the moral indifference of Art originated, I believe, in great measure, with Goethe, and has been propagated chiefly by his too exclusive admirers. I should be content to rest the whole question on a comparison of the moral spirit that prevades the dramas of Goethe and those of Shakespeare. It has been asserted, I believe with truth, that it was the existence of this very theory in Goethe, or rather of that element in him whence this theory was projected, which shuts him out from the highest place as a dramatist, and marks the vast interval between him and Shakespeare. Goethe's moral nature was, it has been said, of a somewhat limp texture, with few strong " natural admirations," so that his dramas are wanting in those moral lights and shadows which exist in the actual world, and give life and outline to the most manly natures. His groups of characters are most of them morally feeble and shadowy. Shake-

speare, on the other hand, being a whole, natural man,
" the moral, imaginative, and intellectual parts of him
do not lie separate," but move at once and all together.
Being wholly unembarrassed with æsthetic theories, his
"poetical impulse and his moral feelings are one." He
does not conceal or explain away the great moral eleva-
tions and depressions that you see in the world. He
paints men and women as they are, with great moral
differences, not withholding admiration from the noble,
contempt and aversion from the base. Therefore,
though we do not say that he is faultless, do not deny
that there are things in him we could wish away, yet,
taken as a whole, there breathes from his works a nat-
ural, healthy, bracing, elevating spirit, not to be found
in the works of Goethe. Every side, every phase of
human nature is there faithfully set down, but to the
higher and better side is given its own natural predomi-
nance. With the largest tolerance ever man had for
all human infirmity, the widest sympathy with all men,
seeing even the soul of good that may lie in things evil,
there is in him nothing of that neutral moral tint, which
is weakness in poetry as truly as in actual life.

Neither do we find in this master-dramatist any trace
of another theory, born of morbid physiology, as the for-
mer of morbid æsthetics, by which character, personality,
the soul are explained away, and all moral energy disap-
pears before such solvents as outward circumstances, an-
tecedent conditions, heredity, and accumulated instincts.
Shakespeare had looked that way too, as he had most
ways ; but he leaves the announcement of this modern
view, or one closely allied to it, to Edmund, one of his
basest characters, and even he scorns it.

If the divorce of poetry from morality will not hold

in the drama, in which alone it can show any semblance of argument, far less can it be applied to poetry in its other forms, epic, lyric, meditative. If it be not the function of poetry in these forms to give beautiful expression to the finer impulses, to the higher side of life, I see not that it has any function at all. If poetry be not a river, fed from the clear wells that spring on the highest summits of humanity, but only a canal to drain off stagnant ditches from the flats, it may be a very useful sanitary contrivance, but has not, in Bacon's words, any " participation of divineness.'

Poets who do not recognize the highest moral ideal known to man do, by that very act, cut themselves off from the highest artistic effect. It is another exemplification of that great law of ethics which compasses all human action " whereby the abandonment of a lower end in obedience to a higher aim, is made the very condition of securing the lower one." For just as the pleasure-seeker is not the pleasure-finder, so he who aims only at artistic effect by that very act misses it. To reach the highest art, we must forget art, and aim beyond it. Other gifts being equal, the poet, who has been enabled to apprehend the highest moral conception, has in that gained for himself a great poetic vantage-ground.

To bring this to a point : The Christian standard we take to be the highest known among men. Must then, you may ask, all great poets, at least in modern times, in order to reach the highest poetic excellence, be Christians ? Goethe, you say, made little of Christianity ; Shelley abjured it : are we on that account to deny that they rank among the great poets of the world?

To this it may be replied, — First, that though they

did not consciously hold it, they could not escape at least some unconscious influence from the religion which surrounded them. Secondly, that had their prejudice against Christianity been removed, could they have frankly owned its divinity, instead of being losers they would have gained hardly less as poets than as men. For lack of this it is that there lie hidden in the human spirit tones, the truest, the most tender, the most profound, which these poets have never elicited.

Let it not be said that I have been advocating sectarian views, — trying to bind poetry to the service of a sect. It is true that poetry refuses to be made over as the handmaid of any one philosophy or view of life or system of belief. But it is equally true that it naturally allies itself only with what is highest and best in human nature ; and in whatever philosophy or belief this is enshrined, thence poetry will draw its finest impulses.

There are only two views with which it has nothing in common. One is the view of life which they hold whose motto is " *Nil admirari.*" With this it can have no fellowship, for it cuts off the springs of emotion at their very sources. The other antipode is the philosophy which denies us any access to truth, except through the senses ; which refuses to believe anything which scalpel, or crucible, or microscope cannot verify ; which reduces human nature to a heap of finely granulated, iridescent dust, and empties man of a soul and the universe of a God. Such a philosophy would leave to poetry only one function, — to deck with tinsel the coffin of universal humanity. This is a function which she declines to perform.

But we need have no fears that it will come to this.

Poetry will not succumb before materialism, or agnosticism, or any other cobweb of the sophisticated brain. It is an older, stronger birth than these, and will survive them. It will throw itself out into fresh forms ; it will dig for itself new channels ; under some form suited to each age, it will continue through all time, for it is an undying effluence of the soul of man.

That this effluence has on the whole been benign in its tendency, who can doubt ? I have wished throughout not to indulge in exaggeration, nor to claim for poetry more than every one must concede to it. Imagination may be turned to evil uses. It may minister, it has sometimes ministered, to the baser side of human nature, and thrown enchantment over things that are vile. But this has been a perversion, which depraves the nature of poetry, and robs it of its finest grace. Naturally it is the ally of all things high and pure ; among these is its home ; its nature is to lay hold of these, and to bring them, with power and attractiveness, home to our hearts. It is the prerogative of poetry to convey to us, as nothing else can, the beauty that is in all nature, to interpret the finer quality that is hidden in the hearts of men, and to hint at a beauty which lies behind these, a light " above the light of setting suns," which is incommunicable. In doing this it will fulfil now, as of old, the office which Bacon assigned to it, and will give some " shadow of satisfaction to the spirit of man, longing for a more ample greatness, a more perfect goodness, and a more absolute variety " than here it is capable of.

CHAPTER II.

CRITICISM AND CREATION.

WE are apt to fancy that the powers which poet and philosopher put forth are of a quite different order from those which we feel in ourselves, and that commonplace people and every-day life have nothing in common with their high functions. It is not so. The most unlettered peasant performs the same kind of mental acts as the poet and the philosopher, only in these last the powers work with a higher energy. Of all men it is true that they feel and energize first, they reflect and judge afterwards. First comes impulse, emotion, active outgoing ; then reflection, analyzing the impulse, and questioning the motive.

Now these two moods of mind, which go on alternately in every human heart, go on in the poet not less, but more, — the same powers are working in him, only in fuller, intenser energy. First comes his creative mood. He has given him a vision of some truth, some beautiful aspect of things, which for a time fills his whole heart and imagination ; he seizes it, moulds it into words, and while he does so his soul is all aglow with emotion, — so strong emotion, that the intellectual power he is putting forth is almost unconscious, almost lost sight of. Then, when the inspiring heat has cooled down, the time of judgment comes on : he contemplates the work of his fervid hours, criticises it, as we say, sees its shortcomings, weighs its value.

This, which goes on in the minds of individual men, who have the creative gift, is seen reflected on a large scale in the literary history of nations and of the race. The world has had its great creative epochs more frequently it has had its great critical ones. The great creative epochs are not those in which criticism most flourishes, neither are the epochs which are most critical those which have most creative force. In nations as in men, the two moods seem to alternate, and, in some degree, to exclude each other.

What happened in Greece we all know. Her creative energy had spent itself, the roll of her great poets was complete, before there appeared anything which can be called criticism. When Aristotle came, and, in his prosaic, methodical way, laid line and plummet to the tragedians, took their dimensions, and drew from these his definitions and canons for tragedy, the tragic, indeed the whole poetic impulse of Greece had exhausted itself.

Then followed the Alexandrian era, — the first epoch of systematic criticism which the world had seen. Behind it lay the whole land which Hellenic genius in its prime had traversed, and had covered with artistic monuments. Looking back on these, the Alexandrian men began to take stock of them, to appraise, arrange, edit them, to extract from them the forms of speech and rules of grammar, — and in fact to construct, as far as they could, a whole critical apparatus. Learned editors, compilers, grammarians, critics, these men were ; but poets, makers, creators, that it was denied them to be. Useful and laborious men, doing work which has passed into the world's mental life, but not interesting, stimulative, refreshing, as the true poets are.

A poet, no doubt, Alexandria had, — the firstfruits of its literature, the most finished specimen of its spirit. In him we have a sample of what the most extensive learning and finished taste, without genius, can do. He wrote, we are told, 800 works, and poems innumerable. All that great talents, vast learning, unwearied industry, and great literary ambition could do, he did. The result is not encouraging. We do not in these latter days desire to see more Callimachi; one Callimachus is enough for the world.

I have alluded to Alexandria and Callimachus, because some seem to think that we in England, as far as poetry is concerned, have now reached our Alexandrian era, that it is in vain we shut our eyes to the fact, that our wisdom is to accept it, and to try to make the best of it.

This is the subject I wish to consider to-day, — Whether, looking back on the course of our poetic history, and considering our present mental condition, there is good reason to believe that our creative, poetic energy has worked itself out, that our Alexandrian era has come.

This rather depressing view of our poetical situation, as though it were the time of Alexandrian decadence, may perhaps seem to receive some countenance from an opinion put forth with much force by a living voice, which most Oxford men have probably heard, and which all are glad to hear, — my friend and my forerunner in this chair, which he so greatly adorned. Mr. Arnold is never so welcome as when he speaks of poetry and literature. Even when we may not agree with all he says, his words instruct and delight us; for every word he speaks on these subjects is living, based on

large knowledge, and on a high standard of excel-
lence.

It must not therefore be supposed that I wish to en-
gage in controversy with my friend, but rather to enter
into a friendly conversation with him on subjects inter-
esting to both of us, if I first remind you of his view,
and then try to supplement what he has said by some
other considerations which, in his zeal for a larger,
more enlightened knowledge, he has perhaps left un-
expressed.

He holds that the one work to which we are at pres-
ent called, both in poetry and in all literature, is the
work of a better, higher, more world-wide criticism,
than any we have as yet known in England. And by
criticism is meant not the old insular British prejudice,
as it has been represented in the *Edinburgh* or the
Quarterly Review, but " the disinterested endeavor to
learn and propagate the best that is known and thought
in the world." Real criticism, he says, is essentially
the exercise of " curiosity as to ideas on all subjects, for
their own sakes, apart from any practical interest they
may serve; it obeys an instinct prompting it to try to
know the best that is known and thought in the world,
irrespectively of practice, politics, and everything of the
kind, and to value knowledge and thought, as they ap-
proach this best, without the intrusion of any other con-
siderations whatever."

This is a view of criticism which, if it has a bearing
on poetry, has a still more obvious bearing on other
forms of literature, and hardly less on science. Crit-
icism in this sense is but one phase, perhaps I should
rather say another name, of that great historic method,
which in our time has entered into and transformed

every province of thought. Taking its stand on the high eminence to which all the past has been leading up, and casting a wide-sweeping eye backward on universal literature, criticism, we are told, sees only two great creative epochs of poetry, one the age of Æschylus and Sophocles, the other the age of Shakespeare.

These two epochs were creative and fruitful, because in both a new and fresh current of ideas was let in on the world. There was a breaking-up of the old confining limitations, an expansion all round of the mental horizon, and this condition of things is the most stimulating and exhilarating of mental influences. This bracing intellectual atmosphere, this fresh movement of ideas, was caused, in the case of Greece, by the national exaltation of mind which followed the overthrow of the Persian, and by the sense of triumph, security, and expanding energy which every Athenian felt, while his country was building up her maritime empire, and Pericles was placing the copestone on the structure.

In Shakespeare's time like causes were at work, and created a similar expansion of men's thoughts. The Renaissance, after having done its work on the Continent, had at last reached the shores of England, and created there the "New Learning." The Mediæval Church fabric had been rent, and new light came in, as the barriers fell down. A new world had arisen beyond the Atlantic, on which the bravest of Englishmen were not ashamed to descend as buccaneers, and to draw fresh life from the wider ocean and larger earth opened to their adventure.

In these two epochs, when great poets were born into the world, the time was propitious, and the result was the great poetic creations which we know. The "men"

and " the moment " had met ; that is the account of it.
Two great creative epochs of poetry vouchsafed to the
world — only two — no third.

We had always fancied that the end of last and the
beginning of this century, the period embraced between
1790 and 1825, had been, in England at least, such a
creative period, that the outburst of native song which
then took place made it one of the world's great poetic
eras.   But it seems that it is not so.

We had imagined that, though the brotherhood of
poets which then arose in England contained no Shake-
speare, yet, taken all together, they formed a band so
original, so energetic, so various, as to have made their
era forever memorable while English literature lasts.
This is a common — I am inclined to think, a not ex-
aggerated — estimate of them.

But the high critical view to which I have been re-
ferring says, No.   And the reason it gives is this.   The
French Revolution, the prime moving force of Europe
during that time, took in France too practical a turn,
was bent too much on political results, and had ceased
to supply that fine atmosphere of universal thought —
" that current of ideas which animate and stimulate the
creative force — such a current as moved the times of
Pindar and of Sophocles in Greece, and of Shakespeare
in England."   In France the force of the Revolution
was expended in carrying out political theories.   At the
same time in England the whole national life was spent
in finding means of resisting those theories, and of
curbing the madness of foreign ideas.   Even the most
thoughtful Englishmen lent themselves to this effort.
Hence, in England, the first quarter of this century was
a period of concentration, of insularity, not of expan-

sion, of thought. This was not a benign atmosphere for creative minds to work in. The men of original genius were given us, but the outward conditions were not given. Therefore we cannot, according to this view, look back with complacency on the poetry which ushered in this century in our own country. And if we cannot so look back on the period before 1825, much less can we do so on anything that has succeeded it. Therefore we must stick to criticism. Criticism is the only function now allowed us. "Criticism first, — a time of true creative activity hereafter, when criticism has done its work."

This is the view which has been advocated. Now consider its results. Had such high critical views been admitted in former times, how would it have thinned the ranks of England's poets! What gaps it would have made in that noble line of singers, —

> "That, on the steady breeze of honor, sail
> In long procession calm and beautiful" !

It is one of the most characteristic things about our literature that the spirit of each time has passed into our poetry. The political changes of each age, the deeds men did, the thoughts they had, the change of manners that was going on, all these acted directly on the imagination of our countrymen, kindled their emotions, and embodied themselves in the poetry of the time.

It has been truly said that "no one poet, however ample his range, represents all the tendencies of his time, but all the poets of any time taken together do." The same writer (Mr. Stopford Brooke) has expressed so well the historical nature of English poetry, as reflecting the life of each age, that I cannot but quote his words : —

" If we want to get a clear idea of any period we must know all the poets, small and great, who wrote in it, and read them altogether. It would be really useful and delightful to take a single time, and read every line of fairly good poetry written in it, and then compare the results of our study with the history of the time. Such a piece of work would not only increase our pleasure in all the higher poetry of the time we study, but would give us grounds for philosophic study, and for greater enjoyment of the poetry of any other time. Above all, it would supply us with an historical element, which the writers of history, even at the present day, have so strangely neglected; the history of the emotions and passions which political changes worked, and which themselves influenced political change; the history of the rise and fall of those ideas, which especially touch the imaginative and emotional life of a people, and in doing so modify their whole development."

It would be easy to illustrate the truth of this, and to show, by a survey of English poetry from Chaucer to our own day, how entirely every change in it reflects some change in national sentiment. I shall take but two instances.

The long struggle between the Stuart kings and the new order of things, from Charles I. till the days of Prince Charles Edward, how faithfully is it reflected in the Jacobite songs and lyrics! At first jaunty, truculent, haughtily anti-plebeian, they then change into a pathetic wail of nameless singers for a lost cause and a departing glory, till at last they lend to the songs of Burns, of Lady Nairne, and of Walter Scott tender tones of imaginative regret for a vanished time.

I suppose no lover of English poetry would willingly

part with what Burns and Cowper have contributed to it. But what would have become of Burns, if, before pouring forth his passion-prompted songs, he had taken counsel with some learned critic, who told him that ere he allowed himself to sing, he must first know the best of what the world had felt and sung before him? Indeed, after he had flung forth in his own vernacular those matchless songs, which have made the whole world his debtor, when he came to know the *literati* of his time, and to read more widely in English literature, he acknowledged that, had he known more, he would have dared less, nor have ventured on such unfrequented by-paths. Wider knowledge, that is, would have paralyzed his singing power.

Again: Cowper was a scholar, and in his youth had seen something of what London could show him. In his manhood, from his Huntingdon seclusion, how much of England's homeliest scenery has he described; how much of England's best life and sentiment at the close of last century has he preserved for us! But had some representative of high criticism come across him, and bidden him, before he essayed his *Task*, know all the best that the world had thought or said on the same subjects, how would the pen have dropped from his sensitive hand, and left the poetic world so much the poorer for his silence!

Gray, on the other hand, had fully laid to heart and acted on the counsels of a refined criticism. He knew whatever of best the world had produced before him. Behind his poetic outcome lay a great effort of thought and criticism, and we have the benefit of it in his scanty and fastidious contribution to English Poetry. I would not willingly underrate the author of the *Elegy* and of the *Ode to Adversity;* but, if the alternative were forced upon us, I do not think that we should be prepared to give up either Burns or Cowper in order to preserve Gray.

It is natural that in a scholarly and academic atmosphere, criticism, knowledge, and appreciation of the best should be highly prized, for this is just that which academic study can give, and which can hardly be got without it. But that which schools and universities cannot give is the afflatus, the native inspiration which originally produced that best. These are powerless to awake the voice of the divine Sibyl, which, " uttering things simple, unperfumed, and unadorned, reaches through myriads of years." If there is one truth which all past experience and all present knowledge teach, it is this : that the creative heat, the imaginative insight, the inspiration, which is the soul of poetry — that all this is something which learning and knowledge may stifle, but cannot generate. That talk about the Muses, and that invocation of their aid, which has long grown vapid and wearisome to us, had in its origin a real meaning. The μῆνιν ἄειδε, θεά, the earliest poets felt as a fact of experience. Something was given them — whence and how they knew not — only it was not their own invention, but given them from without, or from above, in some unnamable way, and utter it they must. Since the days of Homer this feeling of an inspiration from within has dwindled, and literary and artistic efforts have tried to do its work, but in vain. Even till this hour, when poetry is genuine, it originates in a high enthusiasm, a noble passion overmastering the soul.

Though the muse has been " shamed so oft by later lyres on earth," that poets now "dare not call her from

her sacred hill," yet we see the sense of a veritable in-
spiration reappear in Milton in a higher form, other, yet
the same. His " Sing, Heavenly Muse," and " Descend
from Heaven, Urania," " The meaning, not the name,
I call," — these are not empty words, as we know from
what he tells us in prose of the manner and the spirit
in which he prepared himself for song.

Philosophers, who, themselves gifted with imagina-
tion, understand its ways of working, acknowledge that
there is about the origin of the poetic impulse some-
thing which defies analysis, — born, not taught, — inex-
plicable, and mysterious. Plato's few words upon this
in the *Ion* are worth all Aristotle's methodical treatise
on Poetry. To quote from that translation which in
our day has made Plato an English classic, we have
Socrates saying to Ion : " All good poets, epic as well
as lyric, compose their beautiful poems, not as works of
art, but because they are inspired and possessed. . . .
For the poet is a light and winged and holy thing, and
there is no invention in him until he has been inspired.
. . . When he has not attained to this state he is power-
less, and unable to utter his oracles. Many are the
noble words in which poets speak of the actions which
they record, but they do not speak of them by any rules
of art ; they are inspired to utter that to which the
Muse impels them, and that only."

Plato further recognizes the truth that, though the
first and original inspiration is in the poet, yet all who
sympathize with and can rightly interpret him must be
partakers of the same inspiration, though in a subdued
and ever-lessening measure. Thus it is that he " com-
pares the poets and their interpreters to a chain of mag-
netic rings, suspended from one another and from a

magnet. The magnet is the muse, and the large ring which comes next in order is the poet himself; then follow the rhapsodes and actors " (the critics, we might modernize it), " who are rings of inferior power ; and the last ring of all is the spectator" (or the reader of the poems). In these few sentences, making allowance for their antique form, there is more insight into the origin, or first awakening of the poetic impulse, than in anything contained in Aristotle's *Poetics.*

It is a long descent from Plato to Lord Macaulay : but I take the latter as one of the most business-like of modern literary men, who could never be accused of being a victim to transcendentalism. Hear what he says in the introduction to his *Essay on Dryden :* " The man who is best able to take a machine to pieces, and who most clearly comprehends the manner of its working, will be the man most competent to form another machine of similar power. In all the branches of physical and moral science which admit of perfect analysis, he who can resolve will be able to combine. But the analysis which criticism can effect of poetry is necessarily imperfect. One element must forever elude its researches ; and that is the very element by which poetry is poetry."

It is the old story. The botanist can take the flower to pieces, show you the stamens, pistil, calyx, corolla, and all the rest of it, but can he put them together again ? Can he grasp or recreate the mysterious thing which held them together and made the living flower ? No ; the life has escaped his grasp. Now this quick life, this vivid impulse, this unnamable essence which makes poetry to be poetry — these, learning, criticism, study, reflection, may kill, as I have said, but cannot create.

By the flashes of uncritical genius the world has gained its finest truths. When it is working at full power, it leaves behind criticism and all her works. At those moments when it is least conscious, it achieves most. In such rapt moods the poet, carried far out of the ken even of his own intelligence, goes " voyaging through strange seas of thought alone," and overtakes new views, descries far heights of beauty and sublimity, which he in his sober moments can little account for. These are the far fetches of genius, which lie so much beyond its own forecast or deliberate aim, that it is only long after, if ever, that it comes to understand what it has done. This is that which is called truly inspiration.

When Milton flung forth these lines —

> "How sweetly did they float upon the wings
> Of silence through the empty vaulted night,
> At every fall smoothing the raven down
> Of darkness till it smiled,"

do you suppose he could have quite explained his imagery ? If we could call up Shakespeare and place before him the various theories about Hamlet, do you think he would own any one of them as his own? Would he not rather tell you with a smile that those clever fellows, the critics, knew far better than himself the thing that he meant to do ?

But if the spontaneous impulse to soar must be delayed till the poet has looked round and ascertained what soarings have been before attempted, and how much they have achieved, he will wait till the impulse is spent, the buoyancy gone. By all means let young poets cultivate themselves and their powers of expression — take in as much knowledge as they can carry, without being oppressed by it. All the learning they can get, if it be really assimilated, if the native spring of spirit be not overborne, will come in to enrich and expand their imaginative range. But the knowledge, before it can be otherwise than hurtful, must have passed into their being, become entirely spontaneous, a part of themselves. If it be laborious learning, culture always conscious of what other poets have done, it may produce poetry which may please critics, not passion or fervid thought, which will reach the hearts of men. There is no little danger at the present day lest the poetic side of men's natures die of surfeit, be overlaid with a plethora of past literature. In common with many others, I am somewhat weary of criticism. We have heard the best of what she has to say, and would now beg her to stand aside for a season, and give spontaneity its turn.

Men of mature age, academic and literary persons, will probably be found giving other counsel, advising young genius to wait and learn. But these are not the poet's best advisers. If he desires to reach the great mass even of intelligent men, he must remember that they are not learned, and are not to be moved by poetry whose characteristic is its learning. Men who have passed forty will, no doubt, counsel caution and criticism ; but the far larger portion of the world are on the other side of forty, and we elders must regretfully admit that it is among these the poets find their best and most sympathetic audience.

It was not by vast stores of book-knowledge, not by great critical efforts, that the long line of England's poets has been maintained — that unbroken succession which has lasted so many centuries. To them the actual life of men, the face of nature, their own hearts,

were their first and best teachers. To know these in-
timately was their discipline — supplied their material.
Books and book-learning were to them a quite subordi-
nate affair. But the demand for a great critical effort
as the prerequisite of creation seems to put that first
which is not first, and to disallow that instinctive knowl-
edge of man and of nature which is the poet's breath of
life. This view of things probably originates in the
conception of Goethe as the typical poet of the modern
era. Whatever worth it may have in itself, one thing is
certain, that, had it been believed by former generations,
English poetry would have been other, certainly not
better, than it is.

However various the phases of our poetry have been,
they have never been born of criticism, except perhaps
in the days of Pope. If we may judge from all the
past of poetry, criticism must be subordinate to passion,
science to temperament, else the result will be frigid and
without vitality. It remains forever true in the region
of poetry that "immortal works are those which issue
from personal feeling, which the spirit of system has not
petrified."

These last words are from a paper in a recent *Quar-
terly Review*, entitled "A French Critic on Goethe." I
had written nearly all the foregoing before I read that
paper, and when I read it I found in it remarkable con-
firmation of the views I had been trying to express. No
one could doubt the hand from which that paper came;
and, since its first appearance, it has been acknowledged
as Mr. Arnold's. Both the French critic and his Eng-
lish commentator agree in the opinion that of all Goe-
the's works the First Part of *Faust* is his masterpiece.
And the reason they give is this: that, "while it has

the benefit of Goethe's matured powers of thought, of
his command over his materials, of his mastery in plan-
ning and expressing, it possesses an intrinsic richness,
color, and warmth. Having been early begun, *Faust*
has preserved many a stroke and flash out of the days
of its author's fervid youth."

Both the French critic and his commentator agree
that after this " a gradual cooling down of the poetic
fire " is visible, "that in his later works the man of re-
flection has overmastered the man of inspiration." The
conclusion to which the *Quarterly* Reviewer comes on
the whole is that Goethe's preëminence comes not from
his being "the greatest of modern poets," but from his
being "the clearest, largest, most helpful thinker of
modern times." Exactly so. Nothing could more con-
firm what I have been urging throughout than this esti-
mate of Goethe endorsed by two so eminent authorities.
In him we see on a great scale exemplified the tendency
of the critic to mar the poet, of " science to overcome
individuality, of reflection to chill poetic genius, of philo-
sophic thought to prevail over the poetry of passion and
of nature, of the spirit of system to crush or petrify per-
sonal feelings." And this is one of the mental maladies
from which the intellectual health of our times has most
to dread.

There are places where it might be unwise to hazard
thoughts like these, lest we should discourage the im-
portant duty of self-cultivation. But this is not one
of those places. Is there not truth in the charge that
to those who live here permanently there is something
in the atmosphere of the place, call it criticism or what
you will, which too much represses individuality?

I know that Oxford has many aspects, — wears very

different looks, as seen from this side or from that. In the early years of discipleship, or viewed from a distance down long vistas of memory, or revisited after years of absence, she appears, what she truly is, the nurse of all high thoughts, the home of all pure and generous affections. To those who are quite young there is perhaps no spot of English ground which sinks so deeply into the seats of emotion, or enters so intimately into all their study of imagination.

But it is otherwise with older residents. For them the golden exhalations of the dawn are soon turned into the gray light of common day. For those on this side of graduation, whose manhood is harnessed into the duties of the place, what between the routine of work and the necessity of taking a side in public questions, and, above all, the atmosphere of omnipresent criticism in which life is lived here, original production becomes almost an impossibility. Any one who may feel within him the stirring of creative impulse, if he does not wish to have it frozen at its source, must, before he can create, leave the air of academic circles and the distracting talk of literary sets, and retire with his own impulses and thoughts into some solitude, where the din of these will not reach him.

Will young poets excuse me if I make use of a very homely image? They say that among the pea-fowl, the mother-bird, when she would rear her young, retires from farm and thoroughfare, and seeks the most silent places of the wood. There she sits, days and weeks, unseen even by her mate. At length, when the brooding-time is over, and her young are fully fledged, she walks forth some summer morning, followed by her brood, and displays them with pride before human homes. This, I take it, truly represents the way that poetic genius instinctively takes. Vital poems, whether short or long, slight or serious, are born ; not amid literary talk, but in silence and solitude. Goethe, I believe, said that he never could create anything, if he told his purpose to any one before it was completed.

There may be some in this place to whom it will be given to shape the poetry of a new time. If criticism be needed, this generation has done that work to satiety. It has edited and reëdited every great poet; found out all that can be known about each, and a good deal that cannot be known ; has counted and scheduled the percentage of light endings and of weak endings, of end-stopt and run-on verses in every play, has compared, corrected, annotated, with most praiseworthy, and sometimes with most wearisome exactness. It is surely time that this work should cease. For the coming generation we may hope some higher work remains to do — to enjoy the old and to create the new — to use whatever valuable result has been achieved by the laborious processes, and to burn up the heaps of rubbish in a fresh flame of creative impulse. The critic has had his day ; it is time the poet once more should have his. And if the national heart continues to beat strong, if the nation is fired with great, not with ignoble aims, then poets will arise to set to music the people's aspirations, and will " leave the critics well behind them."

If any young spirit feels touched from within by the poetic breath, let him not be scared by the oft-heard saying — that the day of poetry is past. Macaulay indeed has maintained that as " knowledge extends and as the reason develops itself," the imaginative arts decay. It is the literary creed of Mr. Carlyle, several times announced, that the poetic form nowadays is an anachronism, that plain prose alone is welcome to him, that he grudges to see men of genius employ themselves in fiction and versifying, while reality stands in such need of interpreters. " Reality is, as I always say, God's unwritten poem, which it needs precisely that a human genius should write and make intelligible to his less gifted brothers." To discuss these views fully would require several lectures, not the end of one. I can now but throw out a few suggestions.

So far is it from being true that reason has put out imagination, that perhaps there never was a time when reason so imperatively called imagination to her aid, and when imagination entered so largely into all literary and even into scientific products. Imaginative thought, which formerly expressed itself but rarely except in verse, now enters into almost every form of prose except the barely statistical. Indeed, the boundary lines between prose and poetry have become obliterated, as those between prose and verse have become more than ever rigid. Consider how wide is the range of thought over which imagination now travels, how vast is the work it is called upon to do.

Even in the most rigorous sciences it is present, whenever any discoverer would pass beyond the frontiers of the known, and encroach on the unknown, by some wise question, some penetrating guess, which he labors afterwards by analysis to verify. This is what they call the scientific imagination.

Again, what is it that enables the geologist, from the contortions of strata, a few scratchings on rock-surfaces, and embedded fossils here and there, to venture into " the dark backward and abysm of time," and recon-

4

struct and repeople extinct continents? What but a great fetch of imaginative power?

Again, history, which a former age wrote or tried to write with imagination rigorously suppressed, has of late rediscovered what Herodotus and Tacitus knew, that unless a true historic imagination is present to breathe on the facts supplied by antiquary and chronicler, a dead past cannot be made to live again. A dim and perilous way doubtless it is, leading by many a side-path down to error and illusion, but one which must be trod by the genuine historian, who would make the pale shadows of the past live.

It is the same with every form of modern criticism — with the investigations into the origins of language, of society, and of religion. These studies are impossible without an ever-present power of imagination, both to suggest hypotheses and to vivify the facts which research has supplied.

It thus has come to pass that, in the growing subdivision of mental labor, imagination is not only not discredited, but is more than ever in demand. So far from imagination receding, like the Red Indian, before the advance of criticism and civilization, the truth is that expanding knowledge opens ever new fields for its operation. Just as we see the produce of our coal and iron mines used nowadays for a hundred industries, to which no one dreamt of applying them a century ago, so imagination enters to-day into all our knowledge, in ways undreamt of till now. More and more it is felt that, till the fire of imagination has passed over our knowledge, and brought it into contact with heart and spirit, it is not really living knowledge, but only dead material.

You say, perhaps, if imagination is now employed in

almost every field of knowledge, does any remain over to express itself in poetry or metrical language? Is any place left for what we used to know as poetry proper — thought metrically expressed? I grant that the old limits between prose and poetry tend to disappear. If poetry be the highest, most impassioned thoughts conveyed in the most perfect melody of words, we have many prose writers who, when at their best, are truly poets. Every one will recall passages of Jeremy Taylor's writings, which are, in the truest sense, not oratory, but poetry. Again, of how many in our time is this true? You can all lay your finger on splendid descriptions of nature by Mr. Ruskin, which leave all sober prose behind, and flood the soul with imagery and music like the finest poetry.

As the highest instance of all I would name some of Dr. Newman's Oxford sermons. Many of these, instinct as they are with high spiritual thought, quivering with suppressed but piercing emotion, and clothed in words so simple, so transparent, that the very soul shines through them, suggest, as only great poems do, the heart's deepest secrets, and in the perfect rhythm and melody of their words seem to evoke new powers from our native language.

If, then, so much imagination is drained off to enrich other fields of literature ; if, moreover, that peculiar combination of thought and emotion, which is the essence of poetry, now often finds vent in the form of prose, what place, you may ask, still remains for the use of metrical language? Is verse, as a vehicle of thought, any longer genuine and natural? Is it not an anachronism, a mere imitation of a past mode? Have not the old channels which poetry used to fill now gone dry?

Perhaps we may say that it can hardly be denied that some of the old channels are dry, some of the early forms of poetry are not likely to be revivified. Old civilizations do not naturally give birth to epics. Such as they do produce are apt to be not of the genuine, but rather of the imitative sort. Again, of the drama, in its poetic form, it may well be doubted whether it has not gone into abeyance ; whether the world, at least this æon of it, will see another revival of the drama as a living power. Its place has been in a great measure usurped by the modern novel (I wish they would condense their three volumes into one) — the modern novel, which depicts character, groups of men and women, their attitudes, looks, gestures, conversations, all, in fact, which reveals life with a power that versified dialogue can hardly rival. All this may be conceded. And yet there remain large and deep ranges of experience which, just because they are so deep and tender, find no natural and adequate outlet, but in some form of melodious and metrical language. Whether this shall be done by original genius, pouring new life and rhythm into the old and well-used metres, or whether, by striking out novel and untried forms of metre, which may better chime with new cadences of thought, I shall not venture to say.

You ask for reality, not fiction and filigree-work. Well, then, there are many of the most intense realities, of which poetic and melodious words are the fittest, I might say the only vehicle. There is the poetry of external nature ; not merely to paint its outward shows to the eye, but to reproduce those feelings which its beauty awakens. There are those aspects of history in which great national events kindle our patriotism, or striking individual adventures thrill us with a sense of romance. There is the whole world of the affections, those elements of our being which earliest wake and latest die. The deep home affections, the yearnings for those whom no more we see, the unutterable dawnings on the soul, as it looks towards the Eternal, — these which are the deepest, most permanent things in man, though the least utterable in forms of the understanding, how are they to be even hinted at — expressed they can never be — except in a form of words the most rhythmical and musical man can attain to ? All this side of things, which more and more as life advances becomes to us the most real one — to this, poetry is the only form of human speech which can do justice.

Again, there is the wide region of reflective or meditative thought, when the poet, brooding over the great realities of time and eternity, the same which engage the philosopher and the theologian, muses till his heart is hot within him, and the fire burns, and the burning at last finds vent in song. Of the deepest poets it has been truly said that they are

"Haunted forever by the Eternal mind."

To the poet in his brooding mood how often has there been vouchsafed a quick, penetrating glance, a satisfying insight into the heart of things, such as sage and theologian have never attained ? For instance, how many philosophies do we not find condensed into these simple, sincere lines of a poet whom Balliol College reared, and some still there know ? —

"And yet when all is thought and said,
The heart still overrules the head ;
Still what we hope we must believe,
And what is given us receive ;

> Must still believe, for still we hope
> That in a world of larger scope,
> What here is faithfully begun
> Will be completed, not undone."

Lastly, there is religious poetry, the poetry that gives utterance to faith, to devotion, to aspiration. In these, as poetry found its earliest, so, I believe, it will find its latest springs of inspiration. Not only as the life of individual men, but as the life of the race advances, the deepest thoughts, the most earnest emotions, gather round religion and the secrets of which it alone holds the key. And the more we realize the inability of the logical faculty to grasp the things of faith, how it cannot breathe in the unseen world, and falls back paralyzed when it tries to enter it, the more we shall feel that some form of song or musical language is the best possible adumbration of spiritual realities and the emotions they awaken. An expansion of the field of religious poetry this century has seen, since the time when Wordsworth approached the world of nature with a sensitive love and reverence till then unknown, feeling himself and making others feel that the visible light that is in the heavens is akin to the light that lighteth every man, both coming from one centre. This unifying feeling, this more religious attitude seen in men's regard towards the visible world, may we not believe it to be the prelude of a wider unity of feeling, which shall yet take in, not nature only, but all truth and all existence? And if some of our most earnest poets since Wordsworth's day, feeling too sensitively the unbridged gulf between things seen and things unseen, have wasted themselves on intractable problems, and sung too habitually "in sad perplexèd minors;" yet this shall not disturb our faith that the blue heaven is behind the clouds, and that that heaven is the poet's rightful home. As growing time gives men more clearly to discern the real harmony between thought and fact, between the ideal and the actual world, the clouds will pass off the poet's soul, and leave him to sing aloud a free rejoicing worship.

In the hope of that day we live, and, though we may not see it, yet we nothing doubt that come it will.

CHAPTER III.

THE SPIRITUAL SIDE OF POETRY.

WE have been lately told on good authority that it is characteristic of the English poets that they deal mainly with "that great and inexhaustible thing called Life, and that the greatest of them deal with it most widely, most powerfully, most profoundly." Further, it is added that in dealing with life they must deal with it morally; for human life is moral to the very core. Exactly so! What man is, what he does, what he should do, what he may become, what he may enjoy, admire, venerate, love, what he may hope, what is his ultimate destiny, — these things are never absent from the thoughts of great poets, and that not by accident, but from their very essence as poets.

What Horace said of Homer holds even more emphatically of other great ones in the poetic brotherhood : —

> "Qui, quid sit pulchrum, quid turpe, quid utile, quid non,
> Rectius ac melius Chrysippo et Crantore dicit."

As the late Professor Conington translates the lines —

> "What's good, what's bad, what helps, what hurts, he shows,
> Better in verse than Crantor does in prose."

Not that they prove, moralize, or preach; but we learn from being in their company, from the atmosphere which they breathe, and to which they admit us, — learn perhaps more readily, though indirectly, than from the lessons of professed philosophers, moralists, and even preachers.

This truth, that the moral is the essential aspect of life, and that in it poetry has its true home, we are glad to hear reëchoed from quarters whence we should hardly have looked for it. To many it had seemed so obvious that it scarcely needed to be stated — so mere a truism as to be almost a platitude. But of late the theory that poetry and all art is morally indifferent; that vice, if only it be artistically treated; that unmoral or even immoral sides of life, if imaginatively rendered, are as well fitted for poetry as what we have been accustomed to regard as the truest and highest views, — all this has been so often reiterated, and sometimes with so much ability, that one was almost tempted to fancy that this might be the coming faith, and that to hold any other was an old-world prejudice.

Let us then take courage, and accept for the time, as settled, the old conviction that the moral substance of human nature is the soil on which true poetry grows, that the poetry of life must be moral, since life itself is essentially moral. But what do we mean by the moral substance of life ? What is it that gives moral tone and color to the life of each individual man ? Is it not the things he admires, loves, longs for ? the sum, in short, of the desires, affections, hopes, aims, by which he lives ? These make up the moral substance of each man's life ; these create the spiritual air he breathes. But objects, which are adequate to the finer affections, cannot be found within the mere world of sense ; phenomena, however rich and varied, are not enough for any living, feeling man. Even persons, however loved, cannot satisfy him, if these are thought of as only transitory. Some foundation the heart needs to rest on, which shall be permanent, secure, and stable. Where is this element to be found? Not in the maxims of moralists, nor in the abstractions of the schools. " I cannot cordialize with a mere *ens rationis*," said the late Alexander Knox ; and so would say every man with a warm heart throbbing within him. Leave moral abstractions, and categorical imperatives, to the philosopher, who has lived so long by mere intellect, that everything else is dried out of him. But man, as man, needs something more quick and vital, something at least as living as his own beating heart, something akin to his own personality, to commune with. And if man, much more the true poet, who has within him all the elements that make man, only these carried to their highest power.

The truth is that poetry has this in common with religion, that it lives by that which eye hath not seen, nor ear heard. Deny this, and it dies ; confine it to mere appearances, whether phenomena of the outward sense, or of the inner consciousness, and it is dried up at its very source. Religion of course turns the eye directly on the unseen, and the spiritual objects that are there ; poetry, on the other hand, finds its materials in the things seen ; but it cannot deal with these imaginatively, cannot perform on them its finer function, until it draws upon the unseen, and penetrates things visible with a light from behind the veil. So far then poetry and religion are akin, that both hold of the unseen, the supersensible. But we must not press the resemblance too far. Both, it is true, draw upon the invisible, but they turn towards it different sides of our nature, apprehend it by different faculties, use it for different ends. Religion lays hold on the unseen world mainly through conscience and the spiritual affections, and seeks to brmg all that it apprehends to bear on life, conduct, and the soul's health. On this practical end it insists, unless it is a merely sentimental religion. On the other hand, poetry, as poetry, has nothing to do with conduct and action. Contemplation is its aim and end. It longs to see the vision of the beautiful, the noble, and the true ; and that spectacle, when granted, suffices it. Beyond the contemplation of beauty and goodness it does not seek to go. Herein lie the weakness and the temptation not of actual poets only, but of all artistic persons. They feel keen delight in the sight of things noble, are emotionally thrilled by them, strive to find adequate expression for them, and are content to end there. A part of their being, their imagination and emotions, touches the ideal, but their will remains unaffected. Their ideals do not necessarily rule their life. They are content to be sayers of fine things, not doers of them. This, I suppose, is the moral of that early poem of the Laureate's, *The Palace of Art*. Hence perhaps arises the unsatisfactoriness of the lives of so many

"Mighty poets in their misery dead."

The splendid vision they saw contrasts too sadly with the actual lives they lived.

But without pursuing this train of thought, we may observe, that, whenever a poet has attained to a really high impassioned strain, it has not been in virtue of what mere eye or ear discovered, but because, while he saw things visible, and heard things audible, he was haunted by the sense that there was in them something more behind ; and just in proportion as he felt and hinted this something more, the work he has done has risen in true nobility. This will appear more plainly, if we look at the two great fields in which the poet works, the world of Nature, and the world of man.

I. With regard to the first of these, it might seem that any one who has to deal with the visible world should confine himself to its visible features, and not meddle with anything beyond. But a little reflection will show that it is not so. For what is it in Nature that especially attracts the poet, that he is gifted beyond other men to feel, to interpret, and express? Is it not the beauty that is in the face of Nature? Now consider what this beauty is, what it means, how it is apprehended. It is a very wonderful thing, both about ourselves and the world we live in, that, as in our own inward nature, to the gift of life has been added the sense of pleasure, so in the outward world, to the usefulness of it has been added its beauty. The use and the beauty are two aspects of Nature, distinct, yet inseparable. This thought, though not new, has been brought out with such peculiar power by the late Canon Mozley, that in some sort he has made it his own. In that sermon of his on Nature, well known, I doubt not, to many here, he says, "The beauty is just as much a part of Nature as the use; they are only different aspects of the self-same facts." The same laws which make the usefulness make also the beauty. "It is not that the mechanism is painted over, in order to disguise the deformity of machinery, but the machinery itself is the painting; the useful laws compose the spectacle. . . . All that might seem the superfluities of Nature are only her most necessary operations under another view, her ornament is but another aspect of her work; and in the very act of laboring as a machine, she also sleeps as a picture." In the physical world, the laws, their working, and their use, are the domain of science. The beauty which accompanies their working, — this is the special object of the poet, and of the painter.

But consider what this beauty is. Of this that certainly is true which Bishop Berkeley asserted of all outward things — its "esse" is "percipi." Unless it is felt, perceived by an intelligent soul, it does not exist. The forms, the motions, the colors of Nature, taken alone, do not constitute beauty. Not till these enter in and pass through the medium of a feeling heart can the beauty be said to exist. You cannot find it by any mere search into the physical facts, however far back you press your analysis of them. The height, the depth, the expanse, the splendor, the gloom, — these do not in themselves contain it, do not account for it, without the presence of a soul to perceive and feel them, any more than the instrument accounts for the music, without the musician's hand to touch it.

The feeling for the beauty by which the visible world is garmented ranges through many gradations, from a mere animal pleasure up to what may be called a spiritual rapture.

The first and lowest is the mere exhilaration of the animal spirits, stimulated by fresh air, fine weather, blue sky, fine views of sea and land. This need not necessarily be more than an animal enjoyment, an excitement of the bodily nerves, unaccompanied by any fine emotion, or any high thought.

The second stage is that enjoyment which æsthetic natures feel at the sight of gorgeous coloring, or delicate tints, or symmetry of form and outline, the beautiful curve of clouds, their silver lines or rich transparencies. One is almost at a loss to say whether, in this delight, exquisite as it often is, there is necessarily present any spiritual element or not.   Perhaps there is no poet in whom pure sensuous delight in the colors and forms of nature is more prominent than in Keats.   Take his *Ode on Autumn*, for instance.   Here all the sights and sounds of a Devonshire autumn are received into a most responsive soul, and rendered back in most exquisite artistic form.   Or take a well known-passage from the same poet's *Eve of St. Agnes :* —

> " A casement high and triple-arched there was,
>   All garlanded with carven imageries,
>   Of fruits, and flowers, and bunches of knot-grass,
>   And diamonded with panes of quaint device
>   Innumerable of stains and splendid dyes,
>   As are the tiger-moth's deep-damasked wings;
>   And in the midst, 'mong thousand heraldries,
>   And twilight saints, and dim emblazonings,
>   A shielded scutcheon blushed with blood of queens and kings.

> "Full on this casement shone the wintry moon,
>   And threw warm gules on Madeline's fair breast,
>   As down she knelt for heaven's grace and boon;
>   Rose-bloom fell on her hands, together prest,
>   And on her silver cross soft amethyst,
>   And on her hair a glory, like a saint:
>   She seemed a splendid angel, newly drest,
>   Save wings, for heaven: Porphyro grew faint;
>   She knelt so pure a thing, so free from mortal taint."

It is difficult to believe that any poet could enjoy, as Keats did, the sensuous beauty which is in the face of Nature, and in works of Art, and not be carried farther, and led to ask, what does this visible beauty mean, what hint does it give about that universe of which it forms so essential a part?

This leads to the third stage in the upward ascent towards the higher perception of visible beauty.   This is what may be called the moral stage, when some scene of the external world not so much imparts sensuous delight, as awakens within us moral emotion. That it is natural for the outward world to do this is seen in the fact that all languages employ moral or emotional terms to describe, not only the impressions which a scene creates, but the scene itself. Landscapes are universally spoken of as cheerful or melancholy, peaceful or wild, pensive, solemn, or awful. Terms, you will observe, all taken, not from physical, but from moral things. No physical features, height, depth, expanse, contain these qualities in themselves, but they awaken these feelings in us, — why, we know not, but they do. These qualities are not in outward things taken by themselves, nor are they wholly in the soul; but when the outward object and the soul meet, then these emotions awake within us. They are a joint result of the soul of man and the objects fitted to produce them coming in contact. Hence arises that mystical feeling about Nature which forms so large an element in modern poetry; and which, when genuine and not exaggerated, adds to poetry a new charm, because it reveals a real truth as to the relation in which Nature and the human soul stand to each other. Of this feeling Wordsworth's poetry is, of course, the great storehouse. As one sample, out of a thousand, of the vivid way in which a scene may be described by the feeling it awakens, rather than by its physical features, take his poem *Glen Almain or the Narrow Glen.*

In this upward gradation the last and highest stage is, when not merely moral qualities are suggested, but something more than these.

In many persons, and not in poets only, a beautiful sunrise, or a gorgeous sunset, or the starry heavens on a cloudless night, create moral impressions, and something more; these sights suggest to them, if vaguely, yet powerfully, the presence of Him from whom come both Nature and the emotions it awakens. The tender lights that fleet over sea and sky are to them

> "signallings from some high land
> Of One they feel, but dimly understand."

As they gaze, they become aware that they are admitted not only to catch a glimpse into the Divine order and beauty, but to stand, for a time, in greater nearness to Him who makes that order and beauty.

The sublime rapture which it is given to some hearts to feel in the presence of such sights is perhaps nowhere more finely rendered than in a passage of the First Book of *The Excursion*, in which Wordsworth describes the feelings of the Young Wanderer, in presence of a sunrise among the mountains : —

> " For the growing youth
> What soul was his, when from the naked top
> Of some bold headland, he beheld the sun
> Rise up, and bathe the world in light! He looked —
> Ocean and earth, the solid frame of earth,
> And ocean's liquid mass, beneath him lay
> In gladness and deep joy.   The clouds were touched,
> And in their silent faces did he read
> Unutterable love!   Sound needed none,
> Nor any voice of joy; his spirit drank
> The spectacle : sensation, soul, and form
> All melted into him; they swallowed up
> His animal being; in them did he live,
> And by them did he live; they were his life.
> In such access of mind, in such high hour
> Of visitation from the living God,
> Thought was not; in enjoyment it expired.
> No thanks he breathed, he proffered no request;
> Rapt into still communion which transcends
> The imperfect offices of prayer and praise,
> His mind was a thanksgiving to the power
> That made him; it was blessedness and love."

In this fine passage, observe, there is little — hardly one expression (only "the solid frame of earth" and "ocean's liquid mass") — that appeals to the outward eye; no shapes of cloud nor gorgeous gildings; only the feelings and aspirations which these awaken in a pure, high-strung soul. Yet these feelings, once set vibrating, call up more vividly than the most elaborate physical description could have done, the whole outward scene — its colors, its shapes, its glory; and how much more besides?

This is, I believe, characteristic of Wordsworth's best descriptions of Nature, — he touches first the soul, the spirit, evokes at once the moods into which they are thrown by Nature's looks, and through the spirit reaches the eye and the senses more powerfully, after a more ethereal fashion, than if these had been directly appealed to. In this and many another such passage of the same poet is seen the truth of that oft-repeated saying of Mr. Ruskin, that "all great art is the expression of man's delight in the work of God." This is true; it is also true that the sight of natural beauty has no tendency, of itself, to make men religious.

II. Poets there have been who have begun with Nature, whose imagination has been first kindled by the sight of her loveliness. But, if they are really powerful as poets, they cannot be content with mere outward Nature alone, but must pass from it inward to the soul of man. Far more commonly, however, poets begin directly with man, and the heart of man. It is there they find the home of their thoughts, the main region of their song. With man, his affections, his fortunes, and his destiny, they deal directly, and at first hand. Nature, if they touch it at all, is to them only as a back-

5

ground, against which the doings and the sufferings of
man, the great human story, are set off. This is seen
especially in the great dramatists, ancient and modern,
from whose works were you to withdraw all the allu-
sions to Nature, though some of their charm would dis-
appear, yet the greater part of it would remain. When
these poets deal directly with human life and individual
character, it holds in this region, not less but more than
in their dealing with Nature, that it is the continual
reference, tacit or expressed, to a higher unseen order
of things, which lends to all their thoughts about man
their profoundest interest and truest dignity.

> "O Life! O Death, O World, O Time!
> O Grave where all things flow,
> 'Tis yours to make our lot sublime
> With your great weight of woe."

Two thoughts there are, which, if once admitted into
the mind, change our whole view of this life, — the be-
lief that this world is but the vestibule of an eternal
state of being; and the thought of Him in whom man
lives here, and shall live forever. These, as they are
the cardinal assumptions of natural religion, so they are
hardly less, though more unconsciously, the ground-tones
which underlie all the strains of the world's highest
poetry. It makes scarcely more difference in the color
of a man's practical life, whether he really believes these
things to be true, than it does in the complexion of a
poet's work. Even those who can in no sense be called
exclusively religious poets, if they grasp life with a
strong hand, are constrained to take in the sense of
something beyond this life. To say this would, a few
years ago, have sounded a truism. To-day it is neces-
sary once more to reassert it. For there have arisen

among us teachers of great power, who would have us believe that, for artistic purposes at least, human life, with its hopes and fears, its affections and devotions, is a thing complete in itself, — that it can maintain its interest and its dignity, even if confined within this visible horizon, concentrated entirely on this earthly existence. In lieu of the old faith, both religious and poetic, which reached beyond the confines of earth, a new illuminating power has been sought, and is assumed to have been found, in duty to our fellow-men, and to them alone. Duty is not allowed to have an unearthly origin, to strike its root in any celestial soil. A piety without God is now, it would seem, to be the sole light vouchsafed to poor mortals yearning for light. It is to supply to sensitive hearts all " high endeavor, pure morality, strong enthusiasm," and whatever consolation may be possible for them. In opposition to this teaching it is maintained that no poet ever yet has made, or ever can make, the most of human life, even poetically, who has not regarded it as standing on the threshold of an invisible world, as supported by divine foundations. This is true not only of such devout singers as Dante, Milton, Spenser, and Wordsworth ; it holds hardly less of other poets, who may at first sight seem to be more absorbed in the merely human side of things.

As one has lately said, " Shakespeare may or may not have been a religious man ; he may or may not have been a Catholic or a Protestant. But whatever his personal views and feelings may have been, the light by which he viewed life was the light of Christianity. The shine, the shadow, and the colors of the moral world he looked upon were all caused or cast by the Christian Sun of Righteousness." There is hardly a great character in his plays, no pitch of passion, no depth of pathos, where the thought of the other world is not present, to add intensity to what is done or suffered in this.

Look at his finest representations of character, men or women, and it will at once appear how true this is. To take some of the best known passages. When Macbeth is on the verge of his dreadful act, the thought of the future world intrudes —

> " that but this blow
> Might be the be-all and the end-all here, —
> But here upon this bank and shoal of time, —
> We 'd jump the life to come."

When Hamlet's thoughts turn towards suicide, **what is** it " gives him pause " but

> " the dread of something after death,
> The undiscovered country,"

where dreams may come to trouble him ? And in the same play, how the sense of the upright judgment hereafter disturbs the guilty king ! —

> " In the corrupted currents of the world
> Offence's gilded hand may shove by justice;
> . . . but 't is not so above:
> There is no shuffling, there the action lies
> In his true nature; and we ourselves compelled,
> Even to the teeth and forehead of our faults,
> To give in evidence."

Again, Henry V., on the night before Agincourt, when he tries to encourage himself with the thought of all the good deeds he has done to make reparation for the sins of himself and his house, is yet forced to feel that there lies a judgment beyond, whose requirements these things cannot meet : —

> " Five hundred poor I have in yearly pay,
> Who twice a day their withered hands hold up

> Toward heaven, to pardon blood ; and I have built
> Two chantries, where the sad and solemn priests
> Sing still for Richard's soul.   More will I do;
> Though all that I can do is nothing worth,
> Since that my penitence comes after all,
> Imploring pardon."

Even Othello in his deadliest mood has yet some Christian forecastings about him.   His words to Desdemona are —

> "If you bethink yourself of any crime,
>   Unreconciled as yet to heaven and grace,
>   Solicit for it straight.   .   .   .
>   I would not kill thy unprepared spirit ;
>   No ; heaven forfend !   I would not kill thy soul,
>   Think on thy sins."

And all that dreadful scene is full of reverberations from beyond the grave, down to those last words of Othello —

> "when we shall meet at compt,
> This look of thine will hurl my soul from heaven,
> And fiends will snatch at it."

All feel the beauty of Shakespeare's heroines, the variety, the naturalness, the perfection of his portraiture of women.   They are in some sense the crowning grace of his finest dramas.   Shakespeare was no stainless knight, as some of his sonnets too surely witness. But whatever he may himself for a time have been, he never lost his high ideal of what woman is, or may be. Differing, as his best female characters differ, from each other, and beautiful as they all are, in this they agree, that, when they are most deeply moved, their religious feeling comes out most naturally and winningly.   Every one must have observed how in all his most attractive heroines, Shakespeare has made prayer to be not a mere formal office, but the language which, in their

deepest emotion, rises spontaneously to their lips.   You
remember how Imogen, had she been allowed to meet
her lover for a parting interview, would

> "have charged him
> At the sixth hour of morn, at noon, at midnight,
> To encounter me with orisons, for then
> I am in heaven for him."

And they are not less warm in their devotion than true
in their theology.   Justice and mercy are ever in their
thoughts, and while they plead for this, they do not for-
get that.   This is seen in the famous speech of Portia,
in which she discourses so eloquently to the Jew of
" the quality of mercy," ending thus : —

> " Consider this,
> That, in the course of justice, none of us
> Should see salvation: we do pray for mercy;
> And that same prayer doth teach us all to render
> The deeds of mercy."

With still greater emphasis Isabel, she whom Shake-
speare calls

> "a thing
> Ensky'd, and sainted, an immortal spirit,"

pleads for her brother : —

> " Why, all the souls that were, were forfeit once ;
> And he, that might the vantage best have took,
> Found out the remedy.   How would you be,
> If He, which is the top of judgment, should
> But judge you as you are ?   O, think on that ;
> And mercy then will breathe within your lips,
> Like man new made."

Observe that Shakespeare refrains from analyzing, as
is common nowadays, those female characters whom he
loves best, and would have us love; he merely presents
them, true women, yet idealized — moving, speaking,
in the most natural and graceful way.   As our great

modern poet has expressed it, he places each before us
in herself,

"A perfect woman, · · ·
And yet a spirit still, and bright
With something of an angel light."

His analysis, as has been said, he keeps for inferior
characters — for Cressida and Cleopatra. But for the
favorites of his imagination, Portia, Perdita, Imogen,
Cordelia, he has too tender a reverence to treat them
so. And the thing to remark here is, that Shakespeare,
who knew the heart so well, when he would represent
in his heroines the truest, tenderest, most womanly
love, cannot express it without stirring the depths of
their religious nature. It may be said that Shakespeare
merely represented feelings dramatically ; we must not
take them for his own personal convictions. Be it so :
but it is something if he, who of all men knew human
nature best, has shown us that those feelings which
touch on the higher unseen world are the deepest and
truest in the human bosom, and are uttered then only
when men or women are most deeply moved. More-
over, as Gervinus has said, the feelings and sentiments
which rise most frequently to the lips of his purest
characters, and are at every turn repeated, may be fairly
taken to be his own.

It is not, however, in his best characters only that this
is seen : to his worst and most abandoned he has given
very distinctly the sense of " the Deity in their own
bosom," — the forecast of a future judgment.

But we need not dwell longer on the sayings of
Shakespeare's best characters, or even on their always
implied, if not expressed, faith that the world is mor-
ally governed. We have but to ask ourselves, Would

the characters of Desdemona or Cordelia have the same meaning for us, if they were merely images painted on a curtain, which concealed nothing behind it, — if the sufferings and wrongs they endured did not stand out against the light of a really existing and eternal right-eousness? What would our feeling be about the whole spectacle of life with all its enigmas, which Shakespeare places before us, if, as we gazed on it, we felt that it was wholly limited by time, and had no eternal issues? How would the purity, the patience, the self-forgetful-ness he represents affect us, if these qualities were merely foam-flakes on the top of the wave —

"A moment white, then gone forever"?

Further: take even the ordinary moral ideas and affections, which are essential portions of human life, and which govern it, — what would they be, what power would they have, if they depended merely on this visible framework of things; if they were not allied to a higher world, from which they come, to which they tend? Conscience, for instance, as honest hearts feel it, and as Shakespeare described it, what has it to do with a merely material system? Or the emo-tion of awe, — what is there in the merely physical world which has any power or right to evoke it? Or love, — even human love, when it is high, pure, and in-tense, — can it stop within merely temporal bounds? is it not borne instinctively onward to seek for its objects a higher, more stable existence, beyond the reach of earthly vicissitudes?

Again, while it is true that even the most common moral ideas and affections, which all men acknowledge, would be stunted and dwarfed if cut off from a spiritual background, there exists a whole order of moral ideas,

which without that background could not exist at all.
There is a whole range of " delicate and fragile forms of
virtue " which could not grow in the air of ordinary
society, yet in which modern poetry has found its finest
material. The sense of sinfulness, with all that it in-
volves, whence do men get it, but from the sense of
One higher and holier than we ? Repentance, with its
family of gentle graces, compassion for the fallen, sym-
pathy with the wretched, sweet humility, — what would
human life, what would modern poetry be, if these
tender yet unearthly graces were withdrawn from them ?
Aspiration, which gives wings to man's best feelings and
bears them heavenward, — where would this be, if the
human heart were denied all access to an eternal world,
and Him who is the life of it ?

These graces, and many more, are plants which have
their root not in any earthly garden, but in that celes-
tial soil, under that serene sky, which is warmed by the
sunshine of the Divine Spirit. Here we touch the
ground of the profoundest inspiration accessible to man.
If, as we are told, poetry is " the suggestion of noble
grounds for the noble emotions," what emotions so
noble, what grounds so elevated, as those to which de-
vout souls are admitted in communion with their Maker ?
This is a subject merely to hint at, not to dwell on here.
When a man who has vitally felt these moods adds to
them the true poetic gift, we then have the best that
human poetry can do. Then only the soul responds
from its deepest depths, then only are elicited in their
fullest compass " the whole mysterious assemblage of
thoughts and feelings " which the heart has within it,
and to which one object alone is adequate. Such po-
etry is reached by Dante, by Milton, and by Words-

worth, when at the height of their inspiration, — those
consecrated spirits among the poets,

"Haunted forever by the eternal mind."

And yet, truth to tell, one can imagine — indeed, the
spirit craves — something that should transcend even
the highest strains which these have uttered, a poetry in
which deep and fervid devotion, winged with high im-
agination, should relieve the soul's yearnings, in a way
which no human language, save the words of Scripture,
has yet attained to.

The philosophies which have been dominant for the
last thirty years have not been favorable to poetry of
this kind. The system of thought which confines all
knowledge to mere appearances, and all belief to things
which can be verified by physical methods, leaves no
place for it. Such poetry cannot live, any more than
religion, on appearances divorced from substance; it
knows not what to make of phenomena unattached; it
imperatively demands that there shall be a substratum
of reality behind those fleeting images of beauty and of
goodness which it contemplates. How strangely this
philosophy works in the region of poetry, how it sets
head and heart, imagination and conviction, at war, in
those who are enslaved by it, is notably seen in the
experience of the late John Stuart Mill, as recorded in
his autobiography. There came, it will be remembered,
a crisis in his life, when the fabric of happiness, which
he had been rearing up for himself and the world, fell
in ruins about him, and he found himself sunk in hope-
less dejection. This result he ascribes to the all-anni-
hilating power of analysis, which alone of his mental
faculties he had cultivated. He asked himself whether,
if all the social ends he had hitherto aimed at were

achieved, their success would really give him inward satisfaction ; and he honestly answered, No ! He then fell into a prolonged despondency, from which for a time nothing could arouse him. Almost the first thing which came to relieve this mental malady was the study of Wordsworth's Poems, especially the *Lyrical Ballads*. In these he seemed to find the medicine that he needed. Expressing, as they did, " states of feeling, and of thought colored by feeling under the excitement of beauty," they seemed to open to him a perennial source " of inward joy, and of sympathetic and imaginative pleasure, which could be shared by all human beings."

But while Mr. Mill accepted and delighted in the imaginative emotions which Wordsworth awakened, true to the philosophy which he had imbibed from his father, he would not accept the spiritual beliefs, which in Wordsworth supported these emotions. But would Wordsworth's poetry have been possible if, as he looked on the spectacle of the natural and moral universe, he had not apprehended behind it

> " the ever-during power,
> And central peace subsisting at the heart
> Of endless agitation " ?

To be a poet and teacher such as Wordsworth is implies not merely the possession of his great poetic powers, but a firm hold of that moral material out of which such poetry is wrought.

Sometimes, of late years, when our summers have been unusually sunless and cold, we have been told that the cause lay in the icebergs, which, detached in spring from the polar ice, and floating southward into the temperate seas, had chilled our atmosphere.

Some such chill has during the last thirty years fallen on much of our poetry, from the influence of negative philosophies. There have been poets amongst us who, if they had not lived under this cold shadow, possessed gifts which might have carried them to far greater heights than they ever reached. As it is, their poetry, whatever its merits may be, has in it no skylark notes, no tones of natural gladness; still less does it attain to that serener joy, which they know, who, having looked sorrow in the face, and gone through dark experiences, have come out on the farther side. These modern poets have nothing to tell of the peace which

> "settles where the intellect is meek."

They know nothing of

> "Melancholy fear subdued by faith,
>   Of blessed consolations in distress ;
>   Of joy in widest commonalty spread."

These things they cannot know ; because the roots of them lie only in spiritual convictions, from which the philosophy they have embraced has wholly estranged them.

The Experience Philosophy, so long in the air, has put on many forms and taken many names. Whether it call itself Phenomenalism, or Positivism, or Agnosticism, or Secularism, in all its phases it is alike chilling to the soul and to soul-like poetry. No doubt it offers to imagination an ideal, but it is an ideal which has no root in reality. With such an ideal, imagination, which is an organ of the true, not of the false, which is intended to vivify truth, not to create the fictitious, can never be satisfied. Imagination, as has been said, is an eagle, whose natural home is the celestial mountains. Unless it knows these to be, not cloud shadows, but veritable hills, whither it can repair and renew its strength, the faculty pines and dies. If it could not believe that the ideal on which it fixes its eyes, with which it strives to interpenetrate the actual, is truth in its highest essence, imagination would be paralyzed, poetry extinct.

But we need not fear any such catastrophe. Negative philosophies may for a time prevail; but they cannot ultimately suppress the soul, or stifle vivid intuitions which flash up from its depth and witness to its celestial origin. Those "gentle ardors from above," which in better moments visit men, it is the privilege of poetry to seize, and to clothe forever in forms of perfect beauty.

To conclude. There are many ways of looking at life, and each way has an ideal, and a poetry appropriate to it.

There is the view which looks on the world as a place for physical enjoyment, and its ideal is perfect health, bodily vigor, and high animal spirits. And there is a poetry answering to this view, though not a very exalted poetry.

Again, there are views which make intellectual truth, or at least perfect æsthetic beauty, their aim; and under the power of these ideals, poetry no doubt rises to a much higher level. But as such views leave out the deeper part of man, they do not adequately interpret life, or permanently satisfy the heart.

Some there are who, having tried life, and not found in it what they expected, have grown disappointed and cynical, or even defiant and rebellious. And these moods have found poetic utterance in every age, and in every variety of tone. But the poets who have lent their gift to express these feelings only have not much benefited mankind.

Yet others there are who, having looked below the surface, have early learned that, if the world is not meant to give absolute enjoyment, if pain and sorrow are indeed integral parts of it, it yet contains within it gracious reliefs, remedies, alleviations ; and that for many sensitive hearts one of the alleviations is poetry. " We live under a remedial system ; " and poetry, rightly used, not only helps to interpret this system, but itself combines with the remedial tendencies.

Again, there are high-toned spirits which regard the world as a scene made to give scope for moral heroism. Devotion to some object out from self, — to friendship, to country, to humanity, — each of these is a field in which poetry finds full exercise, and on which it sheds back its own consecration. But neither of these last views, noble as they are, can by itself withstand the shock of circumstance, unless it is secured on a spiritual anchorage. The poet who has himself laid hold of the spiritual world, and the objects that are there, is especially fitted to help men to do this. While, in virtue of that insight which great poets have, he reads to men their own thoughts and aspirations, and " comforts and strengthens them by the very reading," he lets down on them a light from above which transfigures them, touches springs of immortality that lie buried within, and sets them murmuring ; opens avenues for the soul into endless existence. Before men, overborne by things seen, he sets an ideal which is real, — an object not for intellect and imagination only, but for the affections, the conscience, the spirit, for the whole of man. When their hearts droop he bids them

> " look abroad,
> And see to what fair countries they are bound."

His voice is a continual reminder that, whether we think of it or not, the celestial mountains are before us, and thither lies our true destiny. And he is the highest poet who keeps this vision most steadily before himself, and, by the beauty of his singing, wakens others to a sense of it.

CHAPTER IV.

THE POET A REVEALER.

HAZLITT has somewhere said that "genius is some strong quality in the mind, aiming at and bringing out some new and striking quality in nature." The same thought seems to have possessed Coleridge, when, in the third volume of *The Friend*, he labors to reconcile Bacon's insistence on observation and experiment, as the tests of truth, with Plato's equal insistence on the truth of ideas, independent of experience. In the " prudens quaestio," says Coleridge, which the discoverer puts to nature, he is unconsciously feeling after and anticipating some hidden law of nature ; and that he does so feel after it till he finds it is in virtue of some mysterious kinship between the guess of the discoverer's mind and the operations of nature.

In the physical world, we observe that those guesses of genius, which are the parents of discovery, are born in gifted minds, here or there, just when some new invention or discovery is required to carry on the course of human affairs. The mariner's compass, whoever may have been its discoverer, was introduced into Europe the century before Vasco da Gama and Columbus undertook their voyages, and, as it would seem, to enable them to do so. Newton wrought out his system of Fluxions, and published his *Principia*, with its announcement of the law of gravitation, at a time when physical inquiry must have remained at a standstill, if these discoveries had been withheld. In the last generation James Watt's great invention, and, within living memory, Robert Stephenson's, appeared just at a time when society was ready to assume a new phase, but could not have assumed it, till these discoveries were perfected.

But there are other social changes, more impalpable, but not less real, more subtle, but piercing deeper, than the physical ones. These last, wrought on the world's surface, are visible and tangible, and all can appreciate them. But the invisible changes wrought in men's minds, the revolutions in sentiment which distinguish one age from another, are so silent and so subtle, that the mere practical man entirely ignores or despises them. Mere sentiment, forsooth! Who cares for sentiment? But let the practical man know, those sentiments he despises are in human affairs more potent than all the physical inventions he so much venerates.

How these changes of feeling arise, from what hidden springs they come, who shall say? But that they do come forth, and make themselves widely felt, and in the end change the whole face of society, none can doubt. They come, as changes in the weather come, as the sky turns from bright to dark, and from dark to bright, by reason of causes which we cannot penetrate, but with effects which all must feel.

"The thoughts they had were the parents of the deeds they did ; their feelings were the parents of their thoughts." So it always has been, and shall be. In the movements of man's being, the first and deepest thing is the sentiment which possesses him, the emotional and moral atmosphere which he breathes. The causes which ultimately determine what this atmosphere shall be are too hidden, too manifold and complex, for us to grasp ;

6

but, among the human agents which produce them, none are more powerful than great poets. Poets are the rulers of men's spirits more than the philosophers, whether mental or physical. For the reasoned thought of the philosopher appeals only to the intellect, and does not flood the spirit; the great poet touches a deeper part of us than the mere philosopher ever reaches, for he is a philosopher and something more, — a master of thought; but it is inspired thought, thought filled and made alive with emotion. He makes his appeal, not to intellect alone, but to all that part of man's being in which lie the springs of life.

If it be true that

    " We live by admiration, hope, and love," —

that the objects which we admire, love, hope for, determine our character, make us what we are, — then it is the poet, more than any other, who holds the key of our inmost being. For it is he who, by virtue of inspired insight, places before us, in the truest, most attractive light, the highest things we can admire, hope for, love. And this he does mainly by unveiling some new truth to men, or, which is the same thing, by so quickening and vivifying old and neglected truths, that he makes them live anew. To do this last needs as much prophetic insight as to see new truths for the first time.

This is the poet's highest office — either to be a revealer of new truth, or an unveiler of truths forgotten or hidden from common eyes. There is another function which poets fulfil, — that of setting forth in appropriate form the beauty which all see, and giving to thoughts and sentiments in which all share beautiful and attractive expression. This last is the poet's artistic function, and that which some would assign to him as his only one.

These two aspects of the poet, the prophetic and the artistic, coexist in different proportions in all great poets; in one the prophetic insight predominates, in another the artistic utterance. In the case of any single poet, it may be an interesting question to determine in what proportions he possesses each of these two qualities. But, without attempting this, it will be enough to show by examples of some of the greatest poets, ancient and modern, that to each has been granted some domain, of which he is the supreme master; that to each has been vouchsafed a special insight into some aspect of truth, a knowledge and a love of some side of life or of nature, not equally revealed to any other; that he has taken this home to his heart, and made it his own peculiar possession, and then uttered it to the world, in a more vivid and a more attractive way than had ever been done before.

To begin with Homer. It was no merely artistic power, but a true and deep insight into human nature, which enabled him to be the first of his race, as far as we know, who saw clearly, and drew with firm hand, those great types of heroic character which have lived ever since in the world's imagination. Achilles, Ulysses, Nestor, Ajax, Hector, Andromache, Priam — these, while they are ideal portraits, are at the same time permanent, outstanding forms of what human nature is. The Homeric vision of Olympus and its immortals, splendid though it be, was still but transient. It had no root in the deepest seats of human nature. For even in his own land a time came when, in the interest of purer morality, Plato wished to dethrone Homer's gods. But his delineation of heroes and heroines remains true to human feeling as it exists to-day. Even

Shakespeare, when, in his *Troilus and Cressida*, he took up those world-old characters, and touched them anew, was constrained to preserve the main outlines as Homer had left them. It is this permanent truthfulness and consistency in the human characters of the *Iliad* which makes one believe, in spite of all the critics, that one master hand was at the centre of the work, drawing those consistent portraits, real yet ideal, which no agglomeration of bards could ever have achieved.

Again, Æschylus and Sophocles were, each in his day, revealers of new and deeper truth to their generation. The Greek world, as it became self-conscious and reflective, had, no doubt, grown much in moral light since the time of Homer, and that light, which their age inherited, these two poets gathered up, and uttered in the best form. But, besides this, they added to it something of their own. In the religion of their poems, though the mythologic and polytheistic conceptions of their country are still present, you can perceive the poet's own inner thought disengaging itself from these entanglements, and rising to the purer and higher idea of the Unity of Zeus, the one all-powerful and all-wise Ruler of heaven and earth; till in Sophocles he stands forth as the "centre and source" of all truth and righteousness.

Then, as to the life of man, we see in Æschylus and in Sophocles the Greek mind for the first time at work upon those great moral problems, which at an earlier date had engaged the Hebrew mind in the Book of Job. The mystery of suffering, especially the suffering of the guiltless, is ever present to them. Popular belief held that such innocent suffering was the mere decree of a dark and unmoral destiny. Æschylus was not content with this, but taught that, when the innocent man or woman suffers, it is because there has been wrong-doing somewhere. He sought to give a moral meaning to the suffering, by tracing it back to sin, if not in the sufferer himself, at least in some one of his ancestors. The father has sinned, the son must suffer. Ὕβρις there has been in some progenitor, ἄτη and ruin fall on his descendants.

Sophocles looks on the same spectacle of innocent suffering, but carries his interpretation of it a step farther, and makes it more moral. Prosperity, he shows, is not always real gain to the individual, but often proves itself an evil by the effects it produces on his character. Neither is adversity entirely an evil, for sometimes, though not always, it acts as a refining fire, purifying and elevating the nature of the sufferer. Its effects, at least in noble natures, are self-control, prudence, contentment, peace of soul. Philoctetes, after being ennobled by the things he had suffered, has his reward even here, in being made the means of destroying Troy, and then returning home, healed and triumphant. Œdipus, in his calm and holy death within the shrine of the Eumenides, and in the honor reserved for his memory, finds a recompense for his monstrous sufferings and his noble endurance. Antigone, though she has no earthly reward for her self-sacrifice, yet passes hence with sure hope — the hope that in the life beyond she will find love waiting her, with all the loved ones gone before.

These few remarks may recall, to some who read them, suggestive thoughts which fell from Professor Jebb in his two concluding lectures on Sophocles, given last summer in the hall of New College, Oxford. And

all who desire to follow out this subject I gladly refer
to the admirable essay on *The Theology and Ethics
of Sophocles*, which Mr. Abbott, of Balliol, has recently
contributed to the book entitled *Hellenica*.

We should not naturally turn to Roman literature to
find the prophetic element.   Speculation and imag-
inative dreaming, whence new thoughts are born, were
alien to the genius of that practical race.   But there is
at least one of Rome's poets who is filled with some-
thing like true prophetic fire.   On the mind of Lucretius
there had dawned two truths, one learned from his own
experience, the other from Greek philosophy; and both
of these inspired him with a deep fervor, quite unlike
anything else to be met with in his country's litera-
ture.   One was the misery and hopelessness of human
life around him, as it still clung to the decaying phan-
toms of an outworn mythology, and groped its way
through darkness with no better guides than these.
The other, gained from the teaching of Democritus
and Epicurus, was the vision of the fixed order of
the Universe, the infinite sweep and the steadfastness
of its laws.   As he contemplated the stately march of
these vast, all-embracing uniformities, he felt as though
he were a man inspired to utter to the world a new
revelation.   And the words in which he does utter it
often rise to the earnestness and the glow of a prophet.
He was, as far as I know, the earliest and most earnest
expounder, in ancient times, of that truth, which has
taken so firm hold of the modern mind.   In the full
recognition by men of the new truth which he preached,
he seemed to himself to see the sole remedy for all the
ills which make up human misery.

Again, Virgil, though with him the love of beauty, as

all know, and the artistic power of rendering it, are paramount, yet laid hold of some new truths, which none before him had felt so deeply. No one had till then conceived so grandly of the growth of Rome's greatness, and the high mission with which heaven had entrusted her. And who else of the ancient poets has felt so deeply, and expressed so tenderly, the pathos of human life, or so gathered up and uttered the most humane sentiment, towards which the world's whole history had been tending — sentiment which was the best flower of the travail of the old world, and which Christianity took up and carried on into the new? In these two directions Virgil made his own contribution to human progress.

If any poet deserves the name of prophet, it is he whose voice was heard the earliest in the dawn of modern poetry. In the *Divine Comedy* Dante gave voice to all the thoughts and speculations, as well as to the action of the stirring thirteenth century. I suppose that no age has ever been summed up so fully and so melodiously, by any singer. On Dante's work, I cannot do better than quote the words in which one of the most accomplished of its interpreters has expressed his feeling regarding it. Dean Church, in his well-known Essay on Dante, has said : —

" Those who have studied that wonderful poem know its austere yet subduing beauty ; they know what force there is in its free and earnest yet solemn verse, to strengthen, to tranquillize, to console. It is a small thing that it has the secret of nature and man ; that a few keen words have opened their eyes to new sights in earth, and sea, and sky ; have taught them new mysteries of sound ; have made them recognize, in distinct image and thought, fugitive feelings, or their unheeded expression by look, or gesture, or motion ; that it has enriched the public and collective memory of society with new instances, never to be lost, of human feelings and fortune ; has charmed ear and mind by the music of its stately march, and the variety and completeness of its plan. But, besides this, they know how often its seriousness has put to shame their trifling, its magnanimity their faint-heartedness, its living energy their indolence, its stern and sad grandeur rebuked low thoughts, its thrilling tenderness overcome sullenness and assauged distress, its strong faith quelled despair and soothed perplexity, its vast grasp imparted harmony to the view of clashing truths.''

To review the great poets of our own country, and consider what new elements of thought and sentiment each in his turn imported into the minds of his country-men, would be an interesting study, but one not to be overtaken in a single essay, if it could be in many. I shall therefore pass at once to that great outburst of song which ushered in the dawn of the present century in England ; and shall try to show, more in detail, some of the original and creative impulses which the poets of that time let loose upon society. This I shall do by taking the examples of two poets of that generation. Other poets, their contemporaries, were not without their share of the prophetic gift; but the two I shall name have exerted an influence, the one wider, the other more deep, and both more distinctly healthful, than any of their brethren.

It was nothing short of a new revelation, when Scott turned back men's eyes on their own past history and national life, and showed them there a field of human interest and a poetic creation which long had lain neglected. Since the days of Shakespeare a veil had been upon it, and Scott removed the veil. Quinet has spoken of the impassable gulf which the age of Louis Quatorze has placed between mediæval France and the modern time. It has parted the literature of France, he says, into two distinct periods, between which no communion is possible. Bossuet, Corneille, Racine, Molière, Voltaire, owe nothing to the earlier thought of France, draw nothing from it. Because of this separation, Quinet thinks that all modern French literature, both prose and poetry, is more real and more fitted to interpret the modern spirit, than if it had grown continuously. We may well doubt this; we may ask whether it has not been the death of French poetry — the cause why modern France possesses so little that to us looks like poetry at all. It would seem as if at one time a like calamity had threatened English literature. In the earlier part of last century, under the influence of Pope and Bolingbroke, a false cosmopolitanism seemed creeping over it, which might have done for our literature what the French wits of the Louise Quartorze age did for theirs. But from this we were saved by that continuity of feeling and of purpose which happily governs our literary not less than our political life. All through last century the ancient spirit was never wholly dead in England, and it would have revived in some way or other. That immense sentiment, that turning back of affection upon the past, was coming — no doubt it would have come — even if Scott had never been born. But he was the chosen vessel to gather up and concentrate within himself the whole force of this retrospective tendency, and to pour it in full flood upon the heart of European society. More profoundly than any other man or poet, he felt the significance of the past, brooded over it, was haunted by it, and in his poems and romances expressed it so broadly, so felicitously, with such genial human interest, that even in his own lifetime he won the world to feel as he did.

One among many results of Scott's work was to turn the tide against the Illumination, of which Voltaire, Diderot, and the host of Encyclopædists were the high priests. Another result was, that he changed men's whole view of history, and of the way in which it should be written; recalled it from pale abstractions to living personalities, and peopled the past no longer with mere phantoms, or doctrinaire notions, but with men and women, in whom the life-blood is warm. If you wish to estimate the change he wrought in this way, compare the historic characters of Hume and Robertson with the life-like portraits of Carlyle and Macaulay. Though these two last have said nasty things of Scott, it little became them to do so; for from him they learnt much of that art which gives to their descriptions of men and scenes and events so peculiar a charm. If we now look back on many characters of past ages, with an intimate acquaintance and a personal affection unknown to our grandfathers, it was Scott who taught us this.

These may be said to be intellectual results of Scott's ascendancy; but there are also great social changes wrought by his influence, which are patent to every eye. Look at modern architecture. The whole mediæval revival, whether we admire it or not, must be credited to Scott. Likely enough Scott was not deeply versed in the secrets of Gothic architecture and its inner proprieties — as, I believe, his own attempts at Abbotsford, as well as his descriptions of castles and churches, prove. But it was he who turned men's eyes and thoughts that way, and touched those inner springs of

interest from which, in due time, the whole movement
came.

Another social result is, that he not only changed
the whole sentiment with which Scotchmen regard their
country, but he awakened in other nations an interest
in it which was till his time unknown. When Scott
was born, Scotland had not yet recovered from the
long decadence and despondency into which she had
fallen, after she had lost her Kings and her Parliament..
Throughout last century a sense of something like deg-
radation lay on the hearts of those who, still loving
their country, could not be content with the cold cosmo-
politanism affected by the Edinburgh wits. Burns felt
this deeply, as his poems show, and he did something in
his way to redress it. But still the prevailing feeling
entertained by Englishmen towards Scots and Scotland
was that which is so well represented in *The Fortunes
of Nigel.* Till the end of the last century, the attitude
of Dr. Johnson was shared by most of his countrymen.
If all this has entirely changed, — if Scots are now
proud of their country, instead of being ashamed of it,
— if other nations look on the land with feelings of
romance, and on the people themselves with respect, if
not with interest, this we owe to Scott, more than to
any other human agency. And not the past only, with
its heroic figures, but the lowly peasant life of his own
time, he first revealed to the world in its worth and
beauty. Jeanie Deans, Edie Ochiltree, Caleb Balder-
stone, Dandie Dinmont, — these and many more are
characters which his eye first discerned in their quiet
obscurity, — read the inner movements of their hearts,
— and gave to the world, a possession for all time. And
this he did by his own wonderful human-heartedness, —

so broad, so clear, so genial, so humorous. More than any man since Shakespeare, he had in him that touch of nature which makes the whole world kin, and he so imparted it to his own creations that they won men's sympathies to himself, not less than to his country and his people. Wordsworth has well called Scott " the whole world's darling." If strangers and foreigners now look upon Scotland and its people with other eyes and another heart, it is because they see them through the personality of Scott, and through the creations with which he peopled the land ; not through the prosaic Radicalism, which since Scott's day has been busily effacing from the character of his countrymen so much that he loved.

I have spoken of how Scott has been a power of social and beneficent influence by the flood of fresh sentiment which he let in on men's minds. But I am aware that to your " practical " man romance is moonshine, and sentiment a delusion. Such an one may, perhaps, be led to esteem them more highly, when he is made aware how much sentiment and romance are worth in the market. The tourists, who from all lands crowd to Scotland every summer, and enrich the natives even in remotest districts, — what was it brought them thither ? What but the spell of Walter Scott ? And, as the late Sir William Stirling Maxwell well expressed it at the Scott Centenary, the fact that Scott has in any of his creations named a farm, or a hill, or a stream, that is to their possessor as good as a new title-deed, which will probably double the marketable value of the spot. So practical a power may poetry become in the affairs of this working world.

I have been speaking of the power poetry has, by

bringing in on men's minds new tides of feeling, to effect great and visible social changes.

I shall now turn to another poet, a contemporary and a friend of Scott's, whose influence has affected a much narrower area, but who within that area has probably worked more deeply. Wordsworth is nothing, if he is not a revealer of new truth. That this was the view he himself took of his office may be gathered from many words of his own. In *The Prelude* he speaks of —

> " the animating faith,
> That poets, even as prophets, · · ·
> Have each his own peculiar faculty,
> Heaven's gift, a sense that fits them to perceive
> Objects unseen before."

And then he goes on to express his conviction that to him also had been vouchsafed

> " An insight that in some sense he possesses
> A privilege, whereby a work of his,
> Proceeding from a source of untaught things,
> Creative and enduring, may become
> A power like one of Nature's."

If Wordsworth was a revealer, what did he reveal?

The subjects of his own poetry, he tells us, are Man, and Nature, and Human Life. What did he teach? What new light did he shed on each of these? He was gifted with soul and eye for nature, which enabled him in her presence to feel a vivid and sensitive delight, which it has been given to few men to feel. The outward world lay before him with the dew still fresh upon it, the splendor of morning still undulled by custom or routine. The earliest poets of every nation, Homer and Chaucer, had, no doubt, delighted in rural sights and sounds, in their own simple, unconscious way. It was Wordsworth's special merit that, coming late in time, when the thick veil of custom and centuries of artificial civilization had come between us and this natural delight, and made the familiar things of earth seem trivial and commonplace, he saw nature anew, with a freshness as of the morning, with a sensibility of soul that was like a new inspiration ; and not only saw, but so expressed it, as to remove the scales from the eyes of others, and make them see something of the fresh beauty which nature wore for himself, — feel some occasional touch of that rapture in her presence, with which he himself was visited. This power especially resides in his *Lyrical Ballads,* composed between 1798 and 1808. Such heaps of comment have recently been written about Wordsworth's way of dealing with nature — and I have made my own contribution to that heap — that I should be ashamed to increase it now ; the more, because in this, as in other good things, our attempts to analyze the gift spoil our enjoyment of it. Two remarks only I shall make, and pass on. First, he did not attempt to describe rural objects, as they are in themselves, but rather as they affect human hearts. As it has been well expressed, he stood at the meeting-point where inflowing nature and the soul of man touch each other, showed how they fit in each to each, and what exquisite joy comes from the contact. Secondly, he did not hold with Coleridge that from nature we " receive but what we give," but rather that we receive much which we do not give. He held that nature is a " living presence," which exerts on us active powers of her own, — a bodily image through which the Sovereign Mind holds intercourse with man.

When face to face with nature, Wordsworth would sometimes seem too much of an optimist. At such times it was that he exclaimed —

> " naught
> Shall e'er prevail against us, or disturb
> Our cheerful faith that all which we behold
> Is full of blessings."

Nature had done so much to restore himself from deep mental dejection, that he sometimes spoke as if she were able to do the same for all men. But, when he so spoke, he forgot how many people there are, whom, either from inward disposition, or from outward circumstances, nature never reaches.

But in the poems which deal with human life and character there is no trace of this optimistic tendency. It has been recently said that " no poet of any day has sunk a sounding-line deeper than Wordsworth into the fathomless secret of suffering that is in no sense retributive." His mind seemed fascinated by the thought of the sorrow that is in this world, and brooded over it as something infinite, unfathomable.

His deepest convictions on this are expressed in these lines —

> " Action is transitory — a step, a blow,
> The motion of a muscle — this way or that —
> 'T is done; and in the after vacancy of thought
> We wonder at ourselves like men betrayed :
> Suffering is permanent, obscure, and dark,
> And hath the nature of infinity.
> Yet through that darkness (infinite though it seems
> And unremovable), gracious openings lie,
> By which the soul — with patient steps of thought,
> Now toiling, wafted now on wings of prayer —
> May pass in hope, and though from mortal bonds
> Yet undelivered, rise with sure ascent
> Even to the fountain-head of peace divine."

This is the keynote of his deepest human poetry. In theory and practice alike he held that it is not in exciting adventure, romantic incident, strange and unusual

mental experience, that the depth of human nature is
most seen, or its dignity.   Along the common high road
of life, in the elemental feelings of men and women, in
the primary affections, in the ordinary joys and sorrows,
there lay for him the truest, most permanent sources of
interest.   His eye saw beneath the outward surface that
which common eyes do not see, but which he was em-
powered to make them see.   The secret pathos, the
real dignity, which lie hid, often under the most un-
promising exteriors, he has brought out, in many of
those narrative poems, in which he has described men
and women, and expressed his views about life in the
concrete more vividly than in his poems that are purely
reflective and philosophical.   Take, for instance, *Ruth*,
The Female Vagrant, *The Affliction of Margaret*, the
Story of Margaret in *The Excursion*, the Story of
Ellen in *The Churchyard among the Mountains*, *The
Brothers*, *Michael*, — above all, *The White Doe of
Rylstone*.   It is noticeable how predominating in these
is the note of suffering, not of action ; and in most of
them, how it is women, rather than men, who are the
sufferers.   This, perhaps, is because endurance seems
to be, in a peculiar way, the lot of women, and patience
has among them its most perfect work.   Human affec-
tion sorely tried, love that has lost its earthly object,
yet lives on, with nothing to support it,

> " solitary anguish,
> Sorrow that is not sorrow, but delight
> To think of, for the glory that redounds
> Therefrom to human kind, and what we are," —

these are the themes over which his spirit broods, spell-
bound as by a strange fascination.   This might be well
illustrated, could I have dwelt in detail on the story of

" Margaret" in the first book of *The Excursion.* Those who are interested in the subject should study that affecting tale, as it is one in which is specially seen Wordsworth's characteristic way of meditating upon, while sympathizing with, human suffering.

The reflection which closes the narrative is peculiarly Wordsworthian. The " Wanderer," seeing the poet deeply moved by the tale, says —

> " My friend ! enough to sorrow you have given,
> The purposes of wisdom ask no more ;
> Be wise and cheerful ; and no longer read
> The forms of things with an unworthy eye.
> She sleeps in the calm earth, and peace is here.
> I well remember, that those very plumes,
> Those weeds, and the high spear-grass on the wall,
> By mist and silent rain-drops silvered o'er,
> As once I passed, did to my heart convey
> So still an image of tranquillity,
> So calm and still, and looked so beautiful,
> Amid the uneasy thoughts that filled my mind,
> That what we feel of sorrow and despair
> From ruin and from change, and all the grief,
> The passing shows of being leave behind,
> Appeared an idle dream, that could not live
> Where meditation was. I turned away
> And walked along my road in happiness."

No poet but Wordsworth would have concluded such a tale with such words. In this " meditative rapture," which could so absorb into itself the most desolating sorrow, there is, it must be owned, something too austere, too isolated, too remote from ordinary human sympathy. Few minds are equal to such philosophic hardihood. Even Wordsworth himself, as he grew older and had experienced sorrows of his own, came down from his solitary height, and changed the passage into a humbler tone of Christian sentiment.

This one story may be taken as a sample of Words-

worth's general attitude towards life, and of the estimate
he formed of things. The trappings, the appendages,
the outward circumstances of men were nothing to him;
the inner heart of the man was everything. What was
a man's ancestry, what his social position, what were
even his intellectual attainments, — to these things he
was almost as indifferent as the writers of the Holy
Scriptures are. There was quite a biblical severity and
inwardness about his estimate of human affairs. It
was the personality, the man within the man, the per-
manent affections, the will, the purpose of the life, on
which alone his eye rested. He looked solely on men
as they are men within themselves. He cared too, I
gather, but little for that culture, literary, æsthetic, and
scientific, of which so much is made nowadays, as though
the possession, or the want of it, made all possible dif-
ference between man and man. This kind of culture
he lightly esteemed, for he had found something wor-
thier than all class culture, often among the lowliest and
most despised. He tells us that he was —

> " Convinced at heart,
> How little those formalities, to which,
> With overweening trust, alone we give
> The name of education, have to do
> With real feeling and just sense ; how vain
> A correspondence with the talking world
> Proves to the most."

It has sometimes been said that Wordsworth's estimate
of men was essentially democratic. Inasmuch as it
looked only at intrinsic worthiness, and made nothing
of distinctions of rank, or of polished manners, or even
of intellectual or æsthetic culture, it may be said to have
been democratic. Inasmuch, however, as he valued only
that which is intrinsically and essentially the best in

men, he may be said to have upheld a moral and spiritual aristocracy; but it is an aristocracy which knows no exclusiveness, and freely welcomes all who will to enter it. No one, indeed, could be farther from flattering the average man by preaching to him equality, and telling him that he is as good as any other man. Rather he taught him that there are moral heights far above him, to which some have attained, to which he too may attain; but that only by thinking lowlily of himself, and highly of those better than himself, only by reverence and by upward looking, may he rise higher.

One thing is noticeable. The ideas and sentiments which fill Wordsworth's mind, and color all his delineations of men and of nature, are not those which pass current in society. You feel intuitively that they would sound strange, and out of place, there. They are too unworldly to breathe in that atmosphere. Hence you will never find the mere man of the world, who takes his tone from society, really care for Wordsworth's poetry. The aspect of things he has to reveal does not interest such men.

Others, however, there are who are far from being worldly-minded, whom nevertheless Wordsworth's poetry fails to reach; and this not from their fault, but from his limitations. His sympathies were deep, rather than keen, or broad. There is a large part of human life which lies outside of his interest. He was, as all know, entirely destitute of humor, — a great want, but one which he shared with Milton. This want, often seen in very earnest natures, shut him out from much of the play and movement that make up life. His plain and severe imagination wanted nimbleness and versatility. Again, he was not at home in the stormy regions of the soul; he stands aloof alike from the Titanic passions, and from the more thrilling and palpitating emotions. If he contemplates these at all, whether in others, or as felt by himself, it is from a distance, viewing the stormy spectacle from a place of meditative calm. This agrees with his saying that poetry arises from emotion remembered in tranquillity. If his heart was hot within him, it was not then that he spake, but when it had had time to grow cool by after reflection. To many sensitive and imaginative natures this attitude is provoking and repellent. Those things about Lucy, I have heard asked, are these all he had to give to the tenderest affection he ever knew? And many turn from them impatiently away to such poems as Byron's on Thyrza, or to his —

> "When we two parted
> In silence in tears,
> Half broken-hearted,
> To sever for years,"

or to the passion of Shakespeare, or to the proud pathos of Mrs. Barrett Browning's sonnets, — tingling through every syllable with emotion. Compared with these, Wordsworth's most feeling poems seem to them cold and impassive, not to say soporific. But this is hardly the true account of them. Byron and such poets as he, when they express emotion, are wholly absorbed in it, lose themselves entirely in the feeling of the moment. For the time, it is the whole world to them. Wordsworth, and such as he, however deeply they sympathize with any suffering, never wholly lose themselves in it, never forget that the quick and throbbing emotions are but "moments in the being of the eternal silence." They make you feel that you are, after all, encompassed by an everlasting calm. The passionate kind of lyric is sure to be the most universally popular. The meditative lyric appeals to a profounder reflectiveness, which is feelingly alive to the full pathos of life, and to all the mystery of sorrow. Which of them is the higher style of poetry I shall not seek to determine. In one mood of mind we relish the one; in another mood we turn to the other. Let us keep our hearts open to both.

In a word, Wordsworth is the prophet of the spiritual aspects of the eternal world; the prophet, too, of the moral depths of the soul. The intrinsic and permanent affections he contemplated till he saw

"joy that springs
Out of human sufferings,"

a light beyond the deepest darkness. In the clearness and the steadfastness with which he was able to contemplate these things, there is something almost superhuman.

It is a large subject on which we have been dwelling, and yet I seem to have only touched the surface of it. Fully to illustrate what contributions of new thought and sentiment Scott and Wordsworth made to their age would require at least a separate treatise for each. And, besides these, there were poets among their contemporaries, who had something of the prophetic light in them, though it was a more lurid light; preëminently the two poets of revolt, Byron and Shelley. It was with something of quite true prophetic fervor that each of these, in his own way, tore off the mask from the social compromises and hollownesses, and denounced the hypocrisies which they believed they saw around them. Neither of them, perhaps, had much positive truth with which to replace the things they would destroy. Byron did not pretend to have. Yet in the far and fierce delight of his sympathy with the tempests and the austere grandeurs of nature, and in the strength with which he portrayed the turbid and Titanic movements of the soul, there was an element of power hitherto unknown in English poetry.

Shelley, again, had a gift of his own altogether unique. He caught and fixed forever movements and hues, both in nature and in the mind of man, which were too subtle, too delicate, too evanescent for any eye but his. He may be said to be the prophet of many shades of emotion, which before him had no language ; the poet, as he has been called, of unsatisfied desire, of insatiable longing. A remedy for all human ills he fancied that he had found in that universal love which he preached so unweariedly. But one may doubt if the love that he dreamt of was substantial, or moral, or self-sacrificing enough to bring any healing.

I refrain from discussing poets who are still living. Else one might have tried to show how the Laureate in some of his works, specially in *In Memoriam*, if he has not exactly imported new truths into his age, has yet so well expressed much of the highest thought that was dawning on men's consciousness, that he has become, in some sort, the first unveiler of it : also, how great inroads he has made into the domain of science, bringing thence truths hitherto unsung, and wedding them to his own exquisite music.

One might have shown, too, how Mr. Browning, disdaining the great highway of the universal emotions, has from the most hidden nooks of consciousness fetched novel situations and hard problems of thought, and in his own peculiar style uttered —

"Things unattempted yet in prose or rhyme."

In the younger poets of the day, as far as I know them, I have not yet perceived the same original prophetic power which has distinguished many of " the dead kings of melody." If it exists, and I have failed to discern it, no one will welcome it more gladly than I. But what seems to me most characteristic in the poetry of the time is, elaborately ornate diction and luscious music, expended on themes not weighty in themselves. Prophet souls, burning with great and new truth, can afford to be severe, plain, even bare in diction. Charged with the utterance of large and massive thoughts, they can seldom give their strength to studied ornamentation. We wait for the day of more substance in our poetry. Shall we have to wait, till the plough-share of revolution has been again driven through the field of European society, and has brought to the surface some subsoil of original and substantive truth, which lies as yet undiscovered ?

CHAPTER V.

" Manner," said Sir James Mackintosh, " is the con-
stant transpiration of character." What manner is to
character and conduct, style is to thought and sentiment,
when these are expressed in literature. We all know
what is meant by saying that a man has a good manner;
and we know too, in some measure, how he has come
by it. It implies first that there exist in his nature
qualities which are admirable, dispositions which are
lovable, and next, that to these has been superadded
courtesy, or the gift of expressing naturally and felici-
tously the feelings that are within him. Where these
dispositions exist, what is needed is that a man during
his pliable youth should have lived in good society.
And by good society we mean not what the world often
calls such, but society where character is true and gen-
uine, where the moral tone is high, and the manners
are refined. It is of course possible, and we sometimes
see, that a man may have good outward manners, which
yet cover a soul inwardly unbeautiful. He may have
adopted the external economy of manners which rightly
belongs to genuine worth, and he may wear these as a
veneer over what is really a coarse and ignoble nature.
And if the polish has been skilfully put on, it requires
a practised eye to detect the deception; but in time it
is detected.

All this may be transferred from character and social

life to literature and its works. A man reveals himself
— what he really is — in many ways ; by his counte-
nance, by his voice, by his gait, and not least by the style
in which he writes. This last, though a more conscious
and deliberate, is as genuine an expression of himself
as anything else that he does.

All literature necessarily implies style, for style is the
reflection of the writer's personality, and literature is
before all things personal. In this indeed lies the dis-
tinction between literature and science, as Dr. Newman
has pointed out. " Science," he says, " has to do with
things, literature with thoughts ; science is universal,
literature is personal ; science uses words merely as
symbols, and by employing symbols can often dispense
with words ; but literature uses language in its full com-
pass, as including phraseology, idiom, style, composition,
rhythm, eloquence, and whatever other qualities are in-
cluded in it." In all literature which is genuine, the
substance or matter is not one thing, and the style an-
other ; they are inseparable. The style is not some-
thing superadded from without, as we may make a
wooden house, and then paint it ; but it is breathed
from within, and is instinct with the personality of the
writer. Genuine literature expresses not abstract con-
ceptions, pure and colorless, but thoughts and things, as
these are seen by some individual mind, colored with all
the views, associations, memories, and emotions which
belong to that mind.

When it is said that one of the chief merits of a style
is to be natural, some are apt to fancy that this means
that it should be wholly effortless and unconscious.
But a little thought will show that this cannot be.
Composition by its very nature implies set purpose, en-

deavor, some measure of painstaking. A few sentences, a few verses, may be struck off in the first heat of impulse. But no continuous essay, no long poem of any merit, can be composed by mere improvisation, or without effort more or less sustained. There are indeed thoughts so simple, that they can be communicated in a style differing little from good conversation, in a few short, transparent sentences. There are other subjects so deep and complex, ideas so novel and abstruse, that the most finished writer cannot express them without much labor, without often retouching his phrases, often recasting his whole mode of expression, ere he can place, in a lucid and adequate way, before the mind of his readers the vision that fills his own. And the result of such elaboration may at last bear the charm of naturalness as much as the easiest, most spontaneous utterance. To use effort, and yet to preserve truth and naturalness, is the main difficulty in all composition. To be able to be natural, yet artistic, it is this which distinguishes true literary genius.

What has just been said is true of all literature, prose as well as poetry. But it applies preëminently to poetry, inasmuch as all poetry worthy of the name is " more intense in meaning, and more concise in style," than prose. If in all real literature the writer's personality makes itself felt, more especially is this true in poetry. Not that the poet necessarily speaks of himself or of his own feelings, but, even in epic narrative and dramatic representation, the personal qualities that are in him are sure to shine through. Some one has defined religion as morality touched with emotion. Much more truly might poetry be said to be thought touched with imagination and emotion. It is the

presence of these two elements, imagination and emo-
tion, informing the poet's thought, — elements which
are essentially personal, — that gives to poetry its chief
attraction, adds to it elevation, intensity, penetrating
power. If then personality is even more characteristic
of poetry than of prose, if poetry is thought and feeling
in their intensest, most condensed power, this implies
that style is more essential to poetry than to prose.

But what do we mean by style? Mr. Matthew Ar-
nold, who, when he speaks of these things, whether we
agree with him or not, is always interesting and at-
tractive, has told us very emphatically what he means
by style. "Style," he says, "in my sense of the word,
is a peculiar recasting and heightening, under a certain
spiritual excitement, a certain pressure of emotion, of
what a man has to say, in such a manner as to add dig-
nity and distinction to it." Again he says, "Power of
style, properly so called, as manifested in masters of
style, like Dante and Milton in poetry, Cicero, Bossuet,
and Bolingbroke in prose, has for its characteristic ef-
fect this, to add dignity and distinction to it." An ad-
mirable definition of certain kinds of style, no doubt.
Dignity and distinction necessarily attend every good
style, but to attain these, it would seem, to judge by
many of the examples which Mr. Arnold cites from Mil-
ton and others, as though he demanded more recasting,
rekneading of expression, than is at all necessary. He
dwells so fondly on Milton's most elaborately wrought
and artistically condensed lines, that one would almost
be led to suppose, what cannot be, that he denies the
highest praise to that most perfect style of all, which
bears with it "the charm of an uncommunicable sim-
plicity." I would therefore take leave to extend the

meaning of poetic style a little wider, and to say that, whenever a man poetically gifted expresses his best thoughts in his best words, there we have the style which is natural to him, and which, if he be a true poet, is sure to be a good style. It may, no doubt, be something very different from the styles which have won the world's admiration in Virgil, in Dante, in Milton. Chaucer has none of that "peculiar kneading and recasting of expression" which these poets have. Yet Chaucer has a style of his own, in which all acknowledge a peculiar charm. Even a poet like Walter Scott, who paid little heed to style, and often worked carelessly, when he chooses to put forth his full power, compensates for the absence of many things by his winsome naturalness. In fact, every great poet has his own individual style, which we recognize at once when we meet with it.

To attempt to characterize the style that is proper to each of the great masters is not my present purpose. But there is one point of view, from which they all appear divided into two great classes as regards style. Some never appear except in their most finished style; they allow nothing to escape them, which has not been touched in their best manner, elaborated with their deftest hand. Of this order are Sophocles, Virgil, Horace, Milton, Gray. These are never seen abroad except in court dress, with ruffles and rapier. On the other hand, Homer, Shakespeare, Cowper, Wordsworth, above all Scott, are often content to work more slackly, and are not ashamed to appear in public with shooting-jacket and hobnailed shoes. Only when their genius is stirred by some great incident, some high thought, some over-mastering emotion, do they rise to their full pitch of power and display their hidden energy. Critics are apt to speak as if this latter class, who do not always walk on the highest levels of style, but sometimes descend nearer to prose, were by that very fact proved inferior to the great masters of style and metre, whose bow is always at the full bend. For my own part I take leave to doubt this canon. Rather, it would seem to be a sign of more spontaneous genius, to be able sometimes to unstring its powers. In a long poem especially, the intervention of barer ground and more level tracts, far from impairing the total effect, affords relief to the mind and makes the surrounding heights stand out more impressively. Such alternations of style reflect the rising and falling, which is incident to the human spirit, more truly than the high pressure of uniformly sustained elevation.

There is one malady to which poetic expression is, by its very nature, peculiarly exposed, and that is conventionalism. Even in the commonest prose writing there are, it is well known, a whole set of stock words and phrases which good taste instinctively avoids. It is not that these were originally bad in themselves, but they have become so worn and faded, that one never hears them without a sense of commonness and fatigue. A good writer keeps clear of such ruts, and finds some simpler and fresher mode of expressing what he has to say. But, if the danger of being entangled in outworn commonplaces besets the prose writer, much more does it waylay the poet. And for this reason: high-pitched imagination and vivid emotion tend, just because they are so vivid and so personal, to groove for themselves channels of language which are peculiar and unique. They shape for themselves a whole economy of diction and rhythm, which, from their very uncommonness, strike the ear and rivet the attention. Such diction and rhythm, admirable in the hands of the original poet who first moulded them for himself, have this drawback, that they lend themselves very easily to imitation. However racy and instinct with meaning a style may at first have been, when once it has got to be the common stock in trade of later and lesser poets, nothing can be more vapid and unreal than it becomes. It requires the shock of some great revolution to sweep this conventional diction into the limbo " of weeds and outworn faces," before the intellectual atmosphere can be left clear for a new and more natural growth of language.

Not once only or twice, in the history of literature, has this malady of conventionalism smitten it to the core. The great Roman poet, perhaps the greatest artist of language the world has seen, created for himself an elaborate rhythm and a high-wrought diction, tessellated with fragments from all former poets, yet worked into an exquisite and harmonious whole, which was simply inimitable. But in the hands of Silius Italicus, Statius, and others, the Virgilian hexameter gives one the sense of a faded imitation, from which the life has gone. Milton, perhaps the next greatest artist of language, moulded for himself a " grand style " of his own, with a similar result. When his blank verse, with its involved and inverted structure, became the heirloom of English poets, it spoiled all our blank verse for nearly two centuries. No meaner hand than that of the great master himself could wield his gigantic instrument. When its tones were recalled in the cumbrous descriptions of Thomson, and in the sonorous platitudes of Young, the result was weariness. Another tyrant, who for several generations dominated English verse, was Pope. What Milton did for blank verse, Pope did for the heroic couplet — left it as a tradition from which no poet of the last century could entirely escape. Gold-smith indeed, in his *Deserted Village*, and Gray in his *Elegy*, returned somewhat nearer to the language of natural feeling. But it was not till Burns and Cowper appeared that poetry was able to throw off the fetters of diction in which Milton and Pope had bound it. Burns and Cowper were the precursors of a revolt against the tyrant tradition, rather than the leaders of it. The return they began towards a freer, more nat-ural diction came from an unconscious instinct for nat-ure, rather than from any formed theory, or from any announced principles, on which they composed. In Burns it may almost be said to have been a happy ac-cident. He had been reared where literary fashions were unknown. His strong intellect naturally loved plain reality, and his whole life was a rebellion against conventions and proprieties, good and bad alike. When his inspiration came, the language he found ready to his hand was, not the worn-out diction of Pope or Shen-stone, but the racy vernacular of his native country. It was well that he knew so little of literary modes, when he began his poetry. For late in life he confessed that, had he known more of the English poets of his time, he would not have ventured to use the homely " Westlau' jingle " which he has made classical. When he did at-tempt to write pure English verse, the result was third-rate conventional stuff. As for Cowper, it was only after a time, and then but in part, that he emancipated himself from the old trammels. In his first volume, published in 1782, containing *Table Talk*, *Progress of Error*, and other pieces, we see his fine wit and deli-cate feeling laboring to express themselves through the forced antithesis and monotonous rhythm of Pope. The blank verse of *The Task* is freer, and more unembarrassed, and yet it contains a strange intermingling of several distinct manners. Almost in the same page you find the stately Miltonic style, with its tortuous involutions employed for homely, even for trivial matters, and then, within a few lines, such passages of playful humor or sweet pensiveness as his address to his "pet hare," or his pathetic allusion to his own spiritual history in the lines beginning

> "I was a stricken deer that left the herd
> Long since."

It is in such passages as these last that Cowper has rendered his best service to English poetry, by showing with what felicitous grace the blank verse lends itself to far other styles than the stately Miltonic movement. And yet towards the end of his life, in his translation of Homer, he returned to the Miltonic manner, and by doing so spoiled his work.

Burns and Cowper then were, as I have said, the forerunners of the revolt against stereotyped poetic diction, not the conscious leaders of it. The end of the old poetic régime came with the great outburst of new and original poetry which marked the last decade of the former century, and the first two decades of the present. It required some great catastrophe to remove the accumulations of used-up verbiage which had so long choked the sources of inspiration, and to cut for the fresh springs of poetic feeling new and appropriate channels. It was as though some great frozen lake, which had already been traversed here and there with strange rents, were suddenly, in one night's thaw, broken up, and the old ice of style, which had so long fettered men's minds, were swept away forever. In the great chorus of song with which England greeted the dawn of this century, individuality had full swing. The exuberance, not to say the extravagance, of young genius was unchecked. His own impulse was to each poet law. Each uttered himself in his own way, in a style of his own, or without style, as native passion prompted. In their work there was much that was irregular, much that was imperfect, but it was young imagination revelling in new-found freedom and strength. Criticism that had insight, — that could be helpful, — there was none extant. For Jeffrey with his *Edinburgh Review* did his little best to extinguish each rising genius as it appeared. Among the host of British poets then born into the world, six, at least, may be named of first-rate power. Each of these shaped for himself a style which was his own, individual, manly, and, with whatever faults, effective. These six were Wordsworth, Coleridge, Scott, Byron, Shelley, Keats. Each of these had his own manner, and we know it. None of them, it is true, always maintained his own highest level of form, rhythm, and diction, as Milton did, as Gray may be said to have done. They were all of them, at times, hasty and even slovenly in style ; but each of them, when he was at his best, when he was grasping with his greatest strength, had substance, — something of his own to say, which he did say in his own manner. Of these six poets only two have left criticism as well as poetry. In two of them, Scott, I mean, and Byron, the absence of criticism is conspicuous. For though Byron did maintain some critical controversy in favor of Pope, yet it is a crude sort of criticism, the offspring rather of prejudice and dislike to some contemporary poets, than of matured

8

judgment. The two younger poets, Keats and Shelley, though they both studied diligently the old poets, announced few principles of criticism. Of all the poets of his time, Scott was the one who set least store by style. He worked always rapidly, often carelessly, writing whole pages, I might almost say cantos, which do not rise above ballad ding-dong. And yet when he put forth his full strength, on a subject which really kindled him, he could rise to a dignity and elevation truly impressive. Though the facility of the octosyllabic couplet often betrayed him into carelessness, yet there are many passages, in which he has made it the best vehicle we possess for rapid and effective narrative — perhaps also for natural description.

The early stanzas of *The Lay*, the opening lines of *Marmion*, the description of Flodden battle, — the most perfect battle-piece which English poetry contains, — these are samples of Scott's style at its best — a style which he has made entirely his own, and in which he has had no equal. Again, in the ballads of *Rosabelle*, and of *The Eve of St. John*, and in some others, he has lifted, as no other poet has done, the old ballad form to a higher power. In all forms of the ballad, and in romantic narrative, if in no other poetic style, Scott stands alone.

Of the six poets above named, two only, as I said, were critics, Wordsworth and Coleridge. These both announced the principles by which they estimated poetry, and — what is noteworthy — their criticism, far from marring the originality of the poetry they composed, only enhanced its excellence. In his own practice, Wordsworth not only rejected the whole of the poetic diction that had been in vogue since the days of Dryden, not only fashioned for himself a style of his own, and forms of expression which his contemporaries derided, but which he maintained to be the natural and genuine language of true thought and feeling — he not only did this, but he gave to the world his reasons for doing so. The two prefaces appended to the *Lyrical Ballads*, in which he attacked the then fashionable poetic diction, and defended the principles on which he himself composed, are so well known that one need only allude to them now. The main positions which he maintained were, first, that poetry should leave the stereotyped phraseology of books, and revert to the language which common men, even peasants, use, when their conversation is animated, and touched by more than ordinary emotion; secondly, that the language of good poetry in no way differs from that of good prose. Even if Wordsworth in some points pressed his theory too far, yet no one who cares for such matters can read the reasoning of these prefaces without instruction.

The two positions which Wordsworth maintained were examined by his friend Coleridge in some chapters of his *Biographia Literaria*, which, as they are not perhaps so well known as they deserve to be, I shall here attempt to summarize.

While upholding most powerfully the genius of Wordsworth as a poet, Coleridge could not accept all the principles which his friend advocated, as a critic. He agreed with Wordsworth in condemning " the gaudy affectation of style which had long passed current for poetic diction," and asserted that, with some few illustrious exceptions, the poetic language in use, " from Pope's translation of Homer to Darwin's *Temple of Nature*, may claim to be poetic, for no better reason than that it would be intolerable in conversation or in prose." He showed, moreover, that the faults which disgusted Wordsworth were as much violations of common-sense and logic, as of poetic excellence. Yet while agreeing with Wordsworth in the object of his attack, he did not approve all the arguments with which Wordsworth had assailed it, or assent to all the articles of the poetic creed which his friend laid down.

In opposition to Wordsworth, Coleridge maintained that the peasantry do not, as Wordsworth held, speak a language better adapted to poetic purposes than that which educated men speak, and that peasants have not the primary feelings and affections simpler, truer, deeper than other men. If Wordsworth had found it so among the Cumberland dalesmen, this arose from exceptional circumstances — circumstances which have now almost disappeared. The peasantry of the midland or southern counties are in no way purer or nobler than men in higher station. Coleridge further protests against Wordsworth's advice to adopt into poetry the language of rustics, only purifying it from provincialisms ; and he maintains that the language of the most educated writers, Hooker, Baker, Burke, is as real as that of any peasant, while it covers a far wider range of ideas, feelings, and experiences. The language of these writers differs far less from the usage of cultivated society, than the language of Wordsworth's homeliest poems differs from the talk of bullock-drivers.

Again, Coleridge will not hear of the doctrine that, between the language of prose and that of metrical composition, there is no essential difference. For, since poetry implies more passion and greater excitement of all the faculties than prose, this excitement must make itself felt in the language that expresses it. Of this excited feeling metre is the natural vehicle — metre, which has it origin in emotion, tempered and mastered by will; or, as Coleridge expresses it, metre, which is the result of the balance which the mind strikes by its voluntary effort to check the working of passion. Hence, as the use of metrical language implies a union of spontaneous impulse and voluntary purpose, both of these elements ought to reflect themselves in the poet's diction. The presence of these two elements, both at a high pitch, must necessarily color the language of the poet, and separate it from that of the prose-writer, which expresses rather the calmer workings of the pure understanding. While thus dissenting from Wordsworth's arguments in the unqualified extent to which he urged them, Coleridge showed that what Wordsworth really meant to enforce was his preference for the language of nature and good sense before all forms of affected ornamentation - - for a style as remote as possible from the false and gaudy splendor which had so long usurped the name of poetry. The thing Wordsworth really desired to see was a neutral style, common to prose and poetry alike, in which everything should be expressed in as direct a way as one would wish to talk, yet in which everything should be dignified and attractive. Such a neutral style Coleridge showed that English poetry already possessed, and he cited examples of it from Chaucer, Spenser, and other poets. This, he believes, is what Wordsworth in his theory was aiming at. But is it not, exclaims Coleridge, surprising that such a theory should have come from — that the establishment of a neutral style should have been advocated by — a poet whose diction, next to that of Shakespeare

and of Milton, was the most individualized and charac-
teristic of all our poets? For in all Wordsworth's most
elevated poems, whether in rhyme or in blank verse, he
rises, says Coleridge, into a diction peculiarly his own —
a style which every one at once recognizes as Words-
worth's. Evidently Coleridge would not have assented
to Mr. Arnold's saying that Wordsworth has no style.
The chapters of the *Biographia Literaria* in which
Coleridge questions Wordsworth's canons of criticism,
and goes on to vindicate the excellence of his poetry,
are well worthy of careful study by all who care for
such matters. Taken along with many fragments scat-
tered throughout the same author's *Literary Remains*,
they form perhaps the finest criticism which our lan-
guage possesses.

It would seem to show that criticism does not neces-
sarily suppress imagination, when we turn to the poetry
of these two poet-critics, and find how high an imagi-
native quality belongs to both. No one whose judgment
is worth anything has ever questioned Wordsworth's
power of imagination, or denied that the substance of
his poetry is preëminently imaginative. But the gift of
style has been denied him, and that by no less an au-
thority than Mr. Arnold. In the fine and suggestive
preface with which Mr. Arnold has introduced his re-
cent admirable *Selections from Wordsworth*, he has said
that Wordsworth has no style; he has fine Miltonic
lines, but he has no assured poetic style of his own, like
Milton. When he seeks to have a style of his own, it
seems, he falls into ponderosity and pomposity. Prob-
ably Mr. Arnold here uses the word "style" in some re-
stricted sense, meaning by it such artistic form as those
writers only display who have fashioned their English

on the model of ancient classic poets. It is true that in this sense Wordsworth has no study of poetic style, but no more had Shakespeare. It may be true that when he seeks to have a style he falls into pomposity. This is just what one would expect — that when a poet seeks to have a style, he should cease to be himself, and should fall into some absurdity. But it is exactly because Wordsworth so seldom sought to have a style, because, when he is most sincere, most fully inspired, he never thought of style, but only of the object before him, because he was so entirely absorbed in the thing he saw, and sought only how most directly to express it — it is this sincerity and wholeness of inspiration that enables him to express his thoughts with the most perfect purity, the most transparent clearness, the most simple and single-minded strength of which the English language is capable. If by poetic style we mean the expression of the best thoughts in the best and most beautiful words, and with the most appropriate melody of rhythm, in this sense Wordsworth, when at his best, has a style of his own, which is perfect after its kind. When at his best, I say; for it cannot be denied that, in the large amount of poetry which he has left, there is a good deal which falls below his highest level.

Take his lyrical pieces, those which are the product of his best decade, between 1798 and 1808. They are so well known that I need hardly allude to them. The lines on *The Cuckoo*, "O blithe newcomer!" "She was a phantom of delight," "I heard a thousand blended notes;" the poems about *Lucy*, *The two April Mornings*, *The Fountain*, *The Solitary Reaper*, *The Poet's Epitaph*, — if these are not poems in a style at once unique and perfect, our language has no such poems. Or turn

to the sonnets.   Among so large a number of these as
Wordsworth composed, there is of course great variety
of excellence.   But it is hardly possible to conceive
more lucid, nervous, or dignified language than that in
which the best of his sonnets are expressed.   Take, for
instance, the morning sonnet on Westminster Bridge,
and the evening one beginning

> "It is a beauteous evening, calm and free."

Can language render sentiment more perfectly than
these do?   In these and a few others, Wordsworth
triumphs over the last difficulty which, from its very
structure, besets the sonnet.   He rises above all sense
of effort — the thought runs off pure and free.   The
series of *Ecclesiastical Sonnets* are far from his best.
They were made to order, rather than by spontaneous
impulse.   Yet even these contain lines so dignified and
distinguished in style that, when once heard, they stamp
themselves on the memory forever.   It is in these we
hear of the shattered tower, which

> "could not even sustain
> Some casual shout that broke the silent air,
> Or the unimaginable touch of time."

In these, that regretful aspiration breathed amid mould-
ering abbeys —

> "Once ye were holy, ye are holy still;
> Your spirit freely let me drink, and live."

In these, too, that fine ejaculation inside of King's Col-
lege chapel, Cambridge —

> "They dreamt not of a perishable home,
> Who thus could build."

Again, spirited narrative was not much in Words-
worth's way, but description was.   In *The White Doe of
Rylstone* the incidents are of little account, the senti-

ment is deep as the world. The first hundred and
seventy lines of that poem, for mellowed diction, for
rhythm and melody appropriate to the meditative and
pensive theme, are a study in themselves. The octo-
syllabic metre has nowhere, that I know, lent itself to
more finely modulated music, as soothing as the murmur
of Wharfe River, by the green holm of Bolton.

Of Wordsworth's blank verse there is much, no doubt,
which may freely be made over to the scourge of the
critic. It is often cumbrous, prolix, altogether prosy.
The last Book of *The Excursion*, for instance, which
tells how the Wanderer and his friends,

> "seated in a ring partook
> The beverage drawn from China's fragrant herb,"

and discussed matters social and educational over their
tea, would have been better written as a pamphlet than
as a poem. Whole pages, too, of *The Prelude* there are,
which are little more than wordy prose cut into ten-
syllable lines. Yet let me whisper to the docile reader,
if not to the self-complacent critic, that, even in the
least effective of Wordsworth's blank verse, he will find
in every page some line, or phrase, or thought, weighty
with individual genius. Even admitting that Words-
worth does, like Homer, sometimes nap, and oftener in
blank verse than elsewhere, yet even in his blank verse,
when he is really possessed by his subject and kindles
with it, he has attained a majesty and a power which
make it more remerberable than any blank verse since
Milton's. Of this kind is the blank verse of *Michael*,
the *Lines on Tintern Abbey*, many a passage in *The
Prelude*, such as the description of a mountain-pass in
the high Alps; of this kind, too, are some of the nar-
rative parts of *The Excursion* — the story of Margaret

in the First Book, the story of Ellen, the village maiden, betrayed and repentant, in the Seventh Book :

> " Meek saint ! by suffering glorified on earth !
> In whom, as by her lonely hearth she sat,
> The ghastly face of cold decay put on
> A sun-like beauty, and appeared divine ! "

It would be easy to go on quoting passages or poems without number, which bear out the assertion that Wordsworth fashioned for himself a style as unlike as possible to the vapid poetic diction which he denounced, but akin to whatever is manliest, noblest, and best in the English poetry of all ages.   Many causes were doubtless at work to put out that outworn poetic language. But no one agency did so much to discredit it as the protest which Wordsworth made against it in his prefaces, and still more by the example of his poems. These have set a standard of what a pure and sincere diction in poetry should be, just as the sermons and other writings of Dr. Newman have done in prose.   Both have alike evoked new power from the English language, and shown what capabilities it possesses of insinuating its tendrils into the deepest and most recondite veins of thought, as well as into the tenderest sentiment by which any spirit of man is visited.

Coleridge we have seen as a critic.   One word about his poetry ; for he is perhaps the finest instance we have in England of the critical and poetical power combined. The editions of his poems usually published contain much that is casual and second-rate, especially among his early poems and his *Religious Musings*.   They contain also something which no other poet could have given.   Of his best pieces it may be said, in the words of a living poet and critic with whom, in this instance,

I am glad to agree, " The world has nothing like them, nor can have ; they are of highest kind, and of their own." These best pieces are *Christabel, The Ancient Mariner,* and *Kubla Khan.* Over this last fragment Mr. Swinburne, who, when he does admire, knows no stint in his admiration, goes into raptures, and exhausts even his eulogistic vocabulary. " The most wonderful of all poems," he calls it. " In reading it," he says, " we are rapt into that paradise where 'music and color and perfume are one;' where you hear the hues, and see the harmonies of heaven. For absolute melody and splendor it were hardly rash to call it the first poem of the language." Especially he dotes over these lines in it :

> "Five miles meandering with a mazy motion
> Through wood and dale the sacred river ran,
> Then reached the caverns measureless to man,
> And sank in tumult to a lifeless ocean;
> And mid this tumult Kubla heard from far
> Ancestral voices prophesying war."

It is not wonderful that a poet, who himself revels in melodious words, should go into ecstasies over a poem which his own favorite devices of alliteration, and assonance, and rhythm have done their best to make a miracle of music. For my part, I cannot compare *Kubla Khan* with *Christabel.* The magical beauty of the latter has been so long canonized in the world's estimate, that to praise it now would be unseemly. It brought into English poetry an atmosphere of wonder and mystery, of weird beauty and pity combined, which was quite new at the time it appeared, and has never since been approached. The movement of its subtle cadences has a union of grace with power, which only the finest lines of Shakespeare can parallel. As we read *Christabel* and a few other of Coleridge's pieces, we recall his own words : —

" In a half-sleep we dream,
And dreaming hear thee still, O singing lark!
That singest like an angel in the clouds."

To leave those few poems, in which Coleridge has touched the supernatural world with so matchless skill, and to come nearer earth, take, as a fine specimen of his style in human things, the opening and closing stanzas of his *Ode on France*. What " a musical sweep " there is in those long-sustained paragraphs ! Coleridge, from his temperament, was not often at the full pitch of his powers; but when he was, he possessed a style which, for inner delicacy and grace, combined with inspired strength and free-sweeping movement, made him one of the few masters of poetic diction, one who, we may be quite sure, will in our language remain unsurpassed. Too early he forsook the Muse, or the Muse forsook him ; and the most subtle imagination of his time was plunged in the Serbonian bog of German metaphysics. Yet in his old age the Muse for brief moments revisited him, and he threw off a few short jets of epigrammatic song, or such lines as those entitled *Youth and Age*, in which we hear once more the old witchery.

Wordsworth and Coleridge were critics and poets at once, and it is because they were so that, in speaking of style, I have dwelt at length on their critical principles and their poetic performance. Byron, on the other hand, was exclusively a poet, and no critic. Of him Mr. Swinburne has truly said that his critical faculty was zero, or even a frightful minus quantity. He had never even attempted to master his art, or to take the measure of himself, and to know the nature of the materials he had to work with. In all that he did he trusted simply to the fiery force that stirred him, and took counsel only with his own fierce Titanic spirit. It is by the vast strength and volume of his powers, rather than by any one perfect work, that he is to be estimated. He does not seem to have had any delicacy of ear for the refinements of metre, or to have studied the intricacies of it. But, when the impulse came, he poured himself forth with wonderful rapidity, home-thrusting directness, and burning eloquence — eloquence that carries you over much that is faulty in structure, and imperfect or monotonous in metre. He himself did not stay to consider the way he said things, so intent was he on the things he had to say. Neither any more does the reader. His cadences were few, but they were strong and impressive, and carried with them, for the time, every soul that heard them. If we look for what is most characteristic, in Byron's poetic style, it is not to his romantic narratives that we turn — to his *Giaours* and his *Laras*. Neither is it to *Childe Harold*, much as it contains of interest, for in the Spenserian stanza Byron was never quite at ease. It was only after attempting many styles, with more or less success, that at last he hit upon a style entirely his own — entirely fitted to express all the various and discordant tones of his wayward spirit. The note which he first struck in *Beppo*, he carried to its full compass in *Don Juan*. In the " ottava rima "— that light, fluent, plastic measure which he made at once and forever his own — he found a fit vehicle for the comic vein that had long slumbered within him, of which in his earlier poems he had given no sign, as well as for the satire that he commanded, a satire sometimes light and playful, oftener scornful and cynical, yet even in the midst of its wildest license and ribaldry, from time to time suspending itself, that the poet may flash out into splendid description, or melt into pathetic retrospect or brief but thrilling regret. For good or for evil, it must be said that all the variety of Byron's moods, and his most characteristic style, are faithfully embodied in the peculiar texture and original versification of *Don Juan*.

Byron, as all know, often affected gloom and played with misanthropy, and his poems reflecting these moods are all, more or less, in a falsetto tone. The sincerest, as they are the most touching poems, expressive of his personal feelings, are the Domestic Pieces and those on *Thyrza*, and sincerity gives to these verses a beauty which, once felt, can never be forgotten. Over blank verse he had no great mastery; and yet he has one poem in this measure, in which he reverts to his early love with a simple sincerity and a piercing pathos which have never been surpassed. In the *Dream*, it is the very artlessness that makes the charm. The lines thrill with intense and passionate sincerity. On the whole, of Byron's style it may be said that, if it has none of the subtle and curious felicities in which some poets delight, it is yet language in its first intention, not reflected over or exquisitely distilled, but, in his strongest moments, coming direct from himself, and going direct to the heart. Placed under the critical microscope, his language, no doubt, shows many flaws and faults, but far beyond any of his contemporaries he has the manly force, the directness, the eloquence which passion gives. Passionate eloquence is the chief characteristic of his style.

Among the poets who appeared in the first two decades of this century, as among all poets, readers will

choose their favorites according to their sympathies.
But putting aside personal preferences, every one must
allow that none of the poets of that time was more
" radiant with genius," and more rich in promise, than
the short-lived Keats. His genius showed itself in a
wonderful power of style, which, after striking many
notes and reflecting many colors, caught from the old
poets he loved, was settling down into a noble style of
his own, when his brief life closed. His first poem,
Endymion, for all its crudeness and extravagance, un-
deniably revealed the vitality of young genius, and re-
claimed for English poetry the original freedom of the
ten-syllable couplet, which had been lost since the days
of Chaucer. The influence of Spenser, who was the
earliest idol of Keats, is strong in his tales, *The Eve of
St. Agnes* and *Isabella.* There is in them, too, some
flavor of the Italian poets, whom he studied much
while he was composing his tales. The " grand style "
of Milton has never been so marvellously reproduced as
in *Hyperion;* but from this great fragment Keats him-
self turned with some impatience, pressing on to utter
himself in a style more genuinely his own. This he
attained in his odes *On a Grecian Urn, To Autumn,
To a Nightingale*, and in a few of his sonnets. In
these he was leaving behind him all traces of early man-
nerism, and attaining to that large utterance, — combin-
ing simplicity with richness, strength with freedom and
grace of movement, — which was worthy of himself.
The odes especially, so finished, so full of artistic beauty,
flow forth into full sonorous harmonies, which leave no
sense of effort. In his later poems, from behind the
love of sensuous beauty, which was the groundwork of
his genius, there was coming out a deeper thoughtful-

ness and humanity, which make us the more regret his
early fate.   Perhaps there is no other instance of so in-
stinctive a yearning towards the old Hellenic life as is
to be seen in Keats.   His thirst for artistic beauty could
find no full satisfaction in the productions of the cold
north, and turned intuitively to the fair creations of the
elder world, as to its native element.   This is the more
remarkable, as we know that Keats was so slenderly
equipped with what is called scholarship that he could
reach the Greek poets only through translations.   His
classical instinct shows itself not only in his love of
Greek subjects and Greek mythology, but in his won-
derful reproduction of Greek form.   As we read such
lines as these :

> " What little town by river or sea-shore,
>   Or mountain-built with peaceful citadel,
>   Is emptied of its folk this pious morn ? "

or these on the nightingale's song :

> " The same that found a path,
> Through the sad heart of Ruth, when, sick for home,
> She stood in tears amid the alien corn " —

we ask, What finished Greek scholar has ever so vividly
recalled the manner of the Greeks ?

To speak of the style of Shelley there is no space
here, and, as comments on his poetry have of late been
so rife, there is the less need.   Suffice it to say that un-
biassed criticism generally admits that his exuberant
power of language often overmastered him, and his de-
light in melodious words tempted him at times to sacri-
fice sense to sound.   Condensation and self-repression
would have improved much that he wrote.   On the
other hand, all must feel that by his subtle sense of
beauty he caught many a vanishing hue of earth and

sky, which no poet before him had noticed, and expressed many a tone of longing and regret, which no language but his has ever hinted.

Fifty years and more have passed since the voices of all the great poets I have named became mute, and in the interval between then and now England has had no lack of poetry. Whether any of it has reached as high a level as the best works of the masters of the former generation, may be doubted. The world is not likely soon again to see another flood of inspiration like that which burst on England with the opening of this century. In the poetry of the last fifty years many notes have been struck, so many and so different, that it would not be easy to characterize them all. On the whole, it may perhaps be said, that two main branches of poetic tendency are discernible, — one which carries on the impulse and the style derived from Keats and Shelley, one which more or less is representative of Wordsworth's influence. Of these two tones the former would seem most to have won the world's ear, and its chief voice is that of the Poet Laureate. Mr. Tennyson is, as all know, before all things an artist; and as such he has formed for himself a composite and richly-wrought style, into the elaborate texture of which many elements, fetched from many lands and from many things, have entered. His selective mind has taken now something from Milton, now something from Shakespeare, besides pathetic cadences from the old ballads, stately wisdom from Greek tragedians, epic tones from Homer. And not only from the remote past, but from the present; the latest science and philosophy both lend themselves to his thought, and add metaphor and variety to his language. It is this elabo-

9

ration of style, this " subtle trail of association, this play of shooting colors," pervading the texture of his poetry, which has made him be called the English Virgil.   But if it were asked which of his immediate predecessors most influenced his nascent powers, it would seem that, while his early lyrics recall the delicate grace of Coleridge, and some of his idyls the plainness of Wordsworth, while the subtle music of Shelley has fascinated his ear, yet, more than any other poet, Keats, with his rich sensuous coloring, is the master whose style he has caught and prolonged.   In part from Shelley, and still more from Keats, has proceeded that rich-melodied and highly colored style which has been regnant in English poetry for the last half century. Tennyson has been the chief artist in it, but it has been carried on by a whole host of lesser workmen.

Beside this, the dominant style, there has lived another, more direct, more plain, more severe, which, without in any way imitating, has represented the influence of Wordsworth. However differing in other respects, Keble, Sir Henry Taylor, Archbishop Trench, and Arthur Clough, each in his own way, represent this second tendency, which I may call the plain-speaking, unornamented, and natural style. There is a passage in Mr. Arnold's preface to his *Selections from Wordsworth*, which all who have read must remember, in which he speaks of Wordsworth's nobly plain manner, " when Nature herself seems to take the pen out of his hand, and to write for him with her own bare, sheer, penetrating power."   But this characteristic, which Mr. Arnold has noted as occasional, occurring in a few poems, such as *The Leech Gatherer* and *Michael*, may be extended to all of best that Wordsworth has done.

It brings out, in fact, the broad and radical distinction, enforced by the late Mr. Bagehot, between pure art and ornate art.

Pure art is that which, whether it describes a scene, a character, or a sentiment, lays hold of its inner meaning, not its surface; the type which the thing embodies, not the accidents; the core or heart of it, not the accessories. As Mr. Bagehot expressed it, the perfection of pure art is " to embody typical conceptions in the choicest, the fewest accidents, to embody them so that each of these accidents may produce its full effect, and so to embody them without effort." Descriptions of this kind, while they convey typical conceptions, yet retain perfect individuality. They are done by a few strokes, in the fewest possible words; but each stroke tells, each word goes home. Of this kind is the poetry of the Psalms and of the Hebrew prophets. It is seen in the brief impressive way in which Dante presents the heroes or heroines of his nether world, as compared with Virgil's more elaborate pictures. In all of Wordsworth that has really impressed the world, this will be found to be the chief characteristic. It is seen especially in his finest lyrics, and in his most impressive sonnets. Take only three poems which stand together in his works, *Glen Almain, Stepping Westward, The Solitary Reaper.* In each, you have a scene and its sentiment, brought home with the minimum of words, the maximum of power. It is distinctive of the pure style that it relies not on side effects, but on the total impression — that it produces a unity in which all the parts are subordinated to one paramount aim. The imagery is appropriate, never excessive. You are not distracted by glaring single lines or too splendid images. There is one tone, and that all-pervading — reducing all the materials, however diverse, into harmony with the one sentiment that dominates the whole. This style in its perfection is not to be attained by any rules of art. The secret of it lies farther in than rules of art can reach ; even in this : that the writer sees his object, and this only ; feels the sentiment of it, and this only ; is so absorbed in it, lost in it, that he altogether forgets himself and his style, and cares only, in fewest and most vital words, to convey to others the vision his own soul sees. This power of intense sincerity, of total absorption in an object which is not self, is not given to many men, not even to men otherwise highly gifted. But without this, the pure style in full perfection is not possible. It comes to this : that in order to attain the truest and best style, a man must, for the time at least, forget style and think only of things. One instance more of that great law of ethics, whereby the abandonment of some lower end, in obedience to a higher aim, is made the very condition of securing the lower one. To employ the pure style in its full power requires the presence of a seer, a prophet-soul ; and prophet-souls are few, even among poets.

The ornate style in poetry is altogether different from this. When a scene, a sentiment, a character, has to be described, it does not penetrate at once, as the pure style penetrates, to the idea which informs the scene, the sentiment, the character ; it does not place the scene before you, impressed by a few words on the mind forever. But it gathers round the scene or the character, which it seeks to delineate, many of the most striking accessories and associations which it suggests, and sets it before you, clad in the richest and most splendid drapery the subject will bear. It sees the informing idea, and expresses it; but by its adjuncts rather than by its bare essence. The vision of the inner reality is not intense enough to make it impatient of accessories and ornamentation. It so delights in imagery, distant allusion, classical retrospect, that the attention is apt to be led off by these, and to neglect the central subject. This ornate style, redundant with splendid imagery, loaded with cloying music, is much in vogue with our modern poets. Mr. Tennyson, who has employed various styles, and sometimes the pure and severe style, has done more of his work in the ornate. As one instance, take his poem on *Love and Duty*. It is intense with passion, the thought is noble and nobly rendered. But after the agony of parting, it occurs to the lover that perhaps the thought of him might still come back, and the poem closes thus :

> "If unforgotten ! should it cross thy dreams,
>   So might it come, like one that looks content,
>   With quiet eyes, unfaithful to the truth,
>   Or point thee forward to a distant light,
>   Or seem to lift a burden from thy heart,
>   And leave thee freer, till thou wake refreshed,
>   Then when the first low matin-chirp hath grown
>   Full quire, and morning driven her plough of pearl
>   Far-furrowing into light the mounded rack,
>   Between the fair green field and eastern sea."

This description of morning is no doubt very pretty, but one has always felt that it might well have been spared, after the passionate parting scene immediately before it.

"A dressy literature, an exaggerated literature, seem to be fated to us. These are our curses, as other times had theirs." With these words Mr. Bagehot closes his essay to which I have alluded. No doubt the multitude of uneducated and half-educated readers, which every day increases, loves a highly ornamented, not to say a meretricious, style, both in literature and in the arts; and if these demand it, writers and artists will be found to furnish it. There remains, therefore, to the most educated the task of counterworking this evil. With them it lies to elevate the thought, and to purify the taste, of less cultivated readers, and so to remedy one of the evils incident to democracy. To high thinking and noble living the pure style is natural. But these things are severe, require moral bracing, minds which are not luxurious, but can endure hardness. Softness, luxuriousness, and moral limpness find their congenial element in excess of highly colored ornamentation.

On the whole, when once a man is master of himself, and of his materials, the best rule that can be given him is, to forget style altogether, and to think only of the thing to be expressed. The more the mind is intent on this, the simpler, truer, more telling the style will be. The advice, which the great preacher gives for conduct, holds not less for writing of all kinds : " Aim at things, and your words will be right without aiming. Guard against love of display, love of singularity, love of seeming original. Aim at meaning what you say, and saying what you mean." When a man who is full of his subject, and has matured his powers of expression, sets himself to speak thus simply and sincerely, whatever there is in him of strength or sweetness, of dignity or grace, of humor or pathos, will find its ways out naturally into his language. That language will be true to his thought, true to the man himself. Free from self-consciousness, free from mannerism, it will still bear the impress of whatever is best in his individuality.

And yet there is something better even than the best individuality — a region of selfless humanity, of pure, transparent ether, into which the best spirits sometimes ascend. In that region there is no trace, no color of individuality any more. The greatest poets, uttering their highest inspirations, there attain a style which is colorless, and speak a common language. It is but in rare moments that even they attain these heights, but sometimes they do attain them.

Πόλλαι μὲν θνητοῖς γλῶσσαι, μία δ' ἀθανάτοισι.

("Mortals speak many tongues, the immortals one."

CHAPTER VI.

THOSE who have read will no doubt remember an essay on Virgil by Mr. Frederick Myers, which appeared in the *Fortnightly Review* of February, 1879. I speak, I believe, the experience of many, when I say that it is long since I have read any piece of criticism with so much interest, I might say delight.

To some the spirit in which it is written may appear too enthusiastic — the style perhaps may be a shade too florid. But it possesses, I think, that one highest merit of criticism — indeed the only thing which makes any criticism worth reading — it is evidently the work of one who has seen more clearly, and felt more vividly, than others have done, the peculiar excellence of Virgil ; and who longs to make others see and feel it.

Speaking of a certain essay on Shakespeare by a Mrs. Montague, Dr. Johnson once said, " No, sir, there is no real criticism in it ; none showing the beauty of thought, as founded on the workings of the human heart." That word of the stern old critic well expresses what is the true function of his own craft, the only thing that makes poetic criticism worth having — when some competent person uses it to explain to the world in general, who really do not see far in such matters, those permanent truths of human feeling on which some great poem is built. For, after all, the reputation which attaches to even the greatest — Homer, Shakespeare, and the like — depends on the verdict of a few. They see into the core of the matter, tell the world what it ought to see and feel; the world receives their saying and repeats it. Mr. Myers has seen anew the truth about Virgil, and expressed it. And, strange to say, this needed to be done, even at this late date, for our age.

This century, as we all know, has seen a great decline in the world's estimate of Virgil. Niebuhr and the Germans began it, and, as usual, England followed suit. Perhaps the thing was inevitable. One reason was, that Virgil could not but suffer from the comparison with Homer, which advancing scholarship brought on. Another reason was, that a civilization which, like our own, has reached a late stage turns with an instinctive relish towards the poets of the early time, still fresh with the dew of youth. To the heat and languor of the afternoon, nothing is so grateful as the coolness and freshness of the dawn. The poetry of an age in many ways so akin to our own as Virgil's was is apt to pall on our taste, and to meet with scanty justice. If from causes like these Virgil's reputation has for a time suffered eclipse, we may hope that the glad deliverance has begun, and that he is now passing back to that serener heaven which rightfully belongs to him. One symptom of a return to a truer judgment of Virgil is to be found in the admirable essay by Mr. Myers of which I have spoken. Another is Professor Sellar's work on Virgil, which has given, probably for the first time in English scholarship, a just and well-balanced estimate of the true nature and excellence of Virgilian poetry.

The truth is, to compare Virgil and Homer, except to contrast them, is a mistake. Who does not at

once feel that of that in which Homer's chief strength
lay Virgil has but a meagre share? Heroic portraiture
was not in his way. He has depicted no characters
which live in the world's imagination, as those of Achilles
and Hector, of Ulysses and Ajax, of Priam and An-
dromache live. To throw himself into the joy of the
onset was so alien to Virgil's whole turn of thought
that one could almost wish that it had been possible
for him to have constructed an Æneid, in which battles
could have been dispensed with. The tenth book of the
Æneid, though it has many vigorous touches, is pale
and ineffectual beside the Homeric battle-pieces. In
the words of a modern poet, Virgil might have said: —

> " The moving accident is not my trade,
>   To freeze the blood I have no ready arts ;
>   'T is my delight alone in summer shade
>   To pipe a simple song for thinking hearts."

In fact, all that forms the charm of Homer's poetry
was simply impossible, and would have been unnatural,
to one living in Virgil's day. The keen morning air,
the strong-beating pulses of youth, unreflecting delight
in all sights of nature, and in all actions of men, could
not belong to a poet living in a civilization that was
old and smitten with decay. But if these things were
denied, other things were given, such as a late time could
give — the mellow, if somewhat sad, wisdom that comes
from a world's experience, the human-hearted sympathy
that, looking back over wide tracts of time on the toils
and sufferings of man, feels the full pathos of the human
story, and yet is not without some consoling hope.

It is well known in what special honor the early
Christian Fathers held Virgil. St. Augustine styled
him the finest and noblest of poets. St. Jerome, who

looked severely on all heathen writers, allows that to read Virgil was a necessity for boys, but complains that even priests in his day turned to him for pleasure.

In the middle age he was regarded by some as a magician ; by others as a prophet or a saint. His form was found sculptured on the stalls of a cathedral among the Old Testament worthies ; in a picture of the Nativity, where David and the prophets are singing round The Child, Virgil is seen leading the concert. His verses are found in the burial-places of the catacombs, associated with the cross and the monogram of our Lord. The power with which he has laid hold of the Christian imagination is proved by nothing more than by the place Dante assigns him in his *Divina Commedia*, as his teacher and his guide to the nether world. You remember the words with which Dante addresses him on his first appearance : —

" Art thou, then, that Virgil — that fountain which pours forth abroad so rich a stream of speech ?   O glory and light of other poets !   May the long zeal avail me, and the great love that made me search thy volume.   Thou art my master and my author ; thou alone art he from whom I took the good style that hath done me honor.[1] "

This general consent of the primitive and the middle ages to adopt Virgil among the possible if not actual saints of Christendom arose, no doubt, from the belief that in his fourth Eclogue he had prophesied the advent of Christ.   Constantine, in his discourse *Ad Sanctos,* quoted it as a prophecy.   Lactantius agreed that it had a Christian meaning.   St. Augustine accepted it as a genuine prophecy, and read in the thirteenth and four-

---

[1] J. Carlyle's Translation of Dante's *Inferno.*

teenth verses of that Eclogue a distinct prediction of
the remission of sins.

This interpretation of the Eclogue, which would
seem to have lingered on till Pope's time, when he
imitated it in his *Messiah*, has for long been discred-
ited.   The Child that was to be born, of which the
Eclogue speaks, whether the son of Pollio, or the
daughter of Augustus, was far enough from being a
regenerator of the world.   While, however, we reject
the grounds which the early Fathers and the men of
the middle age would have given for their belief in
Virgil's religious, even Christian spirit, we need not re-
ject the belief itself.   Though the reason they gave for
it was false, the conception may have been true.   There
is in Virgil a vein of thought and sentiment more devout,
more humane, more akin to the Christian, than is to be
found in any other ancient poet, whether Greek or
Roman.   The religious feeling which Virgil preserved
in his own heart is made the more conspicuous, when we
remember amidst what almost overpowering difficulties
it was that he preserved it.   It was not only that, in
the words of Dante, "he lived at Rome under the good
Augustus in the time of the false and lying gods,"
but he lived at a time when the traditional faith in
these gods was dead among almost all educated men.
As has been lately said, "The old religions were dead
from the Pillars of Hercules to the Euphrates and
the Nile, and the principles on which human society
had been constructed were dead also.   There remained
of spiritual conviction only the common and human
sense of justice and morality; and out of this sense
some ordered system of government had to be con-
structed, under which men could live and labor, and

eat the fruit of their industry. Under a rule of this material kind there can be no enthusiasm, no chivalry, no saintly aspirations, no patriotism of the heroic type." But such was the rule of the Cæsars — "a kingdom where men could work, think, and speak as they pleased, and travel freely among provinces for the most part ruled by Gallios, who protected life and property," and who cared for nothing else. This was the world into which Virgil was born, and it is his unique merit that he in some way maintained within himself a sense of poetry, faith, and devoutness in a time when, if these things were slumbering in the heart of humanity, they were nowhere else apparent.

A man of his spirit must have felt himself lonely enough among the literary men and statesmen whom he met at Rome. Many a secret longing of heart he must have had, for which among them he could find no sympathy. They had ceased to believe in anything divine, probably mocked and ridiculed it. But, whatever else he might have done, a devout soul like Virgil could never do this. A severe and peculiar kind of trial it is for such a spirit to be born into an age, when the old forms of religion, which have sustained former generations, are waxing old and ready to perish. We can imagine that Virgil himself must have felt that those old beliefs had no longer the strength they once had; but his innate modesty and reverence, his love for antiquity and for the scenes of his childhood, his imaginative sympathy, would not suffer him to treat them rudely, but would make him cling to them and make the best of them. In fact, at such a time there are always a few select spirits in whom the inner religious life is sustained by its own strength, or, if fed at all from without, it is fed from sources of which it is unconscious. Instead of deriving nutriment from the old beliefs, it imparts to them from within whatever vitality they still retain. Such we can imagine Virgil to have been. Men of his kind, who still believe that, whatever some scoffers may say, there is "a higher life than this daily one, and a brighter world than that we see," if they fall among a set of acute dialecticians, are often sore bestead to give a reason for the faith that is still in them. If Virgil had been an interlocutor in Cicero's dialogue *De Natura Deorum*, he would probably have cut but a sorry figure against the arguments of Cotta and the sneers of Velleius, and certainly could not have tabled any so clear-cut theory as Stoic Balbus, did. But it is just the very beauty of such spirits, that all the irrefragable arguments and demonstrations of the acutest logicians cannot drive them out of their essential faith in the supernatural and the divine.

Mr. Sellar has truly said that Virgil has failed to produce a consistent picture of spiritual life out of the various elements, the popular, mystical, and philosophical modes of thought, which he strove to combine into a single representation. This may be at once conceded. How could he or any one produce harmony out of elements so discordant as those which his age supplied? But nevertheless, inconsistent, irreconcilable, as these elements are, when they have passed through Virgil's mind one spirit pervades them all. Everywhere we see that the touch of his fine and reverent spirit tends to extract from them a moral, if it cannot reduce them into an intellectual harmony.

What were the elements out of which the very composite Virgilian theology was woven? First, there was

his native love for the old rustic gods whom in his boy-
hood he had seen worshipped by the Mantuan husband-
men — Faunus and Picus, Janus and Pilumnus, and the
like —

"Ye gods and goddesses all! whose care is to protect the fields."

His first impressions were of the country and of coun-
try people, and these Virgil was not worldly enough to
forget amid the life of the city, and the friendship of
the great. His imagination ever reverted to Mincio's
side, and his heart clung with peculiar tenacity to the
recollections of that early time. And therefore we find
that, both in the *Georgics* and in the *Æneid*, he dwells
on the old rustic worships and the local divinities with
something more than a mere antiquarian attachment.
To those primeval traditions, those old-world beliefs
and practices, he adhered, as to his earliest and surest
ground of trust. He felt that to eradicate these would
be to tear up some of the deepest roots of his spiritual
life. Therefore he retained them fondly, and did his
best to reconcile them with the beliefs which his later
culture superinduced.

The second element in Virgil's Pantheon was the
Olympian dynasty of gods, with which the influx of
Greek literature had saturated the whole educated
thought and imagination of Rome. Indeed, the litera-
ture of his day would not have allowed him to reject
this poetic theology. At first sight it might seem that
the Olympian gods had come to Virgil pure and unal-
loyed from Homer. But, when we look more closely,
there is a deep change. Outwardly they may appear
the same, but inwardly the modern spirit has reached
and modified them. Virgil introduces his gods far more
sparingly than Homer; they interfere far less with the

affairs of men. When they do interfere, it is in a gentler
and humaner spirit. It is with pity that they look upon
men slaughtering each other. When Trojans and Ru-
tulians are hewing each other down, and "the gods in
Jove's palace look pityingly on the idle rage of the war-
ring hosts," their feeling is —

"Alas that death-doomed men should suffer so terribly!"

Again, Virgil's Jove is more just and impartial than
Homer's. When Turnus and Æneas contend, he holds
the balance with perfect evenness : —

"Jupiter himself holds aloft his scales, poised and level, and lays
therein
The destinies of the two, to see whom the struggle dooms, and
whose
The weight that death bears down."

When Virgil's gods meet in council, their deliberations
are more dignified ; there is less of the debating agora
in their proceedings. Jupiter addresses them with a
quite Roman majesty ; indeed, approaches more nearly
to a real king of the gods. Monotheism has evidently
colored Virgil's conception of him. Venus appears no
longer as the voluptuous beguiler, but rather as the
mother trembling for her son.

If Virgil cannot altogether hide the follies and vices
of the gods which mythology had given to his hands,
he does his best to throw a veil over them. If Juno's
wrath must still burn implacably, Virgil has for it the
well-known cry of surprise —

"Can heavenly natures hate so fiercely ?"

Thus we see that if the Homeric forms and even some
of the strange doings of the old gods are still retained,
the best ideas and scruples of Virgil's own age enter in
to inform, to modify, and to moralize them.

But, beside the primeval Italian traditions and the Olympian gods, there were probably other extraneous elements, which entered into Virgil's very composite theology. Something, perhaps, he may have gathered from the teaching of the Eleusinian or other mysteries; but of this we know too little to speak with any certainty. Some tincture of Oriental worships, too, is indicated by his mention of the Phrygian goddess Cybele.

Perhaps nowhere in Virgil is the strange medley of faiths forced more disturbingly on our view than in the invocation to the first Georgic. When we read that opening passage, in which Liber and Ceres, Fauni and Dryades, Neptune, producer of the horse; Aristaus, feeder of kine; Pan, keeper of sheep; Minerva, discoverer of the olive; Triptolemus, the Attic inventor of the plough; Silvanus, planter of trees — are all jumbled together, we scarce know what to think of it. When finally Caesar is invoked as a deity — Virgil doubts whether of earth, sky, or sea; surely not of Tartarus, for he would not wish to reign there — we are sorely puzzled, whether we are to regard the whole passage as fictitious and unreal, or as representing a state of belief not impossible to an imaginative mind in Virgil's day, though by us wholly inconceivable. As Mr. Sellar has well said, " it is impossible to find any principle of reconcilement " for such multifarious elements. " Probably not even the poets themselves, least of all Virgil, could have given an explanation of their real state of mind " in composing such a passage. " So far as we can attach any truthful meaning to this invocation, we must look upon it as a symbolical expression of divine agency and superintendence in all the various fields of natural production." Just so. To a reverent mind like Virgil's, unwilling to break with the past, yet accessible to all influences of the present, it may well have been that these multifarious relics of a fading polytheism expressed only the various functions, attributes, or agencies through which worked that Supreme Will, that one Pronoia in which his deeper mind really believed. Something of the same kind is seen in mediæval belief, when the practical faith in elaborate and active angelic hierarchies may have interfered with, though it did not supersede, the true faith in the Divine Unity.

If in the time of Augustus the majority of educated men believed nothing, those religious minds, to whom, as to Virgil, belief was a necessity, were more and more driven towards a monotheistic faith, towards the belief that the essential Being underlying the many forms of religion was One. The whole progress of the world, practical and social, as well as speculative, tended this way. Of intellectual influences making in this direction, the most powerful was Greek philosophy, whether in the shape of Stoicism or of Platonism. Every great poet takes in deeply the philosophy of his time, and certainly Virgil was no exception. Of the three forms of philosophy then current at Rome, the Stoic, the Platonic, and the Epicurean, Virgil began with the last. At Rome he studied under Siron, the Epicurean, and had been profoundly impressed by the great poem of his predecessor, Lucretius, which had expounded so powerfully to the Roman world the Epicurean tenets. For a time he was held charmed by this philosophy; but there were in Virgil's devout and affectionate nature longings which it could not satisfy. When he wrote his Eclogues he may have been a disciple of Epicurus; but in the Georgics we see that, if he still retained the physical views of that sect, he had bidden good-by to their moral and religious teaching. Every one remembers the passage in the second Georgic in which Virgil contrasts the task he had set before himself with the large aim which Lucretius had in view. While according no stinted admiration to the great attempt of Lucretius to lay bare Nature's inner mysteries, he says that he has chosen a humbler path. The import of this passage may be, as the French critic interprets it, to let us know that, after having sounded his own nature, Virgil had found that he was not fitted to persevere in those violent speculations, which had at first seduced his imagination, and that he had decided to abide by the majority, and to share their beliefs; yet not without casting a look of envy and regret at those more daring spirits, who were able to dwell without fear in the calm cold heights of science.

Perhaps another interpretation may be given to this famous passage, which evidently describes a crisis in Virgil's mental life, as well as in the direction of his poetry. After having been fascinated for a time by the seeming grandeur of the Lucretian view of things, he came to a crucial question which meets all thoughtful men in modern as well as in ancient times. He had to ask himself, In what way am I to think of this world; how am I to interpret it? From which side shall I approach it? Shall I think of its central force, its ruling power, under the medium of nature or under that of man? We cannot conceive it barely, absolutely, colorlessly: we must think it under some medium, and these are the only two media possible to us. Between the two we must make our choice. If we take nature for our medium, we see through it vastness, machinery, motion, order, growth, decay. And the contemplation of these things may lead us to think of some great central power, whence all these proceed. Centrality, organization, power,— these are the results which mere nature yields. And if we cannot rest in mere abstractions, we may pass from these to the thought of a Being, who is the spring of all this machinery, the central power of these vast movements, the arranger of these harmonies. Beyond this, by the aid of mere nature, we cannot get. The central power we thus arrive at is characterless, unmoral. Out of nature we can get no morality. "Nature is an unmoral medium." And this is very much all that Lucretius got to, and all that any ever will get to, who start from his point of view and adopt his method.

But take the other medium : start from man — from what is highest and best in him, his moral nature, his moral affections ; make man with these moral affections, which are his proper humanity, our medium, and we are led to a very different result. Interpreting the world and its central power through this medium, we are led not to a mere abstraction, but to think of that ruling Power as a personal and moral Being. That which is chief, highest, central in the universe, cannot possibly be lower than that which is best in man. Using whatever is deepest and best in ourselves as the window through which we look out to what is highest in the universe, in this way alone can we see somewhat into the divine character. This, it may be said, is anthropomorphism ; and that is a big word which scares many. But there is an anthropomorphism which is true, the only true theology — when we refer to God all those moral qualities, — righteous love, righteous hatred, mercy, truth, — of which there are some faint traces in ourselves. High humanity, then, is our guide to God. There is no other medium through which we can see Him as a moral being. Of the two methods, the " physical view," as has been said, " reduces God to a mechanical principle, the human and moral view raises him into a person and a character." The day may come when these two may coalesce and be seen in perfect harmony. But that day is not yet. Till it comes we shall cling to that which is deepest, most essential, and must always be paramount, and regard man's moral nature as the truest key to the interpretation of the universe — as our access to the divine nature.

It is not, of course, meant that Virgil consciously went through any such process of reasoning as this. But he may have been led by half-conscious thoughts, akin to these, to renounce the Lucretian philosophy, and to attach himself to that humbler, more human mode of thought, which breathes through all his poetry. Not but that he once and again reverts in his poems to philosophic speculations. In the song of Silenus, in the sixth Eclogue, he gives us a piece of the Lucretian cosmogony. In the fourth Georgic, when speaking of the wisdom of the bees, he alludes with evident sympathy to the theory, whether learnt from Pythagoras, or Plato, or the Stoics, that all creation, animate and inanimate, is inspired by the breath of one universal soul. To this theory he again returns in the sixth book of the *Æneid,* where Anchises in Elysium expounds it still more earnestly. Yet it is characteristic of Virgil's happy inconsistency, that his pantheism, if he really did in some sense hold it, had not any of the results it frequently has in more consecutive thinkers. It did not in the least obliterate for him moral distinctions, or make him at all less sensitive to the everlasting difference between right and wrong. This is at once apparent in the whole sentiment of the Georgics.

That greatest of didactic poems is Virgil's tribute to his love of Italian scenery, and to his interest in Italian rustics, among whom he had spent his childhood and youth. I cannot now even glance at the many and great beauties of the poem, and at the wonderful way in which, as all travellers testify, it conveys the feeling of the Italian landscape. A young poet, while lately visiting the neighborhood of Mantua, has well expressed this : —

> " O sweetest singer ! stateliest head,
>   And gentlest, ever crowned with bay,
> It seemed that from the holy dead
>   Thy soul came near to mine to-day ;

> "And all fair places to my view
>   Seemed fairer ; — such delight I had,
> To deem that these thy presence knew,
>   And at thy coming oft were glad."

But it is not of this, but of the religious sentiment which pervades the Georgics, that I have now to speak. It is seen not only in that Virgil exhorts the husbandmen to piety —

> "First of all worship the gods " —

and throws himself, as far as he can, into the rustic's reverence for Ceres and other rural deities. This he does. But his religious feeling shows itself in a more genuine and unconventional way.

Virgil's whole view of the relation of man to nature is in marked contrast to that of Lucretius. He felt, as strongly as Lucretius did, that the country is no mere Arcadian paradise ; that nature, if a nurse at all, is a rough and wayward one — often seems to fight against man — is traversed by what seem to us inherent defects and imperfections. Looking on these, Lucretius had maintained that a work, which was so defective, could not be divine: —

> "This universe has by no means been fashioned for us by divine
> Wisdom — with so deep a flaw it stands endowed."

And among the defects he enumerates many features — mountains, seas, the arctic and the torrid zones, and other things, which we now know to be really blessings. Virgil saw and recognized the seeming defects, acknowledges them not less feelingly, but interprets them in a different way. He saw that one end of their existence was to discipline man, to draw out in him the hardy and self-denying virtues, and that, if man so accepted them, they turned to his good.

> "The great sire himself would not have the path of tillage
> To be a smooth one, and first disturbed the fields
> By the husbandman's art, and whetted human wit by many a care,
> Nor suffered heavy sloth to waste his realm."

He regards the husbandman's lot as one full of often thankless toil, of suffering and disappointment. The first days of life are the best:

> "Poor mortals that we are, all the best days of life are the first
> To fly — come on apace diseases and the gloom of age, and suffering
> Sweeps us off, and the unrelenting cruelty of death."

And again in such words as

> "All things are destined to hurry towards decay,"

there is a tone of deep sadness, bordering on despondency; but yet this does not engender in Virgil unbelief or despair, much less anger or revolt. Rather, in view of these acknowledged hardships and evils, he counsels fortitude, patience, watchfulness, self-restraint, reverence. In Virgil's sadness there is no bitterness, but rather a sweet pensiveness, which looks to be comforted. His advice to the husbandman sums itself up into the mediæval motto, " Ora et labora." For nature is not, any more than man, independent. Both are under the control of a heavenly power, a supreme will; and this will ordains that man should by patient toil subdue reluctant nature, and in doing so should find not his sustenance only, but his happiness and peace.

In fine, with regard to the religious sentiment of the *Georgics*, Mr. Sellar thinks that Virgil's faith is purer and happier than that of Hesiod, because it is "trust in a just and beneficent Father, rather than fear of a jealous taskmaster. But he thinks it less noble than the faith of Æschylus and Sophocles, because it is " a passive yielding to the longing of the human heart and to æsthetic emotion, rather than that union of natural piety with insight into the mystery of life" which characterizes the religion of the two great dramatists. Without attempting now to discuss this contrast which Mr. Sellar has drawn, I leave it to the reflections of my readers.

As the *Georgics* are the poem of Italy, so the *Æneid* is the poem of Rome — the epic of the Empire. Patriotism is its keynote, its inspiring motive : pride in the past history of Rome, her present prosperity, her future destiny — all these, strangely interwoven with the fortunes of the Julian House. Yet along with this motive, behind it, in harmony with it, there moves a great background of religious sentiment, so powerful and omnipresent that the *Æneid* may be called a great religious epic.

In Virgil, however it may have been with other Romans, the sense of universal empire, and the belief in the eternal existence of Rome, were not founded on presumption. These things were guaranteed to her by her divine origin, and by the continual presence of an overruling destiny — a Fortuna urbis, Fatum, or Fata, whose behests it was Rome's mission to fulfil. This Fatum was something different from Jupiter. But "Jupiter Capitolinus in ancient, the living emperor in later times, were its visible vicegerents." This mysterious power which ruled the destiny of Rome was neither a personal nor a purely moral power. But in Virgil's view it assumed a beneficent aspect, just as with him the mission of Rome was not merely to conquer the world and rule it, but to bring in law and peace, and to put an end to war — "pacisque imponere morem."

Another religious aspect of the *Æneid* is seen, as the French critic [1] has remarked, in the view taken of the mission entrusted to Æneas. It was not to conquer Italy, but to find there a home and refuge for the outcast deities and penates of Troy. This runs through the poem from end to end. It is seen in the opening lines of it. It is seen in the words which Hector's ghost addresses to Æneas : —

"Troy intrusts to thee now her worship and her gods. Take them
 To share your destiny — seek for them a mighty city."

It is seen at the close, in the words of Æneas himself : —

"I will ordain sacred rites and divinities; let my father-in-law
 Latinus hold to the rule of war."

The Romans would never have tolerated to hear that their ancestors, Latin and Sabine, of whom they were so proud, were conquered by Phrygians, whom they

[1] G. Boissier, *La Religion Romaine.*

despised.   But the East they looked on as the land
of mystery, the birthplace of religion, and they were
not unwilling to receive thence their first lessons in
things divine.   It is as the bearer of the Trojan gods
to Italy that Æneas appears, from first to last.   This
is his main function ; and, this achieved, his mission is
ended, his work done.   At the close of the poem, when
all difficulties are to be smoothed away, the last of
these, Juno's vindictiveness, is appeased when she is
told by Jupiter that her favorite Italians were to be un-
removed, their place and name preserved ; the Trojans
were only to hand on to them their worship and their
name, and then to disappear.

" The Ausonians shall keep their native tongue, their native customs:
  The name shall remain as it is. The Teucrians shall merge in the
        nation they join —
  That and no more ; their rites and worship shall be my gift ;
  All shall be Latins and speak the Latin tongue."

                                        (*Æneid*, xii. 834.)

This view of the mission of Æneas as essentially a
religious one throws, I think, some light on his char-
acter as Virgil portrays it.   That character, as we all
know, has generally been thought uninteresting, not to
say insipid.   Every one has felt the contrast between
him and the hero of the *Iliad*, or even such subordi-
nate characters as Ulysses, Hector, Ajax, and Nestor.
These are living men, full of like passions with our-
selves, only of more heroic mould.   The glow of health
is in their cheek, the strong throb is in their pulses.
Beside them, how pale, washed-out, is the countenance
of Æneas !   He is no doubt, in some sort, a composite
conception — an attempt to embody somewhat diverse
attributes, rather than a man moved by one strong
human impulse.   On one side Æneas represents that

latest product of civilization, the humane man, in whom is embodied "humanitas," as Cicero and Virgil conceived it. On another side, some of his traits are taken from Augustus and meant to recall him. These two elements are both present. But far more potent than either is the conception of him as the man of destiny, whom the fates had called to go forth, he knows not whither, and to seek in some strange land, which the fates would show him, a home for his country's gods and for himself; a sad, contemplative man, to whom the present is nothing, who ever feels that he has a mournful past behind him, and a great destiny before him. He has no strong impulses of his own; natural interests have ceased to move him:

> " In him the savage virtues of the race,
> Revenge and all ferocious thoughts, are dead."

As the French critic has well expressed it, " He has secured from heaven a mission which lies heavy on him; and he accepts it pensively. He toils and endures hardness, to find a resting-place for his penates, a kingdom for his son, a glorious future for his race. Before these great interests his own personality has effaced itself. He obeys the behest of fate in spite of natural reluctance, and sacrifices himself to the commands of heaven." Herein lies the "pietas" which Virgil has made his fixed characteristic. The chief motive-power within him is piety in its widest sense, including all human affections — love to family, love to country, fidelity to the dead; above all, that dependence on a higher power, and that obedience to it, which controls and sanctifies all his actions. To meet these duties, to fulfil the destiny he is called to, is his one absorbing thought. He has no other.

Even that part of his conduct which to moderns seems most unforgivable, his heartless desertion of Dido, is explained by this principle, though it is not justified. Æneas deserts her not from heartlessness, but in obedience to an overmastering call from Heaven. Whatever his attachment may have been, one word brought by Mercury from Jupiter suffices to startle him from his dream. At the god's approach —

> "Art thou not helping to build the walls of lofty Carthage,
>   And in the fondness of weak affection piling up a fair city ! "

he at once awakes and longs to be gone.

> " He is on fire to fly, and leave the too-well-loved city,
>   Astounded at so unlooked-for a warning, and at the command of
>   the gods."

Hence we see why the character of Æneas, as portrayed in the first six books of the *Æneid*, is so much more consistent than it appears to be in the last six. In the former he is entirely the absorbed, devoted man obeying the behests of Heaven. In the latter he has to do the fighting business, to play the part of Achilles or Ajax. When we see him lopping off the heads of the Rutulians, we feel that this is not in keeping with the original conception of him. His bearing becomes unnatural, his words truculent, altogether unlike those of the humane, pensive, contemplative man of the earlier books. But it could not be avoided : the plan of the poem required that he should be the warrior as well as the religious exile; as the warrior, he had bloody work to do, and in describing this Virgil could not be original, but must needs fall back on imitation of the *Iliad* and of the Homeric heroes.

If we cannot get over an impression of baseness in his conduct to the Carthaginian queen, we should remember that in Virgil's intention this but proves the greatness of his self-sacrifice, and the depth of his conviction, that Heaven had called him to another destiny. Had his abandonment of Dido been his own deed it would have been the basest treachery. As it is, that action, though not admirable, is changed in character, when we see it as done at the behest of Heaven, as an act of religious obedience.

> "Cease to inflame by your complaints both yourself and me;
> It is not by my choice I am pursuing Italy."

It makes him, no doubt, less interesting as a man, but it proves more entirely that he is a religious hero inspired by the sense of a divine mission. This was the poet's fundamental conception of him; it was thus he wished to represent him. Unless we continually remember this, we shall not only misinterpret Æneas in his conduct to Dido, but we shall miss the key to his whole character, and to the main purpose of the poem.

It has often been remarked how much more attractive is the character of Turnus than that of Æneas. Turnus and his comrades represent the natural passions, the spontaneous impulses, in a much freer, more human way, than Æneas and his Trojans. The individuality of these last is, as it were, obliterated by the weight of destiny which they feel laid upon them. What is this but to say that in poetry or romance it is much easier to invest with interest an ordinary man, with all the human feelings and infirmities about him, than to portray a religious hero in such wise that, while he commands our reverence, he shall win our affection? If Virgil has failed to do so, and I grant that he has failed, who is there of poets or novelists that in this kind of portraiture has entirely succeeded?

But more than in any other portion of his work, the strength of Virgil's moral and religious feeling comes out in the sixth book of the *Æneid.* His whole conception of the condition of the departed souls is a thoroughly moral one — a projection into the unseen future of the everlasting difference between good and evil. That which lies at the bottom of all the elaborate imagery of the book is the belief that judgment awaits men there for what they have been, and what they have done here; that their works follow them into the unseen state; that the pollution which men have contracted here must be purged away before they can attain to peace. To show in detail how these conceptions pervade that sixth book would require a whole essay devoted to itself, and I cannot do more than allude to it now.

It is not, however, the definite teaching either of the sixth, or of any other book of the *Æneid*, that most clearly reveals the essential piety of Virgil's soul. It is the incidental expressions, the half-uttered thoughts, the sighs which escape him unawares, that show what his habitual feeling about man's life and destiny was — how solemn, how tender, how religious!

Consider the great purity of his mind as seen in his poems. One or two passages only occur in all his works from which the most perfect modesty would shrink. And this in an age when many of the great men of the day were steeped to the lips in impurity. When we first become acquainted with Virgil in boyhood, we are not, of course, aware of this characteristic. It requires larger acquaintance with literature and with the world to make us feel how great is the contrast, in this respect, between Virgil and most of the ancient, and indeed many of the modern, poets. Horace, who lived much in society, was conscious of the rare beauty of Virgil's character, and speaks of him as one of the whitest souls among the sons of men. Indeed, Horace never alludes to Virgil, but his voice hushes itself into a tone of tender reverence unusual with him.

Again, observe how, though Virgil is compelled to speak of war and bloodshed, his soul evidently abhors it. We see this in such lines as

> " The fever of the steel, the guilty madness of battle
> Rages within him."

Again —

> " By degrees crept in an age degenerate and of duller hue,
> And the frenzy for war and the greed of gain."

This sounds strange language from the lips of the great poet of the conquerors of the world, but it was the true language of Virgil's own heart, though not of his people's. Keble has remarked how from the thick of battle and slaughter he turns away to soothe himself with rustic images, as in the description of the conflicts of Æneas in the tenth book of the *Æneid.* Every death is described, not with stern delight, but with a sigh, as of one who felt for the miseries of men. As each warrior falls, Virgil turns aside to recall his home, his family, his peaceful pursuits, as in the well-known —

> " And he dreams in death of his darling Argos."

Note, too, Virgil's unworldliness of spirit. He had evidently no relish for the material splendors that fascinate lower natures. It would seem as if unworldliness were the very condition of all high poetry, and as if a great poet's heart could not be given to those things which the worldling admires. But no one of ancient, and few of modern, poets have shown so decidedly that riches, rank, splendor, have no charm for them. Homer, himself probably a poor man, in his simplicity, looks with evident satisfaction on the riches of the great. Andromache is " rich in gifts ; " Homer's Æneas boasts that his ancestor was " the wealthiest of mortal men." For Virgil

> " the high mansion with proud portals,
> Discharging from all the palace its huge tide of early visitants,"

has no attraction. From the palace of Augustus, and from the home of Maecenas on the Esquiline, he turns away instinctively to the woods and the fields, and to the men who lived among them. The country housewife going about her work pleases him more than the grandest of patrician matrons. Observe his picture, in the eighth book of the *Æneid*, of the thrifty housewife ; how at the mid-hour of the night, " compelled to support life by spinning, she wakes to light the fire that slumbered in the embers, adding night to her day's work, and keeps her handmaids laboring long by the blaze, all that she may be able to preserve her wedded life in purity, to bring up her infant sons." Evidently this was more to his mind than all the Tyrian purple and fretted ceilings of Roman mansions.

Connected with this unworldliness is Virgil's continual remembrance of the poor, and his feeling for the miserable. This he has expressed in one immortal line :

> " Tears there are for human things,
> And hearts are touched by mortal sufferings " —

this is the spirit of all his poetry. If men forget or despise the unfortunate, he is sure that Heaven does not : —

> " If you defy the race of men, and the weapons that mortals wield,
> Yet look to have to do with the gods, who forget not right and
> wrong."

No poet ever less admired mere outward success, and felt more sure that there is a tribunal somewhere which will test men and things by another standard, according to which

> "a noble aim
> Faithfully kept is as a noble deed
> In whose pure sight all virtue doth succeed."

You remember his

> "Learn, O boy! from me what virtue means and genuine toil.
> Let others teach you the meaning of success."

While gentleness and natural piety are Virgil's characteristic virtues, hardly less prized by him is another virtue which might seem opposed to these ; I mean patience, fortitude, manly endurance.

> ' Whate'er betide, every misfortune must be overcome by enduring it " —

this is the undertone of all his morality.

Again, another side of his unworldliness appears in this, that his heart refuses to find full satisfaction in anything here. Not wealth, not honor, not future fame, not the loveliness of nature, not the voice of friend, are enough for him. For, even if for a time they pleased, does he not keenly feel that

> " Poor mortals that we are, our brightest days of life
> Are ever the first to fly " ?

This has been called pessimism in Virgil. It is, however, only his keen feeling of the transitory and unsufficing nature of all earthly things. He does not rail at it, as some poets have done ; he upbraids neither the world nor the power that made it, but accepts it and learns from it reverent patience. And this experience would seem to have wakened within him a longing and aspiration after something purer, higher, lovelier, than

11

anything which earth contains. His poetry has the
tone as of one who, in his own words,

"Was stretching forth his hands with longing desire for the farther
shore."

Therefore, while we may not accept, as former ages did,
the fourth Eclogue as in any sense a prophecy of the
Messiah, we need not be blind to that which it does con-
tain — the hope of better things, the expectation that
some relief was at hand for the miseries of an outworn
and distracted world. This expectation was, we know,
widely spread in Virgil's day, and probably none felt it
more than he. Likely enough he expected that the re-
lief would come from the establishment and universal
sway of Roman Dominion ; but the ideal empire, as he
conceived it, was something more humane and benefi-
cent than anything earth had yet seen — something
such as Trajan may perhaps have dreamed of, but
which none ever saw realized. His conception of the
future work, which he imagined the Empire had to do,
contained elements which belonged to a kingdom not of
this world. Of his enthusiastic predictions regarding
it, we may say, in Keble's words,

"Thoughts beyond their thoughts to those high bards were given."

Taking, then, all these qualities of Virgil together,
his purity, his unworldliness, his tenderness towards the
weak and down-trodden, his weariness of the state of
things he saw around him, his lofty ideal, his longing
for a higher life — in him it may be said that the an-
cient civilization reached its moral culmination. Here
was, as least, one spirit, " who lived and died in faith,"
and kept himself unspotted from the world. It was this
feeling about Virgil, probably, which gave rise to the
legend, that St. Paul on his journey to Rome turned

aside to visit the poet's tomb near Naples, and that, weeping over it, he exclaimed —

> " What a man would I have made of thee,
> Had I found thee alive,
> O greatest of the poets ! "

In the words of the old Latin hymn —

> " Ad Maronis Mausoleum
> Ductus, fudit super eum
> Piae rorem lacrymae ;
> Quem te, inquit, reddidissem,
> Si te vivum invenissem,
> Poetarum maxime ! "

CHAPTER VII.

LYRICAL poetry is poetry in its intensest and purest form. Other kinds of poetry may be greater, more intellectual, — may combine elements more numerous and diverse, and demand more varied powers for their production ; but no other kind contains within the same compass so much of the true poetic ore, of that simple and vivid essence which to all true poetry is the breath of life.

For what is it that is the primal source, the earliest impulse, out of which all true poetry in the past has sprung, out of which alone it ever can spring ? Is it not the descent upon the soul, or the flashing up from its inmost depths, of some thought, sentiment, emotion, which possesses, fills, kindles it — as we say, inspires it ? It may be some new truth, which the poet has been the first to discern. It may be some world-old truth, borne in upon him so vividly, that he seems to have been the first man who has ever seen it. New to him, a new dawn, as it were, from within, the light of it makes all it touches new. In remote times, before poetry had worn itself into conventional grooves, it was only some impulse torrent-strong, some fountain of thought bursting from the deepest and freshest places of the soul, that could cleave for itself channels of utterance. In later times, when a poetic language had been framed, poetic forms stereotyped, and poetry had become an art, or even a literary trade, a far feebler impulse might borrow these forms, and express itself poetically. But originally it was not so. In primitive times, as Ewald says, it was only the marvellous overmastering power, the irresistible impulse of some new and creative thought, which, descending upon a man, could become within him the spirit and impelling force of poetry.

To our modern ears all this sounds unreal, — a thing you read of in æsthetic books, but never meet with in actual life. Our civilization, with its stereotyped ways and smooth conventionalities, has done so much to repress strong feeling; above all, English reserve so peremptorily forbids all exhibition of it, even when most genuine, that, if any are visited by it, they must learn to keep it to themselves, and be content to know " the lonely rapture of lonely minds." And yet even in this century of ours such things have been possible.

A modern poet, whose own experience and productions exemplified his words, has said, " A man cannot say, I will write poetry; the greatest poet cannot say it, for the mind in creation is as a fading coal, which some irresistible influence, like an inconstant wind, awakens to transitory brightness. This power arises from within, like the color of a flower which dims and changes as it is developed, and the conscious portions of our nature are unprophetic either of its approach or of its departure. It is, as it were, the interpenetration of a diviner nature with our own ; but its footsteps are like those of a wind over the sea, which the coming calm erases, and whose traces remain only on the wrinkled sand which paves it. Poetry is the record of the best and happiest moments of the happiest and best minds."

This, if in a measure true of all poetry, is especially

descriptive of lyrical poetry. The thought, sentiment, situation, which shall lay hold of the soul with such intense force and rise to the highest elevation, must be single, solitary. Other thoughts may attach themselves to the ruling one, and contribute to body it forth, but these are merely accessory and subordinate. One ruling thought, one absorbing emotion there must be, if the mind is to be kindled and concentrated into its warmest glow. And what we call a lyric poem is the adequate and consummate expression of some such supreme moment, of some one rapturous mood. Single we said the inspiring mood must be, — whole, unmingled, all-absorbing. When a mood of mind, a thought, a sentiment, or an emotion, or a situation, or an incident, possessing these characters, has filled and overmastered the singer's soul, then the vehicle most fitted to express it is the form of words which we call lyrical or musical.

When and how the adequate utterances of the inward visitation comes is an interesting question, which, however, need not detain us now. There may have been instances in which the poet, in the first flush of emotion, projected it into language perfect and complete. This, however, I should believe, is but rare, and only when the faculty of poetic utterance has been trained to the finest. Far more often, I should believe, a few burning words, a line here and there, have sprung to life in the first moment of excitement, and then have remained in the mind as the keynotes, till afterwards the propitious hour arrives which shall round off the whole thought into perfect language. Other instances there are in which the profound impressions have come and gone, and found no words at the time, but lain long dumb within, till, retouched in some happy moment by memory and imagination, they have taken to themselves wings, and bodied themselves forever in language that renews all their original brightness. This it is of which Wordsworth speaks when he calls poetry "emotion remembered in tranquillity." It is seen exemplified in his own best lyrics, many of which were no doubt born in this way; preëminently is it seen in his master Ode *On Intimations of Immortality.* And if those moments of past fervor, seen through the atmosphere of memory, lose something of their first vividness, they win instead a pensive and spiritual light, which forms I know not how much of their charm.

But however, and whenever, the one inspiring impulse finds words to embody it, one thing is certain, — that embodiment must be in language which has in it rhythm and melody. The expression must be musical, and for this reason. There is a strange kinship between inward fervor of emotion and outward melody of voice. When one overmastering impulse entirely fills the soul, there is a heaving of emotion within, which is in its nature rhythmical, — is indeed music, though unuttered music. And, when this passes outward into expression, it of necessity seeks to embody itself in some form of words which shall be musical, the outward melody of language answering to the already rhythmical and musical volume of feeling that is billowing within. We see this in the fact that, whenever any one is deeply moved, the excitement, passing outward, changes the tones of the voice, and makes them musical. Lyrical poetry is but the concentrating into regular form, and the carrying to higher power, of this natural tendency.

To make the perfect lyric two things must conspire:

an original emotion of more than usual depth, intensity, and tenderness, and a corresponding mastery over language to give it fitting utterance. The light that flashes up in the first creative moment must be so vivid and penetrating, as to fill and illumine every syllable of the language, as the light of the setting sun fills the cloud and transfigures it into its own brightness. When this depth and tenderness of susceptibility meets with perfect power of expression, we have the great lyric poems of the world. Such creations concentrate the largest amount of the true poetic essence into the smallest compass, and project it in the directest form, and with the most thrilling power, of which human language is capable.

Lyric poems are in a special way the creation of youth and the delight of age. Longer poems, the epic, the tragedy, demand more varied and maturer powers, and have generally been composed by men who have reached middle life. The intense glow, the tumultuous rush of feeling, which are the essence of the song, belong preëminently to youth, and can seldom in their first freshness be perpetuated even in those who have carried the boy's heart furthest into manhood. The wear and tear of life, and the continual sight of mortality pressing home, cool down the most ardent glow, and abate the strongest impulse. Hence it is that most of the greatest lyrists have done their pipings before forty; many have ceased to sing even earlier. The songs or lyric poems composed in mature life are mainly such as those which Wordsworth speaks of, — products of emotion remembered in tranquillity. These no doubt have a charm of their own, in which the fervor of early feeling is tempered and mellowed by the ripeness of age.

In the sequel I shall try to illustrate one of the many possible kind of lyrics. There is an obvious division of lyrics suggested by a passage which I recently read in the *Literary Studies* of the late Mr. Walter Bagehot. That very able man, who was long known chiefly as an original writer on political economy, seems to have been even more at home in the deep problems of metaphysics, and amid the fine shades of poetic feeling, than when discussing the doctrine of rent or of the currency. Speaking of lyric poetry, he says, " That species of art may be divided roughly into the human and the abstract. The sphere of the former is of course the actual life, passions, and actions of real men. In early ages there is no subject for art but natural life and primitive passion. At a later time, when, from the deposit of the *débris* of a hundred philosophies, a large number of half-personified abstractions are part of the familiar thoughts and language of all mankind, there are new objects to excite the feelings, — we might even say there are new feelings to be excited ; the rough substance of original passion is sublimated and attenuated, till we hardly recognize its identity." Out of this last state of feeling comes the abstract, or, as I may call it, the intellectual lyric. I propose to dwell now on the former of these two kinds.

There is a very general impression, especially in England, that Burns created Scottish song, and that all that is valuable in it is his work. Instead of saying that Burns created Scottish song, it would be more true to say that Scottish song created Burns, and that in him it culminated. He was born at a happy hour for a national singer, with a great background of song, centuries old, behind him, and breathing from his childhood a very atmosphere of melody. From the earliest times the Scotch have been a song-loving people, meaning by song both the tunes, or airs, and the words. This is not the side which the Scotchman turns to the world, when he goes abroad into it to push his fortune. We all know the character that passes current as that of the typical Scot, — sandy-haired, hard-featured, clannish to his countrymen, unsympathetic to strangers, cautious, shrewd, self-seeking, self-reliant, persevering, difficult to drive a bargain with, impossible to circumvent. The last thing a stranger would credit him with would be the love of song. Yet when that hard, calculating trader has retired from the 'change or the market-place to his own fireside, the thing, perhaps, he loves best, almost as much as his dividends, will be those simple national melodies he has known from his childhood. Till a very recent time the whole air of Scotland, among the country people, was redolent of song. You heard the milkmaid singing some old chant, as she milked the cows in field or byre; the housewife went about her work, or spun at her wheel, with a lilt upon her lips. You might hear in the Highland glen some solitary reaper, singing like her whom Wordsworth has immortalized; in the Lowland harvest field, now one, now another, of the reapers taking up an old-world melody, till the whole band break out into some well-known chorus. The ploughman, too, in winter, as he turned over the green lea, beguiled the time by humming or whistling a tune; even the weaver, as he clashed his shuttle between the threads, mellowed the harsh sound with a song. In former days song was the great amuse-ment of the peasantry, as they of a winter night met for a hamlet-gathering by each other's firesides. This was the usage in Scotland for centuries. Is it certain that the radical newspaper, which has super-seded it, is an improvement?

In general, it may be said that the airs or melodies are older than the words ; almost all the tunes have had at least two sets of words, an earlier and a later ; many of them have outlived more. There is much rather vague discussion as to the source from which the Scottish national tunes came. Some writers would refer them to the First James of Scotland, of whom we are told that he " invented a new, melancholy, and plaintive style of music, different from all others." Some would trace them to the old Celtic music, which has in-filtrated itself unawares from the Highlands into the Scottish Lowlands, and it cannot be doubted that to this source we owe some of our finest melodies. Others would make the Lowland music a Scandinavian rather than a Celtic immigration. Others, with not a little probability, have found a chief origin of it in the plain-song, Gregorian chants, or other sacred tunes of the mediæval Church, still clinging to the hearts and memories of the people, after they had been banished from the churches. Whatever may have been their origin, these old airs or melodies, which have been sung by so many generations, are full of character, and have a marked individuality of their own. They are simple, yet strong ; wild, yet sweet, answering wonderfully to the heart's primary emotions, lending themselves alike to sadness or gayety, to humor, drollery, or pathos, to manly independence and resolve, or to heart-broken lamentation. What musical peculiarities distinguish them I cannot say, knowing nothing of music but only

the delight it gives.   If any one cares to know what
the chief characteristics of Scottish music are, I would
refer him to a publication called *The Thistle*, which is
now being brought out by Mr. Colin Brown, of Glas-
gow.   In that miscellany of Scottish song there is a
disquisition on the nature of the national music, which
seems to me to make the whole matter more plain and
intelligible than any other of the treatises I have met
with.   But whatever may have been the origin, what-
ever may be the characteristics, of the Scottish tunes or
melodies, the thing to be remembered is that, in general,
the musical airs are older than the words which we now
have, and were in a great measure the inspirers of these
words.

About the poetry of the oldest songs, since I cannot
analyze or describe the music, let me say a word or two.
It is songs I speak of now, not ballads.   For though
these two terms are often used indiscriminately, I should
wish to keep them distinct.   A ballad is a poem which
narrates an event in a simple style, noticing the several
incidents of it successively as they occurred; not in-
dulging in sentiment or reflection, but conveying what-
ever sentiment it has indirectly, by the way the facts
are told, rather than by direct expression.   A song, on
the other hand, contains little or no narrative, tells no
facts, or gives, by allusion only, the thinnest possible
framework of fact, with a view to convey some one pre-
vailing sentiment, — one sentiment, one emotion, sim-
ple, passionate, unalloyed with intellectualizing or anal-
ysis.   That it should be of feeling all compact; that the
words should be translucent with the light of the one
all-pervading emotion, this is the essence of the true
song.   Mr. Carlyle well describes it when he says, "The

story, the feeling, is not detailed, but suggested ; not said or spouted in rhetorical completeness and coherence, but sung in fitful gushes, in glowing hints, in fantastic breaks, in warblings not of the voice only, but of the whole mind."

As to the history of these songs, it was only in the last century that men began to think them worth collecting, and only in this century that they have sought to trace their age and history. There are few, if any, entire songs of which we can be sure that they existed, in the form in which we now have them, before the Reformation. Snatches and fragments there are of much older date, some as early as the war of independence, when in the days of Robert Bruce the Scotch sang in triumph —

> "Maidens of England
> Sore may ye mourne
> For your lemmans ye hae lost
> At Bannockburn."

James I., our poet king, is said, besides his graver poems, to have composed songs in the vernacular which were sung by the people; but these have perished, or are now unknown. James V. celebrated his adventures among the peasantry in the somewhat free ballad or song, *The Gaberlunzie Man.*

With the dawn of the eighteenth century there came in Scotland an awakening, some would say a revival, of literature of various kinds. It was at this time that the popular songs, which hitherto had been almost entirely left to the peasantry, first began to be esteemed by the polite, and regarded as a form of literature. The first symptom of this was the publication in 1706 of Watson's collection of Scotch poems, which contained a number of old songs. But that which marked most decisively the turn of the tide in favor of the old popular minstrelsy was the publication by Allan Ramsay of his *Tea Table Miscellany* in 1724. Ramsay was himself a poet and a song-writer, and, living in Edinburgh as a bookseller, undertook to supply the upper ranks with the songs which he had heard in his moorland birthplace. The *Tea Table Miscellany* was intended, as its name suggests, to furnish the more polished circles of Edinburgh, at their social meetings, with the best specimens of their national melodies. Through that collection the homely strains which had been born in cottages, and which described the manners and feelings of peasants, found their way to the drawing-rooms of the rich and refined.

In this collection honest Allan did something to preserve the genuine old ware of our songs, which but for him might have perished. Many old strains he recast after his own taste, substituting for the names of Jock and Jennie, Damon and Phyllis; and for sun and moon, Phœbus and Cynthia. A great deal was, no doubt, done at this time to spoil the genuine old ware by importations of a false classicism from Virgil's Eclogues, or perhaps from Pope's imitations of these. Much was thus irretrievably lost; but we may be glad that so much was allowed to escape the touch of the spoilers.

Ramsay's collection, and other collections which were made early in the eighteenth century, contained many songs which belonged to the seventeenth century, if not to a remoter date; songs which are full of the fine flavor of old vernacular humor and dialect — here and there passing into deep pathos. Such songs are —

"Get up and bar the door," "Tak your auld cloak about ye,"

> "O waly, waly up the bank,
>   And waly, waly down the brae."

These and many more contain all the raciness and melodious feeling of the best songs of Burns.

As a sample of the peculiar manner in which drollery and sentiment are blended often in the same song, take one composed by a Forfarshire laird in the last century, Carnegie of Balnamoon, who, like many of his name, was out with the Prince in the Forty-Five : —

> "My daddie is a cankert carle,
>   He'll no twine wi' his gear;
> My minnie she's a scaulding wife,
>   Hauds a' the house asteer.
>   But let them say, or let them dae,
>   It's a' ane to me,
>   For he's low doun, he's in the brume,
>   That's waitin' on me:
>   Waitin' on me, my love,
>   He's waitin' on me:
>   For he's low doun, he's in the brume,
>   That's waitin' on me.

> "My auntie Kate sits at her wheel,
>   And sair she lightlies me;
> But weel I ken it's a' envy,
>   For ne'er a joe has she.
>   But let them say, or let them dae, etc

>   .   .   .   .

> "Gleed Sandy he cam wast yestreen,
>   And speir'd when I saw Pate;
> And aye sinsyne the neebors round
>   They jeer me air and late.
>   But let them say, or let them dae, etc."

After Ramsay's time the love of Scottish song spread through all ranks in Scotland, and many exquisite melodies, both tune and words, were added to the current stock by distinguished men of the time, and especially by ladies of what Lockhart used to call " the fine old Scottish families." Conspicuous among the lady songstresses stands Lady Grisell Baillie. She was a girl during the troublous times of Charles II. and James II., and died a widow in 1746. By her heroic conduct in preserving the life of her father, the covenanting Earl of Marchmont, she had won the admiration of her countrymen, before she was known as a poetess. To the heroic Christian character which she displayed while still a girl she added the accomplishment of song. One of her songs begins —

"There was ance a may, and she lo'ed na man,"

and it has for a chorus —

"And were na my heart licht I would die."

The song, excellent in itself, was made more famous by being quoted by Robert Burns on a well-known occasion in his later days. Lady Grisell was a native of the Borders, and a large proportion of our best songs, as of our ballads, came from the Border land.

Other Border ladies followed her in the path of song, especially Miss Jane Elliot, of Minto, and Miss Rutherford, of Fairnielee, afterwards Mrs. Cockburn, who lived to be, in her old age, a friend of Scott's boyhood. Each of these made herself famous by one immortal song. Miss Elliot, taking up one old line —

"I've heard the lilting at our ewe milking,"

and a refrain that remained from the lament sung for the Ettrick Forest men who had died at Flodden —

"The flowers o' the Forest are a wed awa,"

sang it anew in a strain which breathes the finest spirit of antiquity. Miss Rutherford, born herself on the edge of Ettrick Forest, took up the same refrain, and adapted it to a more recent calamity which befell, in her own time, many lairds of the Forest, who were overwhelmed with ruin and swept away. The songs of these three Border ladies, while they are true to the old spirit and manner of our native minstrelsy, did something toward refining it, by showing of. how pure and elevated sentiment it might be made the vehicle.

These ladies' songs were first made known to the world by appearing 'in a collection of Scottish songs, ancient and modern, published in 1769 by David Herd, a zealous antiquary and collector. After Ramsay's *Miscellany*, this publication of Herd's marks another epoch in the history of Scottish song. Herd preserved many precious relics of the past, which otherwise would have disappeared. He was indefatigable in searching out every scrap that was old and genuine, and his eye for the genuinely antique was far truer than Ramsay's.

This, however, must be said: he was so faithful and indiscriminate in his zeal for antiquity, that, along with the pure ore, he retained much baser metal, which might well have been left to perish. Not a few of the songs in his collection are coarse and indecent. As has often been said, if we wish to know what Burns did to purify Scottish song, we have only to compare those which he has left us with many which Herd incorporated in his collection, and published not twenty years before Burns appeared.

Scottish song is true pastoral poetry, — truer pastoral poetry is nowwhere to be found. That is, it expresses the lives, thoughts, feelings, manners, incidents, of men and women who were shepherds, peasants, crofters, and small moorland farmers, in the very language and

12

phrases which they used at their firesides. As I have
said elsewhere, the productions, many of them, not of
book-learned men, but of country people, with country
life, cottage characters and incidents, for their subjects,
they utter the feelings which poor men have known,
in the very words and phrases which poor men have
used. No wonder the Scottish people love them; for
never was the heart of any people more fully rendered
in poetry than Scotland's heart in these songs. Like the
homely hodden-gray, formerly the cotter's only wear,
warp and woof, they are entirely homespun. The stuff
out of which they are composed,

> " The cardin o 't, the spinnin o 't,
> The warpin o 't, the winnin o 't,"

is the heart-fibre of a stout and hardy peasantry.

Every way you take them, — in authorship, in senti-
ment, in tone, in language, — they are the creation and
property of the people. And if educated men and high-
born ladies, and even some of Scotland's kings, have
added to the store, it was only because they had lived
familiarly among the peasantry, felt as they felt, and
spoken their language, that they were enabled to sing
strains that their country's heart would not disown. For
the whole character of these melodies, various as they
are, is so peculiar and so pronounced, that the smallest
foreign element introduced, one word out of keeping,
grates on the ear and mars the music. Scottish song
has both a spirit and a framework of its own, within
which it rigorously keeps. Into that framework, these
moulds, it is wonderful how much strong and manly
thought, how much deep and tender human-heartedness,
can be poured. But so entirely unique is the inner
spirit, as well as the outward setting, that no one, not

even Burns, could stretch it beyond its compass, without your being at once aware of a falsetto note.

It was the glory of Burns that, taking the old form of Scottish song as his instrument, he was able to elicit from it so much. That Burns was the creator of Scottish song no one would have denied more vehemently than himself. When he appeared, in 1786, as the national poet of his country, the tide of popular taste was running strongly in favor of Scottish song. He took up that tide of feeling, or rather he was taken up by it, and he carried it to its height. He was nurtured in a home that was full of song. His mother's memory was stored with old tunes or songs of her country, and she sang them to her eldest boy from his cradle-time all through his boyhood. Amid the multifarious reading of his early years, the book he most prized was an old song-book, which he carried with him wherever he went, poring over it as he drove his cart or walked afield, song by song, verse by verse, carefully distinguishing the true, tender, or sublime from affectation and fustian. Thus he learned his song-craft and his critic-craft together. The earliest poem he composed was in his seventeenth summer, a simple love-song in praise of a girl who was his companion in the harvest field. The last strain he breathed was from his deathbed, in remembrance of some former affection.

Yet deep as were the love and power of song, the true lyric throb of heart, within him, it was not as a lyrist or song-writer that he first became famous. The Kilmarnock volume, which carried him at once to the height of poetic fame, contained only three songs, and these, though full of promise, are perhaps not his best. A song which he addressed to an early love,

while he was still young and innocent, composed before
almost any of his other poems, has a tenderness and
delicacy reached in only a few of his later love-songs,
and was the first of his productions which revealed his
lyric genius :

> "Yestreen, when to the trembling string
>   The dance gaed through the lighted ha',
> To thee my fancy took its wing,
>   I sat, but neither heard nor saw;
> Though this was fair, and that was braw,
>   And yon the toast of a' the town,
> I sigh'd, and said among them a',
>   'Ye are na Mary Morison.'

> " O Mary, canst thou wreck his peace,
>   Wha for thy sake wad gladly die?
> Or canst thou break that heart of his,
>   Whase only faut was loving thee?
> If love for love thou wilt na gie,
>   At least be pity to me shown!
> A thought ungentle canna be
>   The thought o' Mary Morison.'

It was during the last eight years of his life that Burns
threw his whole genius into song. Many have been the
lamentations over this. Scott has expressed his regret
that in his later and more evil days Burns had no fixed
poetic purpose, — did not gird himself to some great
dramatic work, such as he once contemplated. Carlyle
has bewailed that " our son of thunder should have
been constrained to pour all the lightning of his genius
through the narrow cranny of Scottish song, — the nar-
rowest cranny ever vouchsafed to any son of thunder."
We may well regret that his later years were so desul-
tory ; we cannot but lament the evil habits to which
latterly he yielded ; we may allow that the supplying
two collections with weekly cargoes of song must have

"degenerated into a slavish labor, which no genius could support." All this may well be granted, and yet we cannot but feel that Burns was predestined, alike by his own native instinct and by his outward circum-stances, to be the great song-maker of his country, — I might say, of the world. Song was the form of lit-erature which he had drunk in from his cradle ; it was a realm with which he was more familiar — into which he had keener insight — than any one else. He had longed from boyhood to shed upon the unknown streams of his native Ayrshire some of the power which gen-erations of minstrels had shed upon Yarrow and Tweed. He tells us in his own vernacular verse that from boy-hood he had

> "Ev'n then a wish (I mind its power),
> A wish that to my latest hour
> Shall strongly heave my breast,
> That I for poor óld Scotland's sake
> Some usefu' plan or book could make,
> Or sing a song at least.'

He had a compassionate sympathy for the old nameless song-makers of his country, lying in their unknown graves, all Scotland over. When he had leisure for a few brief tours, he went to gaze on the places, the names of which were embalmed in their old melodies ; he sought out their birthplaces, and looked feelingly upon the graves where they lie buried, as Wilson beau-tifully says, in kirkyards that have ceased to exist, and returned to the wilderness. The moulds which those old singers had bequeathed him, the channels they had dug, Burns gladly accepted, and into these he poured all the fervor of his large and melodious heart. He perceived how great capabilities lay in the old ver-nacular Lowland dialect, and in the pastoral form and style of the old Scottish songs, availed himself of these, expanded and enriched them; — this he did, but more than this : he entered with his whole soul into the old airs and melodies with which the earliest songs were associated, and these old melodies became his inspirers. He tells us that he laid it down as a rule, from his first attempts at song-writing, to sound some old tune over and over, till he caught its inspiration. He never composed a lyric without first crooning a melody to himself, in order to kindle his emotion, and regulate the rhythm of his words. Sometimes he got an old woman to hum the tune to him ; sometimes the village musician to scrape it on his fiddle, or a piper to drone it on his bagpipe; oftener his own wife sang it aloud to him, with her wood-note wild. And so his songs are not, like many modern ones, set to music ; they are themselves music, conceived in an atmosphere of music, rising out of it, and with music instinct to their last syllable. But the essential melody that was in him might have effected little, if he had not possessed a large background of mind to draw upon ; a broad and deep world of thought and feeling to turn to melody ; a nature largely receptive of all beauty, of all influences from man and the outward world ; most tender sensibility ; vivid and many-sided sympathy with all that breathes ; passionate, headlong impulse, — all these forces acting from behind and through an intellect, perhaps the most powerful of his time, and driving it home with penetrating insight to the very core of men and things. Yet keen as was his intellect, no one knew so well as Burns, that in song-writing intellect must be wholly subordinate to feeling ; that it must be sheathed and gently charmed ; that if for a moment it is allowed to preponderate over feeling, the song is killed. It is the equipoise and perfect intermingling of thought and emotion, the strong sense latent through the prevailing melody, that makes Burns's songs what they are, the most perfect the world has seen. Happy as a singer Burns was in this, that his own strong nature, his birth, and all his circumstances, conspired to fix his interest on the primary and permanent affections, the great fundamental relations of life, which men have always with them, — not on the social conventions and ephemeral modes, which are here to-day, forgotten in the next generation. In this how much happier than Moore or Béranger, or other song-writers of society living in a late civilization! Burns had his foot on the primary granite, which is not likely to move while anything on earth remains steadfast.

Consider, too, the perfect naturalness, the entire spontaneity, of his singing. It gushes from him as easily, as clearly, as sunnily, as the skylark's song does. In this he surpasses all other song-composers. In truth, when he is at his best, when his soul is really filled with his subject, it is not composing at all; the word is not applicable to him. He sings because he cannot help singing, — because his heart is full, and could not otherwise relieve itself.

Consider, again, while his songs deal with the primary emotions, the permanent relations and situations of human nature, how great is the variety of those moods and feelings, how large the range of them, to which he has given voice! One emotion with him, no doubt, is paramount, — that of love. And it must be owned that he allows the amatory muse too little respite. As our eye ranges over his songs, we could wish that, both for his own peace and for our satisfaction, he had touched this note more sparingly.   As Sir Walter says, "There is evidence enough that even the genius of Burns could not support him in the monotonous task of writing love-verses on heaving bosoms and sparkling eyes, and twisting them into such rhythmical form as might suit Scotch reels, ports, and strathspeys."

Yet, allowing all this, when he was really serious, how many phases of this emotion has he rendered into words which have long since become a part of the mother tongue!   What husband ever breathed to his absent wife words more natural and beautiful than those in

> "Of a' the airts the winds can blaw"?

When did blighted and broken-hearted love mingle itself with the sights and sounds of nature more touchingly than in

> "Ye flowery banks o' bonnie Doon,
>   How can ye blume sae fair!
> How can ye chant, ye little birds,
>   And I sae fu' o' care?"

Where is the wooing-match that for pointed humor and drollery can compare with that of Duncan Gray, when "Meg was deaf as Ailsa Craig," and Duncan "spak o' lowpin o'er a linn!"   These are lines that for happy humor none but Burns could have hit off.   Many more of his love-songs are equally felicitous, but there is a limitation.   It has been remarked, and I think truly, of Burns's love-songs that their rapture is without reverence.   The distant awe, with which chivalry approaches the loved one it adores, is unknown to him; it was Scott's privilege above all poets to feel and express this.   Perhaps Burns made some slight approach toward this more refined sentiment in his love-song after the manner of the old minstrels : —

> "My luve is like a red, red rose
> 　That 's newly sprung in June :
> My luve is like a melodie
> 　That 's sweetly play'd in tune."

And again in that early song of his to Mary Morison, which has been already quoted.

Besides those effusions of young ardor in which he generally indulges, how well has he conceived and depicted the sober certainty of long-wedded love in the calm and cheerful pathos of " John Anderson, my jo, John ! "

One emotion, no doubt, was paramount with Burns, and yet how many other moods has he rendered ! What can be simpler, easier, one might think, to compose than such a song as " Should auld acquaintance be forgot " ? Yet who else has done it ? There is about this song almost a biblical severity, such as we find in the words of Naomi, or of one of the old Hebrew patriarchs. For, as has been said, the whole inevitable essential conditions of human life, the whole of its plain, natural joys and sorrows, are described, — often they are only hinted at, — in the Old Testament as they are nowhere else. In songs like *Auld Lang Syne,* Burns has approached nearer to this biblical character than any other modern poet. Again, if wild revelry and bacchanalian joy must find a voice in song, what utterance have they found to compare with " Willie brewed a peck of maut " ? Certainly not the " Nunc est bibendum " of Horace. The heroic chord, too, Burns has touched with a powerful hand in " Scots, wha hae." The great Scotchman, lately departed, has said of it, " As long as there is warm blood in the heart of Scotchmen, or of man, it will move in fierce thrills under this war ode, the best, I believe, that was ever written by any pen." To this oracle I suppose every Scotchman must say, Amen. And yet I have my own misgivings. I think that it is to the charm of music and old associations rather than to any surpassing excellence in the words that the song owes its power. Another mood is uttered, a strange wild fascination dwells, in the defiant Farewell of Macpherson the Highland Reever, who

> " lived a life of sturt and strife,
> And died of treachery ; "

to whose last words Burns has added this matchless chorus : —

> " Sae rantingly, sae wantonly,
> Sae dauntingly gaed he ;
> He play'd a spring and danc'd it round
> Below the gallows tree."

Last of all, I shall name " A man 's a man for a' that," which, though not without a touch of democratic bitterness, contains lines that are for all time : —

> " The rank is but the guinea's stamp ;
> The man 's the gowd for a' that."

These are but a few samples of the many mental moods which Burns has set to melody. He composed in all nearly three hundred songs. Of these from thirty to forty represent him at his best, at the highest floodmark of his singing power. They are perfect in sentiment, perfect in form. Amid all that was sad and heart-depressing in his later years, the making of these songs was his comfort and delight. Besides the solace he had in the exercise of his powers, he found satisfaction in the thought that he was doing something to atone for the waste of the great gifts with which he had been entrusted. Of these three hundred songs some were founded on old words which he took, retouched, or recast; sometimes an old verse or line served as the hint, whence he struck off an original song, far better than the lost one. For others he made new words from beginning to end, keeping to some old tune, and preserving the native pastoral style and vernacular dialect.

Every one of them contains some touch of tenderness or humor, or some delicate grace or stroke of power, which could have come from no other but his master hand. And to his great credit be it ever remembered that in doing this he purified the ancient songs from much coarseness, and made them fit to be heard in decent society. The poems, and even some of the songs, of Burns are not free from grossness, which he himself regretted at the last. But in justice to his memory it should ever be borne in mind how many songs he purged of their coarser element, — how many tunes he found associated with unseemly words, and left married to verses, pure and beautiful, of his own composing. Those old Scottish melodies, said Thomas Aird, himself a poet, "sweet and strong though they were, strong and sweet, were all the more, for their very strength and sweetness, a moral plague, from the indecent words to which many of them had been set. How was the plague to be stayed? All the preachers in the land could not divorce the grossness from the music. The only way was to put something better in its stead. That inestimable something, not to be bought by all the mines of California, Burns gave us. And in doing so, he accomplished a social reform beyond the power of pulpit or parliament to effect."

That which we have seen to be the native quality of Scottish song Burns took up and carried to a higher effect. The characteristics of the best old Scottish songs, and preëminently of the best songs of Burns, are: (1.) Absolute truthfulness; truthfulness to the great facts of life; truthfulness also to the singer's own feelings, — what we mean by sincerity. (2.) Perfect naturalness: the feeling embodies itself in a form and language as natural to the poet as its song is to the bird. This is what Pitt noted when he said of Burns' poems that no verse since Shakespeare's "has so much the appearance of coming sweetly from nature." I should venture to hint, that in this gift of perfect spontaneity Burns was even beyond Shakespeare. (3.) What is perhaps but another form of the same thing, you have in Burns' songs what, in the language of logicians, I would call the "first intention" of thought and feeling. You overhear in them the first throb of the heart, not meditated over, not subtilized or refined, but projected warm from the first glow. (4.) To this effect, his native Scottish vernacular, which no one has ever used like Burns, contributed I know not how much. That dialect, broadening so many vowels and dropping so many consonants, lends itself especially to humor and tenderness, and brings out many shades of those feelings which in English would entirely evaporate. Nothing, I think, more shows the power of Burns than this, that a dialect, which but for him would have perished ere now, he has made classical, — an imperishable portion of the English language. This is but one way of putting a broader and very striking fact; that while everything about Burns would seem to localize and limit his influence, the language he employed, the color-

ing, the manner, the whole environment, — he has in-
formed all these with such strength and breadth of cath-
olic humanity, that of every emotion which he has sung,
his has become the permanent and accepted language
wherever the English tongue is spoken.

Scottish song, I have said, culminated in Burns. I
might have gone further, and said that he gave to the
song a power and a dignity before undreamt of. What
Wordsworth said of Milton's sonnets may equally be
said of Burns' songs — in his hand the thing became a
trumpet —

> " whence he blew
> Soul-animating strains.''

Is there any other form of poetry or of literature
which so lays hold of the heart, — which penetrates so
deep, and is remembered so long ? Although no singer
equal to Burns has arisen in Scotland since his day, or
will again arise, yet, in the generation which followed
him, song in his country gained a new impetus from
what he had done for it. Tannahill, the Ettrick Shep-
herd, Walter Scott, Lady Nairn, Hugh Ainslie, and
many more, each made their contribution to swell the
broad river of their country's song. Other nameless
men there are who will yet be remembered in Scotland,
each as the author of one unforgotten song. Lady
Nairn, I am apt to fancy, is almost our best song-com-
poser since Burns. She has given us four or five songs,
each in a different vein, which might be placed next
after, perhaps even beside, the best of Burns.

Whether the roll of Scottish song is not now closed,
is a thought which will often recur to the heart of those
who love their country better for its songs' sake. The
melodies, the form, the language, the feeling, of those

national lyrics belong to an early state of society.   Can
the old moulds be stretched to admit modern feeling,
without breaking ?   Can the old root put forth fresh
shoots amid our modern civilization ?   Are not school
boards and educational apparatus doing their best to
stamp out the grand old dialect, and to make the coun-
try people ashamed of it ?   Can the leisure and the full-
heartedness, in which song is born, any longer survive,
amid the hurry of life, the roar of railways, the clash of
machinery, the universal devotion to manufacture and
money-making?   I should be loath to answer No ; but
I must own to a painful misgiving, when I remember
that during the present generation, that is, during the
last thirty years, Scotland has produced no song which
can be named along with our old favorites.

I said that Burns had given a voice to a wide range
of emotion, — to many moods ; I did not say to all
moods, — that would have been to exaggerate.   There
is the whole range of sentiment which belongs to the
learned and the philosophic, that which is born of subtle,
perhaps over-refined intellect, which he has not touched.
No Scottish song has touched it.   Into that region it
could not intrude without abrogating its nature and de-
stroying its intrinsic charm.   That charm is that it
makes us breathe a while the air of the mountains and
the moors, not that of the schools.   But Scottish song
is limited on another side, which it is not so easy to ac-
count for.   There is little, almost no, allusion to religion
in it.   It is almost as entirely destitute of the distinct-
ively Christian element, as if it had been composed by
pagans.   Certainly, if we wished to express any pecul-
iarly Christian feeling or aspiration, we should have
to look elsewhere than to these songs.   Had this been

confined to the lyrics of Burns, it might have been ex-
plained by the fact that he, though not without a haunt-
ing sense of religion, lived a life which shut him out
from its serener influences; he never had the "heart
set free," from which alone religious poetry can flow.
But the same want is apparent in almost all Scottish
songs of every age. The Scotch have passed hitherto
for a religious people, and, we may hope, not without
reason. Yet there is hardly one of their popular songs
which breathes any deep religious emotions, which ex-
presses any of those thoughts that wander towards eter-
nity. This is to be accounted for partly by the fact
that the early Scottish songs were so mingled with
coarseness and indecency, that the teachers of religion
and guardians of purity could not do otherwise than
set their face against them. Song and all pertaining to
it got to be looked upon as irreligious. Moreover, the
old stern religion of Scotland was somewhat repressive
of natural feeling, and divided things sacred from things
profane by too rigid a partition; and songs and song-
singing were reckoned among things profane. Yet the
native melodies were so beautiful, and the words, not-
withstanding their frequent coarseness, contained so
much that was healthful, so much that was intensely
human, that they could not be put down, but kept sing-
ing themselves on in the hearts and homes of the people,
in spite of all denunciations. In the old time, it was
often the same people who read their Bibles most, whose
memories were most largely stored with these countless
melodies. As a modern poetess has said,

> "They sang by turns
> The psalms of David, and the songs of Burns."

Lady Nairn, who was a religious person, and yet loved

her country's songs, and felt how much they contain which, if not directly religious, was yet "not far from the kingdom of heaven," desired to remove the barrier; and she sang one strain, *The Land o' the Leal,* which, even were there none other such, would remain to prove how little alien to Christianity is the genuine sentiment of Scottish song, — how easily it can rise from true human feeling into the pure air of spiritual religion. If any Scottish religious teacher of modern times possessed a high spiritual ideal, and could set forth the stern side of righteousness, it was Edward Irving; yet in his devoutest moods he could still remember the melodies and songs he had loved in childhood. With a passage from his sermon on Religious Meditation, I shall conclude: " I have seen Sabbath sights and joined in Sabbath worships which took the heart with their simplicity and thrilled it with sublime emotions. I have crossed the hills in the sober, contemplative autumn to reach the retired, lonely church betimes; and as we descended towards the simple edifice, whither every heart and every foot directed itself from the country around on the Sabbath morn, we beheld issuing from every glen its little train of worshippers coming up to the congregation of the Lord's house, round which the bones of their fathers reposed. In so holy a place the people assembled under a roof, where ye of the plentiful South would not have lodged the porter of your gate; but under that roof the people sat and sang their Maker's praise, ' tuning their hearts, by far the noblest aim,' and the pastor poured forth to God the simple wants of the people, and poured into their attentive ears the scope of Christian doctrine and duty. The men were shepherds, and came up in their shepherd's guise, and the very brute, the shepherd's servant and companion, rejoiced to come at his feet. It was a Sabbath, — a Sabbath of rest! But were the people stupid? Yes, what an over-excited citizen would call stupid; that is, they cared not for parliaments, for plays, routs, or assemblies, but they cared for their wives and their children, their laws, their religion, and their God; and they sang their own native songs in their own native vales, — songs which the men I speak of can alone imagine and compose. And from them we citizens have to be served with songs and melodies, too, for we can make none ourselves."

13

CHAPTER VIII.

SHELLEY AS A LYRIC POET.

So many biographies, records, and criticisms of Shelley have lately appeared that one may take for granted in all readers some general acquaintance with the facts of his life. Of the biographies, none perhaps is more interesting than the short work by Mr. J. A. Symonds, which has lately been published as one of the series, edited by Mr. Morley, *English Men of Letters*. That work has all the charm which intense admiration of its subject, set forth in a glowing style, can lend it. Those who in the main hold with Mr. Symonds, and are at one with him in his fundamental estimate of things, will no doubt find his work highly attractive. Those, on the other hand, who do not altogether admire Shelley's character, or the theories that moulded it, will find Mr. Symonds's work a less satisfactory guide than they could have wished. Of the many comments and criticisms on Shelley's character and poetry, two of the most substantial and rational are an essay by Mr. R. H. Hutton, and one by the late Mr. Walter Bagehot. These two friends had together in their youth felt the charm of Shelley, and each in his riper years has given his estimate of the man and of his poetry. We all admire that which we agree with; and nowhere have I found on this subject thoughts which seem to me so adequate and so helpful as those contained in these two essays, none which give such insight into Shelley's abnormal character, and into the secret springs of his inspiration. Of the benefit of these thoughts I shall freely avail myself, whenever they seem to throw light upon my subject.

The effort to enter into the meaning of Shelley's poetry is not altogether a painless one. Some may ask, Why should it be painful? Cannot you enjoy his poems merely in an æsthetic way, take the marvel of his subtle thoughts, and the magic of his melody, without scrutinizing too closely their meaning or moral import? This, I suppose, most of my hearers could do for themselves, without any comment of mine. Such a mere surface, dilettante way of treating the subject might be entertaining, but it would be altogether unworthy of this place. All true literature, all genuine poetry, is the direct outcome, the condensed essence, of actual life and thought. Lyric poetry for the most part is — Shelley's especially was — the vivid expression of personal experience. It is only as poetry is founded on reality that it has any solid value; otherwise it is worthless. Before, then, attempting to understand Shelley's lyrics, I must ask what was the reality out of which they came — that is, what manner of man Shelley was, what were his ruling views of life, along what lines did his thoughts move?

Those who knew Shelley best speak of the sweetness and refinement of his nature, of his lofty disinterestedness, his unworldliness. They speak too of something like heroic self-forgetfulness. These things we can in a measure believe, for there are in his writings many traits that look like those qualities. And yet one receives with some reserve the high eulogies of his friends; for we feel that these were not generally men whose moral estimates we can entirely accept, and there were incidents in his life which seem somewhat at variance with the qualities they attribute to him. When Byron speaks of his purity of mind, we cannot but doubt how far Byron can be accepted as a good judge of purity.

One of his biographers has said that in no man was the moral sense ever more completely developed than in Shelley, in none was the perception of right and wrong more acute. I rather think that the late Mr. Bagehot was nearer the mark when he asserted that in Shelley conscience, in the strict meaning of that word, never had been revealed — that he was almost entirely without conscience. Moral susceptibilities and impulses, keen and refined, he had. He was inspired with an enthusiasm of humanity after a kind; hated to see pain in others, and would willingly relieve it; hated oppression, and stormed against it ; but then all rule and authority he regarded as oppression. He felt for the poor and the suffering, and tried to help them, and willingly would have shared with all men the vision of good which he sought for himself. But these passionate impulses are something very different from conscience. Conscience first reveals itself, when we become aware of the strife between a lower and a higher nature within us — a law of the flesh warring against the law of the mind. And it is out of this experience that moral religion is born, the higher law leading us to One whom that law represents. As Canon Mozley has said, " it is an introspection on which all religion is built — man going into himself and seeing the struggle within him ; and thence getting self-knowledge, and thence the knowledge of God." But Shelley seems to have been conscious of no such strife, to have known nothing of the inward struggle between flesh and spirit. He was altogether a child of impulse — of impulse, one, total, all-absorbing. And the impulse that came to him he followed whithersoever it went, without questioning either himself or it. He was preëminently τοῖς πάθεσιν ἀκολουθητικός, one who followed his passions unquestioningly ; and Aristotle, we know, tells us that such an one is no fit judge of moral truth. But this peculiarity, which made him so little fitted to guide either his own life or that of others, tended, on the other hand, to make him preëminently a lyric poet. How it fitted him for this we shall presently see. But abandonment to impulse, however much it may contribute to lyrical inspiration, is a poor guide to conduct ; and a poet's conduct in life, of whatever kind it be, quickly reacts on his poetry. It was so with Shelley.

It would be painful to revert to unhappy incidents, and as needless as painful. But when one reads in Mr. Symonds's book that Shelley's youth was "strongly moralized," some incidents of his early years rise to mind which make ordinary persons ask, with wonder, what sort of morality it was wherewith he was "moralized."

Partisans of Shelley will, I know, reply, " You judge Shelley by the conventional morality of the present day, and, judging him by this standard, of course you at once condemn him. Do you not know that it was against these very conventions, which you call morality, that Shelley's whole life was a protest? He was the prophet of something truer or better than this." But was Shelley's revolt only against the conventional morality of his own time, and not rather against the fundamental morality of all time? Had he merely cried out against the

stifling political atmosphere and the dry, dead ortho-
doxy of the Regency and the reign of George IV., and
longed for some ampler air, freer and more life-giving,
one could well have understood, even sympathized with,
him. His rebellion, however, was not against the limita-
tions and corruptions of his own day, but against the
moral verities which two thousand years have tested, and
which have been approved not only by eighteen Chris-
tian centuries, but no less by the wisdom of Virgil and
Cicero, of Aristotle and Sophocles. Shelley may be
the prophet of a new morality; but it is one which never
can be realized till moral law has been obliterated from
the universe, and conscience from the heart of man.

That he possessed many noble traits of character,
none can gainsay; and yet it is impossible, when reading
his life and his poetry, not to feel that his nature must
have been traversed by some strange deep flaw, marred
by some radical inward defect. In some of his gifts and
impulses he was more — in other things essential to
goodness, he was far less — than other men; a fully
developed man he certainly was not. I am inclined to
believe that, for all his noble impulses and aims, he was
in some way deficient in rational and moral sanity.
Many will remember Hazlitt's somewhat cynical de-
scription of him; yet, to judge by his writings, it looks
like truth. He has "a fire in his eye, a fever in his
blood, a maggot in his brain, a hectic flutter in his
speech, which mark out the philosophic fanatic. He
is sanguine-complexioned and shrill-voiced." This is
just the outward appearance we could fancy for his
inward temperament. What was that temperament?

He was entirely a child of impulse, lived and longed
for high-strung and intense emotion — simple, all-absorb-

ing, all-penetrating emotion, going straight on in one direction to its object, hating and resenting whatever opposed its progress thitherward. The object which he longed for was some abstract intellectualized spirit of beauty and loveliness, which should thrill his spirit, unceasingly, with delicious shocks of emotion.

This yearning, panting desire is expressed by him in a thousand forms and figures throughout his poetry. Again and again this yearning recurs —

> "I pant for the music which is divine,
>   My heart in its thirst is a dying flower ;
> Pour forth the sound like enchanted wine,
>   Loosen the notes in a silver shower ;
> Like a herbless plain for the gentle rain
>   I gasp, I faint, till they wake again.

> "Let me drink the spirit of that sweet sound ;
>   More, O more ! I am thirsting yet ;
> It loosens the serpent which care has bound
>   Upon my heart to stifle it ;
> The dissolving strain, through every vein,
>   Passes into my heart and brain."

It was not mere sensuous enjoyment that he sought, but keen intellectual and emotional delight — the mental thrill, the glow of soul, the "tingling of the nerves," that accompany transcendental rapture. His hungry craving was for intellectual beauty, and the delight it yields ; if not that, then for horror ; anything to thrill the nerves, though it should curdle the blood, and make the flesh creep. Sometimes for a moment this perfect abstract loveliness would seem to have embodied itself in some creature of flesh and blood ; but only for a moment would the sight soothe him — the sympathy would cease, the glow of heart would die down — and he would pass on in hot, insatiable pursuit of new rapture. "There is no rest for us," says the great preacher,

" save in quietness, confidence, and affection." This was not what Shelley dreamed of, but something very different from this.

The pursuit of abstract ideal beauty was one form which his hungry, insatiable desire took. Another passion that possessed him was the longing to pierce to the very heart of the mystery of existence. It has been said that before an insoluble mystery, clearly seen to be insoluble, the soul bows down and is at rest, as before an ascertained truth. Shelley knew nothing of this. Before nothing would his soul bow down. Every veil, however sacred, he would rend, pierce the inner shrine of being, and force it to give up its secret. There is in him a profane audacity, an utter awelessness. Intellectual Αἰδώς was to him unknown. Reverence was to him another word for hated superstition. Nothing was to him inviolate ; all the natural reserves he would break down. Heavenward, he would pierce to the heart of the universe and lay it bare ; manward, he would lay bare the inner precincts of personality. Every soul should be free to mingle with any other, as so many raindrops do. In his own words,

> " The fountains of our deepest life shall be
> Confused in passion's golden purity."

However fine the language in which such feelings may clothe themselves, in truth they are wholly vile ; there is no horror of shamelessness which they may not generate. Yet this is what comes of the unbridled desire for " tingling pulses," quivering, panting, fainting sensibility, which Shelley everywhere makes the supreme happiness. It issues in awelessness, irreverence, and what some one has called " moral nudity."

These two impulses both combined with another passion he had — the passion for reforming the world. He had a real, benevolent desire to impart to all men the peculiar good he sought for himself — a life of free, unimpeded impulse, of passionate, unobstructed desire. Liberty, Equality, Fraternity — these of course; but something far beyond these — absolute Perfection, as he conceived it, he believed to be within every man's reach. Attainable, if only all the growths of history could be swept away, — all authority and government, all religion, law, custom, nationality, everything that limits and restrains — and if every man were left open to the uncontrolled expansion of himself and his impulses. The end of this process of making a clean sweep of all that is, and beginning afresh, would be that family ties, social distinctions, government, worship, would disappear, and then man would be king over himself, and wise, gentle, just, and good. Such was his temperament, the original emotional basis of Shelley's nature ; such, too, some of the chief beliefs and aims towards which this temperament impelled him. And certainly these aims do make one think of the "maggot in the brain." But a temperament of this kind, whatever aims it turned to, was eminently and essentially lyrical. Those thrills of soul, those tingling nerves, those rapturous glows of feeling, are the very substance out of which high lyrics are woven.

The insatiable craving to pierce the mystery of course drove Shelley to philosophy for instruments to pierce it with. During his brief life he was a follower of three distinct schools of thought. At first he began with the philosophy of the senses, was a materialist, adopting Lucretius as his master, and holding that atoms are the only realities, with, perhaps, a pervading life of nature to mould them — that from atoms all things come, to atoms return. Yet even over this dreary creed, without spirit, immortality, or God, he shouted a jubilant " Eureka," as though he had found in it some new glad tidings.

From this he passed into the school of Hume — got rid of matter, the dull clods of earth, denied both matter and mind, and held that these were nothing but impressions, with no substance behind them. This was a creed more akin to Shelley's cast of mind than materialism. Not only dull clods of matter, but personality, the " I " and the " thou," were by this creed eliminated, and that exactly suited Shelley's way of thought. It gave him a phantom world.

From Hume he went on to Plato, and in him found still more congenial nutriment. The solid, fixed entities — matter and mind — he could still deny, while he was led on to believe in eternal archetypes behind all phenomena, as the only realities. These Platonic ideas attracted his abstract intellect and imagination, and are often alluded to in his later poems, as in *Adonais*. Out of this philosophy it is probable that he got the only object of worship which he ever acknowledged, the Spirit of Beauty — Plato's idea of beauty changed into a spirit, but without will, without morality ; in his own words —

> " That Light whose smile kindles the universe,
> That Beauty in which all things work and move,
> That Benediction which the eclipsing curse
> Of birth can quench not, that sustaining Love
> Which, through the web of being blindly wove
> By man and beast and earth and air and sea,
> Burns bright or dim, as each are mirrors of
> The fire for which all thirst.''

To the moral and religious truths which are the back-bone of Plato's thought he never attained. Shelley's thought never had any backbone. Each of these successively adopted philosophies entered into and colored the successive stages of Shelley's poetry; but through them all his intellect and imagination remained unchanged.

What was the nature of that intellect? It was wholly akin and adapted to the temperament I have described as his. Impatient of solid substances, inaccessible to many kinds of truth, inappreciative of solid, concrete facts, it was quick and subtle to seize the evanescent hues of things, the delicate aromas which are too fine for ordinary perceptions. His intellect waited on his temperament, and, so to speak, did its will — caught up, one by one, the warm emotions as they were thrown off, and worked them up into the most exquisite abstractions. The rush of throbbing pulsations supplied the materials for his keen-edged thought to work on, and these it did mould into the rarest, most beautiful shapes. This his mind was busy doing all his life long. The real world, existence as it is to other minds, he recoiled from — shrank from the dull gross earth which we see around us — nor less from the unseen world of Righteous Law and Will which we apprehend above us. The solid earth he did not care for. Heaven — a moral heaven — there was that in him which would not tolerate. So, as Mr. Hutton has said, his mind made for itself a dwelling-place, midway between heaven and earth, equally remote from both, some interstellar region, some cold, clear place

"Pinnacled dim in the intense inane,"

which he peopled with ideal shapes and abstractions,

wonderful or weird, beautiful or fantastic, all woven out
of his own dreaming phantasy.

This was the world in which he was at home; he was
not at home with any reality known to other men. Few
real human characters appear in his poetry; his own
pulsations, desires, aspirations, supplied the place of
these. Hardly any actual human feeling is in them;
only some phase of evanescent emotion, or the shadow
of it, is seized — not even the flower of human feeling,
but the bloom of the flower, or the dream of the bloom.
A real landscape he has seldom described, only he has
caught his own impression of it, or some momentary
gleam, some tender light, that has fleeted vanishingly
over earth and sea. Nature he used mainly to cull
from it some of its most delicate tints, some faint
hues of the dawn or of the sunset clouds, to weave in
and color the web of his abstract dream. So entirely
at home is he in this abstract shadowy world of his own
making, that, when he would describe common visible
things, he does so by likening them to those phantoms
of the brain, as though with these last alone he was
familiar. Virgil likens the ghosts by the banks of Styx
to falling leaves —

> "Quam multa in silvis autumni frigore primo
> Lapsa cadunt folia."

Shelley likens falling leaves to ghosts. Before the wind
the dead leaves, he says,

> "Are driven, like ghosts from an enchanter fleeing."

Others have compared thought to a breeze. With
Shelley the breeze is like thought; the pilot spirit of
the blast, he says,

> "Wakens the leaves and waves, ere it hath past,
> To such brief unison as on the brain

> One tone which never can recur has cast
>   One accent, never to return again."

We see thus that nature, as it actually exists, has little place in Shelley's poetry. And man, as he really is, may be said to have no place at all.

Neither is the world of moral or spiritual truth there — not the living laws by which the world is governed — no presence of a Sovereign Will, no all-wise Personality, behind the fleeting shows of time. The abstract world, in which his imagination dwelt, is a cold, weird, unearthly, unhuman place, peopled with shapes which we may wonder at, but cannot love. When we first encounter these, we are fain to exclaim, Earth we know, and heaven we know, but who and what are ye? Ye belong neither to things human nor to things divine. After a very brief sojourn in Shelley's ideal world, with its pale abstractions, most men are ready to say with another poet, after a voyage among the stars —

> "Then back to earth, the dear green earth;
>   Whole ages though I here should roam,
>   The world for my remarks and me
>   Would not a whit the better be:
>   I've left my heart at home."

In that dear green earth, and the men who have lived or still live on it, in their human hopes and fears, in their faiths and aspirations, lies the truest field for the highest imagination to work in. That is, and ever will be, the haunt and main region for the songs of the greatest poets. The real is the true world for a great poet, but it was not Shelley's world.

Yet Shelley, while the imaginative mood was on him, felt this ideal world of his to be as real as most men feel the solid earth, and through the pallid lips of its phantom people and dim abstractions he pours as warm a flood of emotion, as ever poet did through the rosiest lips and brightest eyes of earth-born creatures. Not more real to Burns were his Bonny Jean and his Highland Mary, than to Shelley were the visions of Asia and Panthea, and the Lady of the Sensitive Plant, while he gazed upon them. And when his affections did light, not on these abstractions, but on creatures of flesh and blood, yet so penetrated was his thought with his own idealism, that he lifted them up from earth into a rarefied atmosphere, and described them in the same style of imagery and language as that with which he clothes the phantoms of his mind. Thus, after all, Shelley's imagination had but a narrow tract to range over, because it took little or no note of reality, and because, boundless as was his fertility and power of resource within his own chosen circle, the widest realm of mere brain-creation must be thin and small, compared with the realities which exist both in the seen and the unseen worlds.

This is the reason why most of Shelley's long poems are such absolute failures, while his short lyrics have so wonderful a charm. Mere thrills of soul were weak as connecting bonds for long poems. Distilled essences and personified qualities were poor material, out of which to build up great works. These things could give neither unity, nor motive power, nor human interest to long poems. Hence the incoherence which all but a few devoted admirers find in Shelley's long poems, despite their grand passages and their splendid imagery. In fact, if the long poems were to be broken up and thrown into a heap, and the lyric portions riddled out of them and preserved, the world would lose nothing, and would get rid of not a little superfluity. An exception to this judgment is generally made in favor of the *Cenci ;* but that tragedy turns on an incident so repulsive that, notwithstanding its acknowledged power, it can hardly satisfy any healthy mind.

On the other hand, single thrills of rapture, which are insufficient to make long poems out of, supply the very inspiration for the true lyric. It is this predominance of emotion, so unhappy to himself, which made Shelley the lyrist that he was. When he sings his lyric strains, whatever is least pleasing in him is softened down, if it does not wholly disappear. Whatever is most unique and excellent in him comes out at its best — his eye for abstract beauty, the subtlety of his thought, the rush of his eager pursuing desire, the splendor of his imagery, the delicate rhythm, the matchless music. These lyrics are gales of melody blown from a far-off region, that looks fair in the distance. To enjoy them it may perhaps be as well not to inquire too closely what is the nature of that land, or to know too exactly the theories and views of life of which these songs are the effluence. If we come too near, we may find that there is poison in the air. Many a one has read those lyrics, and felt their fascination, without thought of the unhappy experience out of which they have come. They understood " a beauty in the words, but not the words." I doubt whether any one after very early youth, any one who has known the realities of life, can continue to take Shelley's best songs to heart, as he can those of Shakespeare or the best of Burns. For, however we may continue to wonder at the genius that is in them, no healthy mind will find in them the expression of its truest and best thoughts.

Other lyric poets, it has been said, sing of what they

feel. Shelley in his lyrics sings of what he wants to
feel. The thrills of desire, the gushes of emotion, are
all straining after something seen afar, but unattained,
something distant or future; or they are passionate
despair, — utter despondency for something hopelessly
gone. Yet it must be owned that those bursts of pas-
sionate desire after ideal beauty set our pulses a-throb-
bing with a strange vibration, even when we do not
really sympathize with them. Even his desolate wails
make those for a moment seem to share his despair who
do not really share it. Such is the charm of his im-
passioned eloquence, and the witchery of his music.

Let us turn now to look at some of his lyrics in de-
tail.

The earliest of them, those of 1814, were written
while Shelley was under the depressing weight of mate-
rialistic belief, and at the time when he was abandoning
poor Harriet Westbrook. For a time he lived under
the spell of that ghastly faith, hugging it, yet hating it;
and its progeny are the lyrics of that time, such as
Death, Mutability, Lines in a Country Churchyard.
These have a cold, clammy feel. They are full of
" wormy horrors," as though the poet were one,

> "who had made his bed
> In charnels and on coffins, where black Death
> Keeps record of the trophies won from Life,"

as though, by dwelling amid these things, he had hoped
to force some lone ghost

> "to render up the tale
> Of what we are."

And what does it all come to? What is the lesson he
reads there?

> "Lift not the painted veil which those who live
> Call life. . . . Behind lurk Fear

> And Hope, twin destinies, who ever weave
>   Their shadows o'er the chasm, sightless and drear."

That is all that the belief in mere matter taught Shelley, or ever will teach any one.

As he passed on, the clayey, clammy sensation is less present. Even Hume's impressions are better than mere dust, and the Platonic ideas are better than Hume's impressions. When he came under the influence of Plato his doctrine of ideas, as eternal existences and the only realities, exercised over Shelley the charm it always has had for imaginative minds; and it furnished him with a form under which he figured to himself his favorite belief in the Spirit of Love and Beauty, as the animating spirit of the universe — that for which the human soul pants. It is the passion for this ideal which leads Alastor through his long wanderings to die at last in the Caucasian wilderness, without attaining it. It is this which he apostrophizes in the *Hymn to Intellectual Beauty*, as the power which consecrates all it shines on, as the awful loveliness to which he looks to free this world from its dark slavery. It is this vision which reappears in its highest form in *Prometheus Unbound*, the greatest and most attractive of all Shelley's longer poems. That drama is from beginning to end a great lyrical poem, or I should rather say a congeries of lyrics, in which perhaps more than anywhere else Shelley's lyrical power has highest soared. The whole poem is exalted by a grand pervading idea, one which in its truest and deepest form is the grandest we can conceive — the idea of the ultimate renovation of man and of the world. And although the powers, and processes, and personified abstractions, which Shelley invoked to effect this end, are ludicrously inadequate, as

14

irrational as it would be to try to build a solid house out of shadows and moonbeams, yet the high ideal imparts to the poem something of its own elevation. Prometheus, the representative of suffering and struggling humanity, is to be redeemed and perfected by union with Asia, who is the ideal of beauty, the light of life, the spirit of love. To this spirit Shelley looked to rid the world of all that is evil, and to bring in the diviner day. The lyric poetry, which is exquisite throughout, perhaps culminates in the song in which Panthea, one of the nymphs, hails her sister Asia, as

> "Life of Life! thy lips enkindle
>   With their love the breath between them;
> And thy smiles, before they dwindle,
>   Make the cold air fire; then screen them
> In those looks, where whoso gazes
> Faints, entangled in their mazes.

> " Child of Light! thy limbs are burning
>   Through the vest which seems to hide them;
> As the radiant lines of morning
>   Through the clouds, ere they divide them;
> And this atmosphere divinest
> Shrouds thee wheresoe'er thou shinest.

> "Lamp of Earth! where'er thou movest,
>   The dim shapes are clad with brightness,
> And the souls of whom thou lovest
>   Walk upon the winds with lightness,
> Till they fail, as I am failing,
> Dizzy, lost, yet unbewailing."

The reply of Asia to this song is hardly less exquisite. Every one will remember it : —

> "My soul is an enchanted boat,
>   Which, like a sleeping swan, doth float
> Upon the silver waves of thy sweet singing;
>   And thine doth like an angel sit
>   Beside the helm, conducting it,

Whilst all the winds with melody are ringing;
  It seems to float ever, forever,
  Upon the many-winding river,
  Between mountains, woods, abysses,
  A paradise of wildernesses!
Till, like one in slumber bound,
Borne to the ocean, I float down, around
Into a sea profound of ever-spreading sound.

"Meanwhile thy spirit lifts its pinions
  In music's most serene dominions,
Catching the winds that fan that happy heaven.
  And we sail on, away, afar
  Without a course, without a star,
But, by the instinct of sweet music driven;
  Till through Elysian garden islets
  By thee, most beautiful of pilots,
  Where never mortal pinnace glided,
  The boat of my desire is guided:
Realms where the air we breathe is love,
Which in the winds on the waves doth move,
Harmonizing this earth with what we feel above."

In these two lyrics you have Shelley at his highest
perfection. Exquisitely beautiful as they are, they are,
however, beautiful as the mirage is beautiful, and as un-
substantial. There is nothing in the reality of things
answering to Asia. She is not human, she is not di-
vine. There is nothing moral in her — no will, no
power to subdue evil; only an exquisite essence, a melt-
ing loveliness. There is in her no law, no righteous-
ness; something which may enervate, nothing which
can brace the soul.

Perfect as is the workmanship of those lyrics in *Pro-
metheus* and of many another, their excellence is less-
ened by the material out of which they are woven be-
ing fantastic, not substantial truth. Few of them lay
hold of real sentiments which are catholic to humanity.
They do not deal with permanent emotions which be-

long to all men and are for all time, but appeal rather
to minds in a particular stage of culture, and that not a
healthy stage. They are not of such stuff as life is
made of. They will not interest all healthy and truth-
ful minds in all stages of culture, and in all ages. To
do this, however, is, I believe, a note of the highest or-
der of lyric poem.

Another thing to be observed is, that while the im-
agery of Shelley's lyrics is so splendid and the music
of their language so magical, both of these are at that
point of over-bloom which is on the verge of decay.
The imagery, for all its splendor, is too ornate, too re-
dundant, too much overlays the thought, which has not
strength enough to uphold such a weight of ornament.
Then, as to the music of the words, wonderful as it is,
all but exclusive admirers of Shelley must have felt at
times, as if the sound runs away with the sense. In
some of the *Prometheus* lyrics the poet, according to Mr.
Symonds, seems to have " realized the miracle of mak-
ing words, detached from meaning, the substance of a
new ethereal music." This is, to say the least, a dan-
gerous miracle to practise. Even Shelley, overborne
by the power of melodious words, would at times seem
to approach perilously near the borders of the unintel-
ligible, not to say the nonsensical. What it comes to,
when adopted as a style, has been seen plainly enough
in some of Shelley's chief followers in our own day.
Cloyed with overloaded imagery, and satiated almost to
sickening with alliterative music, we turn for reinvigo-
ration to poetry that is severe, even to baldness.

The *Prometheus Unbound* was written in Italy, and
during his four Italian years Shelley's lyric stream
flowed on unremittingly, and enriched England's poetry

with many lyrics unrivalled in their kind, and added to its language a new power. These lyrics are on the whole his best poetic work. To go over them in detail would be impossible, besides being needless. Perhaps his year most prolific in lyrics was 1820, just two years before his death. Among the products of this year were *The Sensitive Plant, The Cloud, The Skylark, Love's Philosophy, Arethusa, Hymns of Pan, and of Apollo*, all in his best manner, with many besides these. About the lyrics of this time two things are noticeable : more of them are about things of nature than heretofore, and several of them revert to themes of Greece.

Of all modern attempts to renovate Greek subjects, there are, perhaps, none equal to these, unless it be one or two of the Laureate's happiest efforts. They take the Greek forms and mythologies, and fill them with modern thought and spirit. And perhaps this is the only way to make Greek subjects real and interesting to us. If we want the very Greek spirit we had better go to the originals, not to any reproductions.

It is thus he makes Pan sing —

> "From the forests and highlands
>   We come, we come;
> From the river-girt islands,
>   Where loud waves are dumb,
>   Listening to my sweet pipings.
>
> .   .   .   .
>
> "Liquid Peneus was flowing,
>   And all dark Tempe lay
> In Pelion's shadow, outgrowing
>   The light of the dying day,
>   Speeded with my sweet pipings.
> The Sileni, and Sylvans, and Fauns,
>   And the nymphs of the woods and waves,
> To the edge of the moist river-lawns,

And the brink of the dewy caves,
And all that did then attend or follow,
Were silent with love, as you now, Apollo,
With envy of my sweet pipings.

"I sang of the dancing stars,
I sang of the dædal earth,
And of Heaven and the giant wars,
And Love, and Death, and Birth,
And then I changed my pipings —
Singing how down the vale of Menalus
I pursued a maiden and clasped a weed :
Gods and men, we are all deluded thus !
It breaks in our bosom, and then we bleed:
All wept, as I think both ye now would,
If envy or age had not frozen your blood,
At the sorrow of my sweet pipings."

Of the lyrics on natural objects the two supreme ones
are the *Ode to the West Wind* and *The Skylark.*   Of
this last nothing need be said.   Artistically and poet-
ically it is unique, has a place of its own in poetry ; yet
may I be allowed to express a misgiving, which I have
long felt, and others too may feel ?   For all its beauty,
perhaps one would rather not recall it, when hearing
the skylark's song in the fields on a bright spring morn-
ing.   The poem is not in tune with the bird's song
and the feelings it does and ought to awaken.   The
rapture with which the strain springs up at first dies
down before the close into Shelley's ever-haunting mel-
ancholy.   Who wishes, when hearing the real skylark,
to be told that —

" We look before and after,
And pine for what is not:
Our sincerest laughter
With some pain is fraught " ?

If personal feeling must be inwrought into the living

powers of nature, let it be such feeling as is in keeping with the object, appropriate to the time and place. In this spirit is the invocation with which Shelley closes his grand *Ode to the West Wind*, written the previous year, 1819 —

"Make me thy lyre, even as the forest is :
   What if my leaves are fallen like its own !
The tumult of thy mighty harmonies

" Will take from both a deep autumnal tone,
   Sweet though in sadness. Be thou, spirit fierce,
My spirit ! be thou me, impetuous one !

" Drive my dead thoughts over the universe
   Like withered leaves, to quicken a new birth ;
And, by the incantation of this verse,

" Scatter, as from an unextinguished hearth
   Ashes and sparks, my words among mankind !
Be through my lips to unawakened earth

"The trumpet of a prophecy ! O Wind,
   If Winter comes, can Spring be far behind ? "

This ode ends with some vigor, some hope ; but that is not usual with Shelley. Every one must have noticed how almost habitually his intensest lyrics — those which have started with the fullest swing of rapture — die down, before they close, into a wail of despair. It is as though, when the strong gush of emotion had spent itself, there was no more behind, nothing to fall back upon, but blank emptiness and desolation. It is this that makes Shelley's poetry so unspeakably sad — sad with a hopeless sorrow that is like none other. You feel as though he were a wanderer who has lost his way hopelessly in the wilderness of a blank universe. True is Carlyle's well-known saying, " his cry is like the infinite inarticulate wailing of forsaken infants." In the

wail of his desolation there are many tones — some
wild and weird, some defiant, some full of desponding
pathos.

The *Lines written in Dejection*, on the Bay of Naples,
in 1818, are perhaps the most touching of all his wails,
the words are so sweet, they seem, by their very sweet-
ness, to lighten the load of heart-loneliness : —

> " I see the Deep's untrampled floor
>   With green and purple seaweeds strown;
> I see the waves upon the shore,
>   Like light dissolved in star-showers, thrown:
> I sit upon the sands alone;
>   The lightning of the noon-tide ocean
> Is flashing round me, and a tone
>   Arises from its measured motion,
> How sweet! did any heart now share in my emotion.

> ' Alas! I have nor hope, nor health,
>   Nor peace within, nor calm around,
> Nor that content, surpassing wealth,
>   The sage in meditation found.
>   .   .   .   .   .
> " Yet now despair itself is mild,
>   Even as the winds and waters are;
> I could lie down like a tired child,
>   And weep away this life of care
> Which I have borne, and yet must bear,
>   Till death like sleep might steal on me,
> And I might feel in the warm air
>   My cheek grow cold, and hear the sea
> Breathe o'er my dying brain its last monotony."

Who that reads these sighing lines but must feel for
the heart that breathed them! Yet how can we be
surprised that he should have felt so desolate ? Every
heart needs some stay. And a heart so keen, a spirit
so finely touched, as Shelley's, needed, far more than
narrow and unsympathetic natures, a refuge amid the
storms of life. But he knew of none. His universe

was a homeless one; it had no centre of repose. His universal essence of love, diffused throughout it, contained nothing substantial — no will that could control and support his own. While a soul owns no law, is without awe, lives wholly by impulse, what rest, what central peace, is possible for it? When the ardors of emotion have died down, what remains for it, but weakness, exhaustion, despair? The feeling of his weakness awoke in Shelley no brokenness of spirit, no self-abasement, no reverence. Nature was to him really the whole, and he saw in it nothing but " a revelation of death, a sepulchral picture, generation after generation disappearing, and being heard of and seen no more." He rejected utterly that other " consolatory revelation which tells us that we are spiritual beings, and have a spiritual source of life " and strength, above and beyond the material system. Such a belief, or rather no belief, as his, can engender only infinite sadness, infinite despair. And this is the deep undertone of all Shelley's poetry.

I have dwelt on his lyrics because they contain little of the questionable elements which here and there obtrude themselves in the longer poems. And one may speak of these lyrics without agitating too deeply questions which at present I would rather avoid. Yet even the lyrics bear some impress of the source whence they come. Beautiful though they be, they are like those fine pearls which, we are told, are the products of disease in the parent shell. All Shelley's poetry is, as it were, a gale blown from a richly dowered but not healthy land; and the taint, though not so perceptible in the lyrics, still hangs more or less over many of the finest. Besides this defect, they are very limited in their range of influence. They cannot reach the hearts of all men. They fascinate only some of the educated, and that probably only while they are young. The time comes when these pass out of that peculiar sphere of thought, and find little interest in such poetry. Probably the rare exquisiteness of their workmanship will always preserve Shelley's lyrics, even after the world has lost, as we may hope it will lose, sympathy with their substance. But better, stronger, more vital far are those lyrics which lay hold on the permanent, unchanging emotions of man — those emotions which all healthy natures have felt, and always will feel, and which no new deposit of thought or of civilization can ever bury out of sight.

CHAPTER IX.

THE POETRY OF THE SCOTTISH HIGHLANDS. — OSSIAN.

IT was towards the end of August when I bethought me of my Oxford audience, and of what I should say when next I met them. Around me was the flush of the heather on all the braes; before me the autumn lights and shadows were trailing over the higher Bens. With the power of the hills thus upon him, who could turn to books? It seemed impossible for me to fix on any subject which was not in keeping with the sights on which my eyes were resting the while.

And then I thought of the countless throng of strangers from England and from all lands, who at that moment were crowding all the tourist thoroughfares of the Highlands, visiting the usual lochs and glens, and climbing, perhaps, some of the more famous mountains. And I could not but feel how rarely any one of these penetrates beyond the mere shell of what he sees, or gets a glimpse into the heart of that mountain vision which passes before him. It cannot be that they should. They hurry for a week or ten days, which are all they have leisure for, along the beaten tracks; they catch from the deck of a crowded steamer or the top of a stage coach, rapid views of mountains, moors, and sea-lochs, which may for a moment please the eye and refresh the spirit. But it is not thus that the mountain solitudes render up their secret, and melt into the heart.

A momentary glance at the pine woods of Rothiemur-
chus, and the granite cliffs of the Cairngorm, snatched
from a flying railway-train is better than Cheapside;
that is all. Even those more fortunate ones who can
pass a month at a shooting lodge in some Highland glen,
or by some blue sea-loch, are for the most part so ab-
sorbed in grouse-killing or deer-stalking, that they have
seldom eye or ear for anything beside.

Those only have a chance of knowing what the real
Highlands are who go with hearts at leisure to see and
to feel, and who "go all alone the while;" some adven-
turous wanderer, who has had the gentle hardihood to
leave the crowded tourist-paths, with their steamers and
hotels, and setting his face, unattended, to the wilder-
ness, has been content to shelter for nights together be-
neath some huge boulder-stone, or in a cave, or under
the roof of crofter, keeper, or shepherd; or some deer-
stalker who has lain for hours in the balloch or hill-pass,
waiting till the antlered stag came by; or the grouse-
shooter, who, when wearied with a whole day's walk-
ing, has sat down towards evening on some western hill-
side, and watched the sun going down to the Atlantic
Isles. At such seasons the traveller and the sportsman,
while his eye went dreaming over the dusky waste, and
ear and heart were awake to receive the lonely sounds
of the desert, and to let these, and the great silence
that encompasses them, melt into his being; at such
seasons it was, that he perhaps became aware how vast
a world of unuttered poetry lies all dumb in those great
wildernesses — poetry of which the best words of the
best poets, who have essayed to give voice to it, are but
a poor, inadequate echo.

Some features of that country's scenery, and some

human feelings and habits which it has fostered, have expressed themselves in songs of the native Gaelic-speaking bards, which for force and vividness no foreign language can equal. To succeed, however imperfectly, in conveying even a faint notion of this Gaelic poetry, might be serviceable in several ways.

As modern civilization has, whether for good or evil, willed that all the Scottish Highlands shall be a vast playground or hunting-field for the rich Southron, it might, perhaps, be well that the Southron should know something more of the land and of the people amid which he takes his summer pastime. The character of the land appeals to every eye; less apparent, but not less marked and interesting, is the character of the people, whose forefathers, ages ago, gave names to its mountains and glens, which they still retain. To know something about their native poetry might help strangers to understand better, and appreciate more highly, the noble qualities that lie hidden in these Scottish Gael. There are facts in their history, and traits in their character, which might benefit even the most self-complacent stranger, if he could learn to know and sympathize with them. Besides, to us here, accustomed to read the great standard poets and to measure all poetry by their model, it may be some advantage to turn aside and look at a poetry wholly unlike that of England, Rome, or Greece; a poetry which is as spontaneous as the singing of the birds and the beating of men's hearts; a poetry which is, in a great measure, independent of books and manuscripts; a poetry which, if narrower in compass and less careful in finish, is as intense in feeling, and as true to nature and to man, as anything which the classical literatures contain.

It is strange to think how long, and up to how late a date, the whole world of the Scottish Gael lay outside of the political and the intellectual life not only of England, but even of their neighbors, the Scottish Lowlanders. From the time, A. D. 1411, when on the field of Harlaw it was finally decided that Saxon, not Celt, should rule in Scotland, down to the time of Montrose and Claverhouse, that is for two centuries and a half, the Highlanders lay little heeded within their own mountains, except when they descended in some marauding raid upon the Lowland plains ; or when one or another of the Royal Jameses plunged into the mountains to hang some rebellious chief, and quell his turbulent clan. The first appearance of the clans in modern history took place when they rose in defence of the dethroned Stuarts, and enabled Montrose to triumph at Inverlochy, and Viscount Dundee at Killiecrankie. When they rose again, for the same cause, in the Fifteen and the Forty-five, especially in the latter, they so alarmed the minds of English politicians, that in the rebound after the victory of Culloden these exacted from the helpless Gael a bloody vengeance, which is one of the darkest pages in England's history. During the century when the Gael were throwing themselves with all their native ardor into the political struggle, they were making no impression on England's literature. This was first done nearly twenty years after the Forty-five, when James MacPherson published his translation of the so-called Epics of Ossian.

Of the great storm of controversy which MacPherson's Ossian awakened, I shall say nothing at present. But whether we regard the Ossianic Poems as genuine productions of the ancient Gael, or fabrications of Mac-

Pherson, there cannot be a doubt that in that publication the Gael for the first time put in their claim to be recognized on the field, not only of England's but of Europe's literature. Henceforth Highland scenery and Celtic feeling entered as a conscious element into the poetry of England and of other nations, and touched them with something of its peculiar sentiment. How real and penetrating this influence was, hear in the eloquent words of Mr. Arnold in his suggestive lectures on Celtic Literature. " The Celts are the prime authors of this vein of piercing regret and passion, of this Titanism in poetry. A famous book, MacPherson's Ossian, carried in the last century this vein like a flood of lava through Europe. I am not going to criticise MacPherson's Ossian here. Make the part of what is forged, modern, tawdry, spurious, in the book, as large as you please ; strip Scotland, if you like, of every feather of borrowed plumes which, on the strength of MacPherson's Ossian, she may have stolen from that *vetus et major Scotia* — Ireland ; I make no objection. But there will still be left in the book a residue with the very soul of the Celtic genius in it ; and which has the proud distinction of having brought this soul of the Celtic genius into contact with the nations of modern Europe, and enriched all our poetry by it. Woody Morven, and echoing Lora, and Selma with its silent halls ! We all owe them a debt of gratitude, and when we are unjust enough to forget it, may the Muse forget us ! Choose any one of the better passages in MacPherson's Ossian, and you can see, even at this time of day, what an apparition of newness and of power such a strain must have been in the eighteenth century."

In his work on *The Study of Celtic Literature,* from

which I have just quoted, Mr. Arnold lays his finger with his peculiar felicity on the Celtic element which exists in the English nature, and shows how it is the dash of Celtic blood in English veins, which has given to it some of its finest, if least recognized, quality; how the commingling of Celtic sentiment and sensibility with Saxon steadiness and method has leavened our literature. I know nothing finer in criticism than the subtle and admirable tact with which he traces the way in which the presence of a Celtic sentiment has heightened and spiritualized the genius of our best poets, has added to the imagination of Shakespeare a magic charm, not to be found even in the finest words of Goethe. This line of thought, true and interesting as it is, has reference to the unconscious influence of the Celtic spirit on Englishmen, who never once, perhaps, thought or cared for anything Celtic. It would be a humbler and more obvious task to trace how the direct and conscious infiltration of the Celtic genius, from the time of MacPherson's Ossian, has told on our modern poets. But from this I must refrain to-day; and in what remains confine myself strictly to the Gael of the Scottish Highlands and their poetry.

I shall not venture to speak of the Celts in general, much less of that very abstract thing called " Celtism." For Celt is a wide word, which covers several very distinct and different peoples. What is true of the poetry of Wales is not true of the poetry of Ireland. What is true of the poetry of Ireland cannot be said of the poetry of the Scottish Gael. In all our talk about Celts, let us never forget that there are two main branches of the great Celtic race — the Cymri and the Gael. Each of the two great branches had its own distinct cycle of legends — or myths, if you choose — on which were founded their earliest heroic songs or ballads. The story of Arthur and his knights sprang from the Cymri, and had its root probably in some vicissitudes of their early history, when the Saxons invaded their country and drove them to the western shores of Britain. Latin chroniclers and French minstrels, at a later day, took up the story of their doings, and handed it on, transformed in character, and invested with all the hues of mediæval chivalry. It is, in fact, an old Cymric legend, seen by us through the haze which centuries of chivalric sentiment have interposed. But, however transfigured, vestiges of the Arthurian story linger to this day in all lands where descendants of the Cymri still dwell — in Brittany, in Cornwall, in Wales, in the old Cymric kingdom of Strath-Clyde. Merlin lies buried at Drummelzier-on-Tweed ; Guenevre at Meigle, close to the foot of the so-called Grampians ; Arthur's most northern battle was fought, according to Mr. Skene, near the foot of Loch Lomond. But there all traces of Arthur cease ; beyond the Highland line he never penetrated.

That Highland line, namely the mountain barrier which stretches from Ben Lomond in a northeastern direction to the Cairngorms and the Deeside Mountains, encloses a whole world of legend as native to the Gael of Scotland and Ireland as the Arthurian legend is to the lands of the Cymri. Where Arthur's story ends, that of Fion and his Feinne begins.

Within that mountain barrier, all the Highlands of Perthshire, Inverness-shire, and Argyll are fragrant with memories of an old heroic race, called the Feinne, or Fianntainean. Not a glen, hardly a mountain, but

15

contains some rock, or knoll, or cairn, or cave, named from the Fenian warriors, whose memories people those mountains like a family of ghosts. The language of the native Gael abounds with allusions to them ; their names are familiar in proverbs used at this hour.

Who were these Feinne ? To what age do they belong ? Mr. Skene, our highest authority on all Celtic matters, replies that they were one of those races which came from Lochlan, and preceded the Milesian Scots, both in Erin and in Alban. Lochlan is the most ancient name of that part of North Germany which lies between the mouths of the Rhine and the Elbe, before the name was transferred to Scandinavia. From that North German sea-board came the earliest race that peopled Ireland and Alban or the Scottish Highlands. During their occupation, Ireland and the north of Scotland were regarded as one territory, and the population passed freely from one island to the other at a time " when race, not territory, was the great bond of association." Hence it came that the deeds and memories of this one warrior race belong equally to both countries. Each has its songs about the Fenian heroes ; each has its local names taken from these, its " Fenian topography." The question, therefore, often agitated, whether the Fenian poetry belongs by right to Ireland or to Scotland, is a futile one. It belongs equally to both, for it sprang from the doings and achievements of one warrior race, which occupied both lands indifferently. I leave Ireland to speak for itself, as it does very effectually through the lectures of the late Professor O'Curry, and other native writers. In the Western Highlands, to quote the words of Mr. Skene, " the mountains, streams, and lakes, are everywhere redolent of names connected with the heroes and actions of the Feinne, and show that a body of popular legends, whether in poetry or prose, arising out of these, and preserved by oral recitation, must have existed in the country, where this topography sprang up." But whether the events associated with particular local names originally happened in Scotland or in Ireland must be left undetermined.

That songs about the Feinne, which had never been committed to writing, had been preserved from time out of mind by oral recitation among the native Gael, no candid man who has examined the question can doubt. The great Dr. Johnson would not believe this on any evidence. But as one among innumerable witnesses tells us, "It was the constant amusement or occupation of the Highlanders in the winter time to go by turns to each other's houses in every village, either to recite, or hear recited or sung, the poems of Ossian, and other songs and poems." Almost all the native Gael could recite some parts of these, but there were professed Seannachies, or persons of unusual power of memory, who could go on repeating Fenian poems for two or three whole nights continuously. I have myself known men who have often heard five hundred lines of continuous Fenian poetry recited at one time.

A little after the middle of the last century, when James MacPherson began his wanderings in search of these songs, the Highlands were full of such Ossianic poetry, and of men who could recite it. I am not going to retail the oft-told history of MacPherson's marvellous proceedings, much less to plunge into the interminable jungle of the Ossianic controversy. Those who may desire to see the facts clearly stated will find this done

in Mr. Skene's Introduction to the book of the Dean
of Lismore, published in 1862, also in the very clear
and candid Dissertation prefixed by Dr. Clerk to his
new and literal translation of the *Gaelic Ossian,* pub-
lished in 1870. A condensed view of the present state
of the question will be found in a paper published in
Macmillan's Magazine for June, 1871. Since this last
date, new contributions have been made to the subject,
especially by the publication of Mr. J. F. Campbell's
Book of the Feinne, in which he advocates a view en-
tirely opposed to that taken in the three publications
already named. Without at all entering into the con-
troversy, I shall just note the crucial point round which
the whole question turns. MacPherson published in
1762 an English translation of *Fingal,* an epic which
he attributed to Ossian. The next year, 1763, he pub-
lished *Temora,* another Ossianic epic. The genuineness
of the two epics was immediately challenged. Mac-
Pherson never published the Gaelic originals while he
lived, but he left them in manuscripts, which after many
vicissitudes were published by the Highland Society in
1807. Of the Gaelic Ossian, published by the Highland
Society, a new translation, much more literal and exact
than MacPherson's was made by Dr. Clerk of Kilmal-
lie, in 1870. There they now lie side by side, the
Gaelic Ossian and the two English versions, that of
MacPherson and that by Dr. Clerk; and the question
now is, which is the original, the Gaelic or the Eng-
lish? Mr. Skene and Dr. Clerk strongly maintain that
the Gaelic shows undoubted signs of being the original,
and the English of being a translation. These two are
among the most eminent Gaelic scholars now alive. On
the other hand, Mr. J. F. Campbell, an ardent collector

of Gaelic tales and antique things, if not so critical a
Gaelic scholar as the two former, contends as strongly
for the English being the original, from which he says
the Gaelic has evidently been translated.   Again, sup-
posing, with Mr. Skene and Dr. Clerk, that the Gaelic
is the original, who composed the Gaelic?   Among
those who agree in holding the Gaelic to be the original,
there are two divergent opinions as to the composers of
it.   Some hold that the Gaelic was mainly the compo-
sition of MacPherson and some of his friends, who in-
corporated into it here and there certain ancient frag-
ments, but composed the larger portion of it themselves.
It is further alleged that when the Gaelic had been
thus composed, MacPherson rendered it into the stately,
if sometimes tawdry English, which we know as *Ossian.*
Others maintain that by far the larger portion of the
Gaelic is ancient, and that MacPherson supplied only a
few passages here and there to link together his ancient
originals.   Hardly any one, however, is prepared to
argue that the long epics of *Fingal* and *Temora* came
down from a remote antiquity in the exact form in
which MacPherson published them.   The piecing to-
gether of fragments often ill-adjusted and incongruous
is too evident to allow of such a supposition.

The English and the Gaelic Ossian, as I said, lie be-
fore us.   Is it too much to hope that criticism may yet
decide the question? that some Gaelic Porson or Bent-
ley may yet arise, who shall apply to the documents the
best critical acumen, and pronounce a verdict which
shall be final, as to which of the two is the original,
which the translation ?   If some one were to assert that
he had discovered a lost book of Homer, and were to
publish it with an English translation, the resources of

Greek scholarship are quite competent to settle whether the Greek were authentic or a forgery. Why should not Gaelic scholarship achieve as much?

But even if we were to cancel all that has passed through MacPherson's hands, whether Gaelic or English, enough still is left of Ossianic poetry, both in the Dean of Lismore's book, that dates from early in the sixteenth century, and also in the gleanings of other collectors, whose honesty has never been questioned, to prove that the whole Highlands were formerly saturated with heroic songs about the Feinne, and to enable us to know what were the characteristics of this Fenian poetry. I believe that the last reciters of Ossianic songs have scarcely yet died out in the remoter Hebrides.

Who was this Ossian, and when did he live? His exact date, even his century, no one can determine; but fragments, which are undoubtedly genuine, refer to a very dim foretime, even to the centuries when Christianity was yet young, and was struggling for existence against old Paganism, in Erin and in Alba.

The conception of Ossian, not only in MacPherson, but in the oldest fragments and in universal Highland tradition, is one and uniform. He is the proto-bard, the first and greatest of all the bards. Himself the son of the great Fenian king Fionn, or Finn, and a warrior in his youth, he survived all his kindred, and was left alone, blind and forlorn, with nothing, but the memories of the men he loved, to solace him. There he sits in his empty hall, with the dusky wilderness around him, listening to the winds that sigh through the gray cairns, and to the streams that roar down the mountains. No longer can he see the morning spread upon the hilltops, nor the mists as they come down upon their flanks. But in these

mists he believes that the spirits of his fathers and his
lost comrades dwell, and often they revisit him waking
or in dreams. One only comfort is left him, Malvina,
the betrothed of his hero son, Oscar, who had early fallen
in battle; and the best consolation she can minister
is to raise her voice in the joy of song. As the sightless
old man sits in the last warmth of the setting sun, the
days of other years come back to him, and he is fain to
sing a tale of the times of old. And his song is of his
father Fionn, the king of the Fenians, and of his deeds
of prowess, when he led his peers to battle against the
invading hosts of Lochlan. Those peers were the " great
Cuchullin with his war chariot, the brown-haired and
beautiful Diarmid, slayer of the boar by which himself
was slain, the strong and valiant Gaul, son of Morni,
the rash Conan — a Celtic Thersites — the hardy Ryno,
the swift and gallant Cailta." These all stand out be-
fore the imagination of the Gael, as individual in their
deeds and their characters, as did the Homeric heroes
before the minds of the Greeks. All of them died
before Ossian, and, most pathetic of all, Oscar, his own
son, the pride and hope of the Feinne, died, treacher-
ously slain in the first bloom of his youth and valor.

As a sample of the average Ossianic style, let me give
a few lines of one of those fragments which MacPher-
son published in 1760. These he put forth before he
knew they would have any literary value, and before he
brought out his epics; so that, as Mr. Skene says, there
is little reason to doubt that they are genuine ancient
fragments. The one I am about to give he afterwards
incorporated as an episode in the first book of *Fingal*,
but this version is the literal unadorned rendering of
Dr. Clerk.

A warrior, called Du-chomar, meets a maiden, called
Morna, alone on the hill, and thus addresses her : —

> " 'Morna, most lovely among women,
>   Graceful daughter of Cormac,
>   Why by thyself in the circle of stones,
>   In hollow of the rock, on the hill alone ?
>   Streams are sounding around thee;
>   The aged tree is moaning in the wind;
>   Trouble is on yonder loch ;
>   Clouds darken round the mountain tops ;
>   Thyself art like snow on the hill —
>   Thy waving hair like mist of Cromla,
>   Curling upwards on the Ben,
>   'Neath gleaming of the sun from the west;
>   Thy soft bosom like the white rock
>   On bank of Brano of foaming streams.'

> " Then said the maid of loveliest locks,
>   ' Whence art thou, grimmest among men ?
>   Gloomy always was thy brow ;
>   Red is now thine eye, and boding ill.
>   Sawest thou Swaran on the ocean ?
>   What hast thou heard about the foe ? "

He replies that he has seen or heard nothing, and then
goes on : —

> " ' Cormac's daughter of fairest mien,
>   As my soul is my love to thee.'
>   .   .   .   .   .
>   ' Du-chomar,' said the gentle maiden,
>   ' No spark of love have I for thee ;
>   Dark is thy brow, darker thy spirit;
>   But unto thee, son of Armin, my love,
>   Brave Cabad, Morna cleaves to thee.
>   Like gleaming of the sun are thy locks,
>   When rises the mist of the mountain.
>   Has Cabad, the prince, been seen by thee,
>   Young gallant, travelling the hills?
>   The daughter of Cormac, O hero brave,
>   Waits the return of her love from the chase."

> " ' Long shalt thou wait, O Morna,'
>   Said Du-chomar, dark and stern —

' Long shalt thou wait, O Morna,
  For the fiery son of Armin.
  Look at this blade of cleanest sweep —
  To its very hilt sprang Cabad's blood.
  The strong hero has fallen by my hand;
  Long shalt thou wait, O Morna.
  I will raise a stone o'er thy beloved.
  Daughter of Cormac of blue shields,
  Bend on Du-chomar thine eye ;
  His hand is as thunder of the mountains.'

" Has the son of Armin fallen in death ? '
  Exclaimed the maiden with voice of love.
  Has he fallen on the mountain high,
  The brave one, fairest of the people ?
  Leader of the strong ones in the chase,
  Foe, with cleaving blows for ocean strangers ?
  Dark is Du-chomar in his wrath ;
  Bloody to me is thy hand ;
  Mine enemy thou art, but reach me the sword—
  Dear to me is Cabad and his blood.' "

He gives her the sword, she plunges it in his breast.
Falling, he entreats her to draw the sword from his
wound.   As she approaches he slays her.

One of the standing arguments used by Dr. Johnson
and others to prove that MacPherson's *Ossian* was a
shameless imposture was the generosity of heart, the
nobility of nature, and the refined and delicate senti-
ment, attributed in these poems to Fingal and his com-
rades ; if they lived when they were said to have lived,
they must, it was alleged, have been ferocious savages.
This, no doubt, was a natural objection.   But one fact
is worth a world of such hypotheses.   Here is the
description of Finn, as it is found in one of the frag-
ments of Ossianic song, about which no doubt can be
raised, for it has been preserved in the book of the
Dean of Lismore, and that was written about A. D. 1520.
The fragment when thus written down by the Dean was

attributed to Ossian, who then was reckoned a poet of
unknown antiquity.   The following is the bare literal
translation of it : —

> "Both poet and chief,
>   Braver than kings,
>   Firm chief of the Feinne,
>   Lord of all lands.
>   Foremost always,
>   Generous, just,
>   Despising a lie.
>   Of vigorous deeds
>   First in song,
>   A righteous judge,
>   Polished in mien,
>   Who knew but victory.
>   All men's trust,
>   Of noble mind,
>   Of ready deeds,
>   To women mild.
>   Three hundred battles
>   He bravely fought.
>   With miser's mind
>   Withheld from none.
>   Anything false
>   His lips never spake.
>   He never grudged,
>   No, never, Finn,
>   The sun ne'er saw king
>   Who him excelled.
>   Good man was Finn,
>   Good man was he ;
>   No gifts were given
>   Like his so free."

This may not be very fine poetry, but it is an image
of noble manhood.

As a sample of an Ossianic battle-picture, take the
well-known description of the chariot of Cuchullin.   The
passage has by MacPherson been incorporated into his
first book of *Fingal*, but later authorities refer it to a

different era and cycle of events. However this may be, there is no doubt that the passage is very ancient, for it has been recovered from old Highlanders, who never read a word of MacPherson's *Ossian*, nor heard of it. I give the translation, not of MacPherson, but the much more literal one lately done by Dr. Clerk.

Swaran, King of Lochlan (Scandinavia), has invaded Erin, and sent forward a scout to reconnoitre, and bring him word of the movements of the Irish host. This is the description, with which the scout returns, of the chariot and the appearance of Cuchullin, leader of the warriors of Ulster : —

> " Rise, thou ruler of the waves,
>   True leader of dark-brown shields,
>   I see the sons of Erin and their chief,
>   A chariot — the greatest chariot of war —
>   Moving over the plain with death,
>   The shapely swift car of Cuchullin.
>   Behind, it curves downward like a wave,
>   Or mist enfolding a sharp-cragged hill;
>   The light of precious stones is about it,
>   Like the sea in the wake of a boat at night.
>   Of shining yew is the pole of it;
>   Of well-smoothed bone the seat.
>   It is the dwelling-place of spears,
>   Of shields, of swords, and of heroes.
>
> " On the right side of the great chariot
>   Is seen a horse, high-mettled, snorting,
>   Lofty-crested, broad-chested, dark,
>   High-bounding, strong-bodied son of the mountain,
>   Springy, and sounding his hoof :
>   The spread of his forelock on high
>   Is like mist on the dwelling of deer;
>   Shining his coat, and swift
>   His pace — Si-fadda his name.
>
> " On the other side of the car
>   Is an arch-necked snorting horse :

Thin-maned, free-striding, deep-hoofed,
Swift-footed, wide-nostrelled son of the mountain,
Du-sron-gel the name of the gallant steed.
Full a thousand slender thongs
Fasten the chariot on high ;
The hard bright bit of the bridle
In their jaws is covered white with foam,
Shining stones of power
Wave aloft with the horses' manes —
Horses like mist on the mountain side,
Which onward bear the chief to his fame.
Keener their temper than the deer,
Strong as the eagle their strength,
Their noise is like winter fierce
On Gormal smothered in snow.

" In the chariot is seen the chief,
True, brave son of the keen-cutting brand,
Cuchullin of blue-dappled shields,
Son of Semo, renowned in song.
His cheek like the polished yew ;
Clear, far-ranging his eye,
Under arched, dark, and slender brow ;
His yellow hair, down-streaming from his head,
Falls round the glorious face of the man,
As he draws his spear from his back."

Then addressing Swaran, the scout exclaims —

" Flee thou great ruler of ships,
Flee from the hero who comes right on,
As a storm from the glen of torrents."

If any one were carefully to compare Dr. Clerk's
version just given with that of MacPherson, he could
not fail to observe that, whenever they differ, the former
is more exact and graphic, preserving all the edges,
whereas the latter is vague, less definite, more declama-
tory. And this, as far as I have observed, is character-
istic of MacPherson's translations throughout. He at-
tains rhythmical flow, stateliness, sometimes sublimity,
of language ; but for these he sacrifices the realistic

force, the sharpness of outline, and the vivid exactness which belong to the Gaelic, and are faithfully preserved in Dr. Clerk's rendering. If this is true, it has a very close bearing on the question whether MacPherson's English or his Gaelic *Ossian* is the original.

Perhaps I ought to refrain from quoting, or even from alluding to, a passage so familiar to all readers of Ossian as the address or hymn to the Sun. But it is so remarkable in itself, and is of such undoubted antiquity, having been recovered from many other sources besides MacPherson, that I shall venture to presume on the ignorance of at least some of my readers, and once more to quote it.

Dr. Clerk's literal, word for word, translation of it runs thus —

> " O thou that traveliest on high
> Round as the warrior's hard full shield,
> Whence thy brightness without gloom,
> Thy light that is lasting, O sun!
> Thou comest forth strong in thy beauty,
> And the stars conceal their path;
> The moon, all pale, forsakes the sky,
> To hide herself in the western wave;
> Thou, in thy journey, art alone;
> Who will dare draw nigh to thee ?
> The oak falls from the lofty crag;
> The rock falls in crumbling decay ;
> Ebbs and flows the ocean;
> The moon is lost aloft in the heaven ;
> Thou alone dost triumph evermore,
> In gladness of light all thine own.

> " When tempest blackens round the world,
> In fierce thunder and dreadful lightning,
> Thou, in thy beauty, lookest forth on the storm,
> Laughing mid the uproar of the skies.
> To me thy light is vain,
> Never more shall I see thy face,

Spreading thy waving golden-yellow hair,
In the east on the face of the clouds,
Nor when thou tremblest in the west,
At thy dusky doors, on the ocean.

"And perchance thou art even as I,
    At seasons strong, at seasons without strength,
Our years, descending from the sky,
    Together hasting to their close.
Joy be upon thee then, O sun!
Since, in thy youth, thou art strong, O chief."

This hymn to the Sun marks the highest pitch
reached by the Ossianic poetry; if I may venture to say
so, only a little below the description of the sun in the
19th Psalm.

That sensitiveness to the powers of nature said to be
characteristic of the Celtic race appears very impress-
ively stamped on the Ossianic remains.   One might go
on quoting, by the hour, passages in which the old poet,
or poets, have rendered the changing aspects of the
mountains, the ocean, and the sky.   But, instead of
this, I shall give a specimen from a poem which be-
longs to an older legend even than any of the Fenian
cycle.

The subject of it is this.   There was in Ulster a cer-
tain Deirdre, the most beautiful woman of her time —
a Celtic Helen, only as faithful as Helen of Troy was
faithless.   Conor, King of Ulster, loved her, but she
preferred Naisi, one of his chiefs ; and Naisi married
Deirdre, and fled with his two brothers and many of his
clan to the coast of Argyll.   A long time they lived
there in happiness, these three sons of Uisnach, with
their people, and Naisi and Deirdre were supreme among
them.   At length Conor summoned them back to Erin,
and they, by some spell, felt constrained to return.

The king, finding that Deirdre was as beautiful as ever, treacherously slew her husband and his brothers, but Deirdre would not yield, and died, it is said, on the grave of the sons of Uisnach.

The following poem is her lament, as she sailed away to Erin, and looked back on the lovely shores of **Argyll,** which she felt she had left forever : —

> " Beloved land, that Eastern land,
>   Alba with its wonders,
>   O that I might not depart from it,
>   But that I go with Naisi.
>   .   .   .   .   .   .
>
> " Glen Massan, O Glen Massan !
>   High its herbs, fair its boughs,
>   Solitary was the place of our repose
>   On grassy Invermassan.
>
> " Glen Etive !   O Glen Etive !
>   There was raised my earliest home.
>   Beautiful its woods at sunrise,
>   When the sun struck on Glen Etive.
>
> " Glen Urchay !   O Glen Urchay !
>   The straight glen of smooth ridges.
>   No man of his age was more joyful
>   Than Naisi in Glen Urchay.
>
> " Glendaruadh !   O Glendaruadh !
>   Each man who dwells there I love.
>   Sweet the voice of the cuckoo on bending bough,
>   On the hill above Glendaruadh.
>
> " Beloved is Draighen and its sounding shore,
>   Beloved the water over the clear pure sands.
>   O that I might not depart from the east,
>   Unless I go with my beloved."

All the places here mentioned are well-known **scenes** in Argyll, beloved to this day by the natives — **pleasant** memories to many a stranger.   This is the earliest poem which celebrates the beauty of those West Highland shores, and it is said to be one of the oldest poems in the Gaelic tongue. It is found in a manuscript of the year 1238, and who can say how long before that it had travelled down, living only on the lips of men?

I wish I could go on to give more specimens of this ancient poetry, for there are many more to give. This only must be said: that the people who in a rude age could create poetry like that, and could so love it as to preserve it from generation to generation in their memories, merit surely some better fate than the contempt and ill-treatment they have too often received from their prosaic Saxon neighbors.

I have throughout indicated that I regard the body of Ossianic poetry, which belongs to the Scottish Highlands, and partly also to Ireland, as a genuine ancient growth. Even were we to set down all that MacPherson published as fabricated by himself, we should still have in the fragments preserved in the Dean of Lismore's book, in those collected by the Highland Society, and in pieces gathered by other collectors of undoubted veracity, enough to prove that it belonged to a remote antiquity. How remote I do not venture to say, only I am inclined to believe that it belonged to a time far back beyond the mediæval age. Neither have I said a word as to the existence of one Ossian.

Mr. Skene has distinguished three separate and successive stages in the creation of this poetry. At each stage it assumed a different form. In its oldest form there are pure poems of a heroic character, each poem complete in itself, and formed on a metrical system of alliteration and of rhyme, or correspondence of vowels. For the other two forms I must refer to Mr. Skene's

Introduction. The poems of the oldest form are attributed to one mythic poet; but, whether one or many, it is natural to suppose that there must originally have been one master-spirit, who struck the key-note of a poetry containing so much that was original, exalted, and unique.

What the characteristic faults of the Gael are, we have been well told by Dr. Arnold, and many other writers. It is more to our purpose now to note their characteristic excellences, as these appear in their native poetry.

The exquisite, penetrating sensibility which has been so often noted as the basis of Celtic character is fully reflected in these Ossianic poems. Quickness to see, quickness to feel, lively perceptions, deep, overpowering, all-absorbing emotions, these, the exact opposite of the Saxon temperament, tough, heavy, phlegmatic, are nowhere more conspicuous than in the Scottish Gael, and in that early poetry which rose out of their deepest nature, and has since powerfully reacted on it. This liveliness of eye and sensitiveness of heart have been noted as main elements of genius, and no doubt they are.

One side of their sensibility is great openness to joy — a sprightly, vivacious nature, loving dance and song. The other side is equal openness to melancholy, to despondency. Gleams intensely bright, glooms profoundly dark, exaltations, depressions — these are the staple of the Gael's existence, and of his poetry.

Turned on human life, this high-toned sensibility makes the Gael, in poetry as well as in practice, venerate heroes, cling to the heroic through all vicissitudes; though the heroes fall, die, and disappear, still he remains faithful to their memories, loves these, and only these. This fervid devotion to the memory of all the Fenian warriors whom he had known is a characteristic note in Ossian, but it becomes quite a passionate tenderness towards " the household hearts that were his own," towards his father Fion, his brother Fillan, his son Oscar. The laments he pours over this latter exceed in their piercing tenderness anything in Greek or Roman poetry, and recall some Hebrew strains.

These feelings of devotion to their chiefs, and tenacity of affection to their kindred, which we find in their most ancient poetry, reappear in the Gael throughout all their history, down to the present hour.

Again, this same sensibility made a lofty ideal of life quite natural to the Gael, even before Christianity had reached him ; made his heart open to admire the generous and the noble, and imparted a peculiar delicacy to his sentiments, and courtesy to his manners, — qualities which, even after all he has undergone, have not yet forsaken him. These qualities enter largely into the Ossianic ideal. It is wonderful how free from all grossness these poems are, how great purity pervades them. There is, of course, the dark side to this picture : ferocity of vengeance when enraged, recklessness of human life. As the counterpart of his devotion to the high and the heroic is the Gael's aversion to the commonplace routine of life ; his contempt for the mechanical trades and arts. To this day the native Gael in his own glens thinks all occupations but that of the soldier, the hunter, and, perhaps, the shepherd, unworthy of him. He carries down to the present hour something of the Ossianic conception, which recognizes only the warrior and the hunter.

Turned upon nature, their open sensibility is quick to seize the outward aspect of things, but does not rest there, cannot be satisfied with a homely realism ; is not even content with the picturesque appearances, but penetrates easily, rapidly, to the secret of the object, finds its affinity to the soul ; in fact, spiritualizes it. This is that power of natural magic, which Mr. Arnold makes so much of in his book on Celtic literature. The impressionable Gael was, from the earliest time, greatly under the power of the ever-changing aspects of earth and sky. The bright side is in his poetry ; the sunrise on the mountains, the sunset on the ocean, the softness of moonlight, all are there touched with exceeding delicacy. But more frequently still in Ossian, as befitted his country and his circumstances, the melancholy side of nature predominates. His poetry is full of natural images taken straight from the wilderness ; the brown heath, the thistle-down on the autumn air, the dark mountain cairns, the sighing winds, the movements of mist and clouds, silence and solitude — these are forever recurring in impressive monotone. Even to this day, when one is alone in the loneliest places of the Highlands, in the wilderness where no man is, on the desolate moor of Rannoch, or among the gray boulders of Badenoch, — when

> "the loneliness
> Loadeth the heart, the desert tires the eye" —

at such a time, if one wished a language to express the feeling that weighs upon the heart, where would one turn to find it ? Not to Scott ; not even to Wordsworth — though the power of hills was upon him, if upon any modern. Not in these, but in the voice of Cona alone would the heart find a language that would relieve it.   It is this fact, that there is something which is of the very essence of the Highland glens and mountains, something unexpressed by any modern poet, but which the old Ossianic poetry alone expresses ; this, if nothing else, would convince me that the poetry which conveys this feeling is no modern fabrication, but is native to the hills, connatural, I had almost said, with the granite mountains among which it has survived.

Lastly, this sadness of tone in describing nature is still more deeply apparent, when the Gaelic poet touches on the destiny of his race.   That race, high-spirited, impetuous, war-loving, proud, once covered a great portion of Europe.   As one has said, it shook all empires, but founded none.   For ages it has been pushed westward before a younger advancing race, till for many ages the Gael has retained only the westernmost promontories and islands.   To these they still cling, as limpets cling to their rocks; and they feel, as they gaze wistfully on the Atlantic ocean, that beyond it the majority of their race has already gone, and that they, the remnant, are doomed soon to follow, or to disappear.

> " Cha till, cha till, cha till mi tuille."
> " I return, I return, I return no more."

This is the feeling deepest in the heart of the modern Gael ; this is the mournful, ever-recurring undertone of the Ossianic poetry.   It is the sentiment of a despairing and disappearing race, a sentiment of deeper sadness, than any the prosperous Saxon can know.

Two facts are enough to convince me of the genuineness of the ancient Gaelic poetry.   The truthfulness with which it reflects the melancholy aspects of Highland scenery. the equal truthfulness with which it expresses the prevailing sentiment of the Gael, and his sad sense of his people's destiny. I need no other proofs that the Ossianic poetry is a native formation, and comes from the primeval heart of the Gaelic race.

CHAPTER X.

MODERN GAELIC BARDS AND DUNCAN MACINTYRE.

To those who feel that poetry is a thing older than all manuscripts and books, and that in its essence it is independent of these, it is I know not how refreshing to turn from the poetry that is confined to books to the song-lore of the Gael. They find there a poetry which, both in its ancient and in its modern forms, was the creation of men who were taught in no school but that of nature; who could neither read nor write their native Gaelic; who, many of them, never saw a book or a manuscript; who had no other model than the old primeval Ossianic strains which they had heard from childhood; and who, when inborn passion prompted, sang songs of natural and genuine inspiration. What they composed they never thought of committing to writing, for writing was to them an art unknown. The great body of Highland poetry, both in old and in modern times, has come down to us preserved mainly by oral tradition. This is a fact which can be proved, let learned criticism say what it will. I have already spoken of that great primitive background of heroic songs and ballads, known as the Ossianic poetry, which had lived for centuries only on the lips of men, before it was committed to writing. That was the nurse and school by which all after Gaelic poets were formed. To-day let us turn to the post-Ossianic, or modern poetry of the Gael, which reaches from the middle age almost down to our own time.

" In a land of song like the Highlands," says one who knew well what he spoke of, " every strath, glen, and hamlet had its bard. In the morning of my days," he goes on to say, writing in 1841, " it was my happy lot to inhale the mountain air of a sequestered spot, whose inhabitants may be designated children of song, in a state of society whose manners were little removed from that of primitive simplicity. I had many opportunities of witnessing the influence of poetry over the mind, and I found that cheerfulness and song, music and morality, walked almost always hand in hand." Making allowance for the warmth of feeling with which a man looks back on a childhood spent among the mountains, these words are, I believe, true. One may be forgiven if one doubts, whether School Boards and the Code with its six Standards, which have superseded this state of things, and are doing their best to stamp out the small remains of Gaelic poetry, are wholly a gain.

The writer from whom I have quoted, Mr. John Mackenzie, was a native of the west coast of Ross, to whom those who still cherish Gaelic poetry owe a great debt; for in 1841 he published his *Beauties of Gaelic Poetry*, which is a collection of the best pieces of the best modern Gaelic bards. They are but a sample of what might have been dug from a vast quarry, but they are a good sample. In many cases he had to gather the poems of some of the best bards, not from any edition of their works, or even from manuscripts, but from the recitation of old people, who preserved them in memory. Mackenzie's book contains more than thirty thousand lines of poetry on all kinds of subjects, from the long heroic chant about

"Old unhappy far off things,
And battles long ago!"

down to the

"More humble lay,
Familiar matter of to-day."

To this book and its contents I shall confine myself, while speaking of the modern poetry of the Gael.

The book is divided into three parts. First, a few poems of the mediæval time, which form a sort of link between the Ossianic and the modern poetry. The second, and by far the largest part, consists of the poems of well-known bards from the Reformation down to the present century. The names of these are given with their works, and with some account of their lives. The third portion consists of short popular songs well known among the people, but without the name of the authors attached to them.

Of the early or pre-Reformation poems given by Mackenzie, two only seem to be of undoubted antiquity, one a poem called *The Owl*, and another, *The Aged Bard's Wish*. In the former, an old hunter, who is ill-treated by his young wife, and is turned by her out of doors at night, tells all his grievances to an owl. The most interesting thing about it is the mention he makes of all the mountain places, where he used in happier days to hunt the wolf or the deer. Singing four hundred years ago, he mentions the mountains that cluster round Ben Nevis, and the waterfalls by Loch Treig, by the same names which they bear to-day. The other ancient poem, called *The Aged Bard's Wish*, is of unknown date, but certainly belongs to the pre-Reformation period. It is beautiful in its composition, melodious in its language, and pervaded not at all by the spirit of the warrior, and only in a slight degree by that of the hunter, but rather by the pastoral sentiment. This is a distinct advance on the poems of the Ossianic era. Here are some stanzas from Mackenzie's literal prose translation, and these will show its tone: —

" Oh, lay me near the brooks, which slowly move with gentle steps ; under the shade of the budding branches lay my head, and be thou, O sun, in kindness with me. . . .

"I see Ben-Aid of beautiful curve, chief of a thousand hills; the dreams of stags are in his locks, his head in the bed of clouds.

" I seen Scorn-eilt on the brow of the glen, where the cuckoo first raises her tuneful voice ; and the beautiful green hill of the thousand pines, of herds, of roes, and of elks.

" Let joyous ducklings swim swiftly on the pool of tall pines. A strath of green firs is at its head, bending the red rowans over its banks.

" Let the swan of the snowy bosom glide on the top of the waves. When she soars on high among the clouds she will be unencumbered.

" She travels oft over the sea to the cold region of foaming billows; where never shall sail be spread out to a mast, nor an oaken prow divide the wave. . . .

" Farewell, lovely company of youth! and you, O beautiful maiden, farewell. I cannot see you. Yours is the joy of summer; my winter is everlasting.

"Oh, place me within hearing of the great waterfall, where it descends from the rock; let a harp and a shell be by my side, and the shield that defended my forefathers in battle.

"Come friendlily over the sea, O soft breeze, that movest slowly, bear my shade on the wind of thy swiftness, and travel quickly to the Isle of Heroes,

"Where those who went of old are in deep slumber, deaf to the sound of music. Open the hall where dwell Ossian and Daol. The night shall come, and the Bard shall not be found."

Several things about this poem are noteworthy. Here you have a vein of fine and delicate sentiment in a Gaelic poem composed centuries before MacPherson appeared. Then observe that, though pastoral life has come in, Christianity is yet unknown, or, at least, unbelieved by this dweller beside Loch Treig. His desire is that his harp, a shell full of wine, and his ancestral shield should be laid by his side; and then that his soul, which he believed to be of the nature of wind, should be borne by its kindred winds, not to heaven, but to Flath-Innis, the Isle of the Brave, the Celtic Paradise, where Ossian and Daol are. Lastly, note the peculiar love of nature, and that magical charm with which it is touched.

Of those thirty bards, whose poems Mackenzie has preserved, I might give the names and a few facts about the lives and compositions of each; but this, which is all I could do within my prescribed space, would not greatly edify any one. I might tell you of Mary MacLeod, the nurse of five chiefs of MacLeod, and the poetess of her clan; of Ian Lom MacDonald, the first Jacobite bard, who led Montrose and his army to Inverlochy, pointed out the camping ground of the Campbells, then mounted the ramparts, watched the battle, and sang a fiery pæan for the victory; of Alastair MacDonald, the second great Jacobite bard, who joined Prince Charlie's army, shared his disaster, and preserved the memory of that time in songs of fervid Jacobite devotion.

But I should do little good by giving you merely bare lists of names, facts, and a few notions, about Rob Donn, or Mackay, the poet of the Reay Country, a bitter and powerful satirist; about Dougal Buchanan, the earnest and solemn religious poet of Rannoch; and William Ross, the sweet lyrist of Gairloch in Ross, and many more.

If any one desires to know further about these bards of the Gael, let me refer him to the brief biographies given of each of them, in the book I have already spoken of, Mackenzie's *Beauties of Gaelic Poetry*, and also to the very animated commentary on the contents of that book, contained in Professor Blackie's interesting work on *The Language and Literature of the Scottish Highlands.*

One characteristic of these Gaelic bards must be mentioned. They were most of them satirists as well as lyrists and eulogists. It was a true instinct which made the Chief of MacLeod forbid his poetic nurse to sing praises of himself and his family, for he said the bard who is free to praise is also free to blame. Enthusiastic admiration and love have as their other side equal vehemence of hatred. And this bitter side of the poetic nature found full vent in the poetry of many Highland bards. Biting wit, invectives often exceeding all bounds — these, but not humor, characterize the Gael. Humor, which is a quieter, more kindly quality, generally comes from men fatter, better fed, in easier circumstances than most of the Highland poets were. Satire abounds in both the MacDonalds, above all in Rob Donn, who carries it often to coarseness. It is not wanting in the kindlier nature of the poet of whom I shall now speak; for I think I cannot do better than take as a sample of the whole Bardic brotherhood one whom I have most studied, and who is, I believe, recognized as among the very foremost, if not quite the foremost, of the Highland minstrels.

Any one who of late years has travelled by the banks of Loch Awe must have remarked by the wayside, a short distance above Dalmally, a monument of rude unhewn stones cemented together. It stands very near the spot where, as his sister tells, Wordsworth, in his famous tour, first caught sight across the loch of the ruined Castle of Kilchurn, and shouted out impromptu the first three lines of his *Address to the Castle* —

> " Child of loud-throated war, the mountain stream
>   Roars in thy hearing, but thine hour of rest
>   Is come, and thou art silent in thine age."

That monument has been raised to the memory of the
Bard of Glenorchy, Duncan MacIntyre, or " Donacha
Ban nan Oran," Fair Duncan of the Songs, as he is
familiarly called by his Highland countrymen. If ever
poet was a pure son of nature, this man was. Born in
a lonely place, called Druimliaghart (pronounced Drum-
liarst), on the skirts of the Monadh Dhu, or the Forest
of the Black Mount, of poor parents, he never went to
school, never learnt to read or write, could not speak
English, knew but one language, his own native Gaelic.
His only school was the deer forest, in which he spent
his boyhood. His lessons were catching trout and
salmon with his fishing rod, shooting grouse and stalk-
ing deer with his gun. His mental food was the songs
of the mountains, especially the great oral literature of
the Ossianic minstrelsy. He tells us that he got "a
part of his nursing " at the shealings ; and I remember
once, in a walk through the mountains of the Black
Forest, beside a grass-covered road that leads down to
Loch Etive, having the ruins of a shealing both pointed
out to me in which Duncan Ban used to spend his early
summers. Those shealing times, when the people from
the glens drove their black cattle and a few small sheep
to pasture for the summer months on the higher Bens,
are still looked back to by the Highlanders as their
great season of happiness, romance, and song. With
the shealings for his summer, Drumliarst for his winter
home, Duncan had just reached manhood when the ris-
ing of the clans and the Forty-five broke out. Like all
true Highlanders, his heart was with the Stuarts, but,

as he lived on the lands of the Earl of Breadalbane, he was obliged to serve on the Hanoverian side, as a substitute for a neighboring Tacksman. This man supplied Duncan with a sword, which, in the rout of Falkirk, Duncan treated as Horace did his shield, and either lost or flung away. His earliest poem was composed on this battle, and in it he describes with evident relish the disgraceful retreat, hinting that, had he been on the Prince's side, he would have fought with more manhood. The man for whom Duncan served as a substitute refused to pay the sum promised, because the sword had been lost; so the bard took his revenge by writing a satiric poem on the sword and its owner. Fletcher, for that was the man's name, fell upon the poet and thrashed him with his walking-stick, telling him to go and make a song upon that. But Duncan had a friend in the Breadalbane of the day, who came to his aid, and forced Fletcher to pay down the money to the man who had risked his life on his account. This first poem soon became known, and made Duncan famous, and Fletcher despised.

Early in life the bard married a young girl of somewhat higher station and richer parents than himself. There is nothing more pleasing in the loves of any of the poets than this courtship. In a beautiful lyric called *Mairi Bhan-og*, or " Fair young Mary," he tells how he wooed and won her. Her home was within less than a mile from his own, but their conditions in life were so different, that for long he despaired. Her father was baron bailiff, or under factor, and a freeholder, and she had some cows and calves of her own for a dowry. He was the son of poor people, and had no patrimony. He tells how he used from his own door to watch her, as

she went about her household work, and how, when at
last he ventured to address her, the kindness of her
demeanor gave him confidence.   After praising her
beauty, he says, the thing that most took him was her
firmness in good, and her manners, that were ever
so womanly.   And he concludes with a fine delicacy,
wishing to take her away and hide her in some place,
where decay or change might never reach her.   This
song, we are told, is regarded, " on account of its com-
bined purity and passion, its grace, delicacy, and tender-
ness," as the finest love song in the Gaelic language.

After his return from soldiering, his patron, Lord
Breadalbane, made Duncan his forester, first in Coire
Cheathaich (pronounced Hyaich), or the Misty Corrie,
in the forest of Maam-lorn, at the head of Glen Lochy;
then on Ben Doran, a beautifully-shaped hill at the head
of Glenorchy, looking down that long glen towards
Loch Awe.   For a time, too, he served the Duke of
Argyll, as his deer forester on the Buachaill Etie or the
Shepherds of Etive, gnarled peaks facing towards both
Glen Etive and Glencoe.

Duncan has made famous Coire Cheathaich and Ben
Doran by two of his best poems.   The poem on Coire
Cheathaich has been translated by a living poet, Mr.
Robert Buchanan, in his book called *The Land of Lorne.*
His version gives a very good notion of it, with its
minute realistic description : —

> "My beauteous corrie! where cattle wander;
>   My misty corrie! my darling dell!
>   Mighty, verdant. and covered over
>   With tender wild flowers of sweetest smell;
>   Dark is the green of thy grassy clothing,
>   Soft swell thy hillocks, most green and deep,
>   The cannach flowing, the darnel growing,
>   While the deer troop past to the misty steep."

But of all Duncan Ban's poems the most original, the most elaborate, and the most famous is that on Ben Doran. It consists of five hundred and fifty-five lines, and is unique in its plan and construction. It is adapted to a pipe tune, and follows with wonderful skill all the turns, and twirls, and wild cadences of the pibroch. It falls into eight parts, alternating with a sort of strophe and antistrophe, one slow, called urlar, in stately trochees ; another swift, called siubhal, in a kind of gallopping anapests.

In Ben Doran, as in Coire Cheathaich, the bard dwells with the most loving minuteness on all the varied features and the ever-changing aspects of the mountain, which he loved as if it were a living creature and a friend. But besides this, in no poem on record have the looks, the haunts, the habits, and the manners of the deer, both red and roe, been pictured so accurately and so fondly, by one who had been born and reared among them, and who loved them as his chosen playmates.

Professor Blackie has made a very spirited rendering into English of this most difficult poem, to which I would advise any one to turn who cares for poetry fresh from nature. I venture at present to give some passages from a translation I made years ago, to beguile hours of lonely wandering among the Highland hills. Be it remembered, however, how different a thing is a wild Celtic chant, adapted to the roar and thunder of the bagpipe, from a literary performance meant only to be read by critical eyes in unexcited leisure. Here is the opening stave : —

> "Honor o'er all Bens
> On Bendoran be!
> Of all hills the sun kens,
> Beautifullest he ;

> Mountain long and sweeping,
> Nooks the red deer keeping,
> Light on braesides sleeping;
>   There I 've watched delightedly.
> Branchy copses cool,
> Woods of sweet grass full,
> Deer herds beautiful,
>   There are dwelling aye.
> Oh! blithe to hunting go,
>   Where white-hipped stag and hind,
> Upward in long row,
>   Snuff the mountain wind;
> Jaunty follows sprightly,
>   With bright burnished hide,
> Dressed in fashion sightly,
>   Yet all free from pride."

The poem is, as I have said, made for a pibroch tune, and is, like the pibroch, full of repetitions. It returns again and again upon the same theme, but each time with variations and additions. Thus the grasses and plants and bushes that grow on Ben Doran are more than once described, as if the poet never tired of thinking of them. The red-deer, stag and hind, with their ways; the roe-deer, buck and doe, with their ways; each is several times dwelt on at length.

I shall now give a specimen of the description of each kind of deer. Here is a picture of the red-deer hind, and of the stag, her mate : —

> "Hark that quick darting snort!
>   'T is the light-headed hind,
> With sharp-pointed nostril
>   Keen searching the wind;
> Conceited, slim-limbed,
>   The high summits she keeps,
> Nor, for fear of the gun-fire,
>   Descends from the steeps.
> Though she gallop at speed
>   Her breath will not fail,
> For she comes of a breed
>   Were strong-winded and hale.

" When she lifteth her voice,
　　What joy 't is to hear
The ghost of her breath,
　　As it echoeth clear.
For she calleth aloud,
　　From the cliff of the crag,
Her silver-hipped lover,
　　The proud antlered stag.
Well-antlered, high-headed,
　　Loud-voiced doth he come,
From the haunts he well knows
　　Of Bendoran, his home.

" Ah! mighty Bendoran!
　　How hard 't were to tell,
How many proud stags
　　In thy fastnesses dwell.
How many thy slim hinds,
　　Their wee calves attending,
And, with white-twinkling tails,
　　Up the Balloch ascending,
To where Corrie-Chreetar
　　Its bield is extending.

" But when the mood takes her
　　To gallop with speed,
With her slender hoof-tips
　　Hardly touching the mead,
As she stretcheth away
　　In her fleet-flying might,
What man in the kingdom
　　Could follow her flight ?
Full of gambol and gladness,
　　Blithe wanderers free,
No shadow of sadness
　　Ever comes o'er their glee.
But fitful and tricksy,
　　Slim and agile of limb,
Age will not burden them,
　　Sorrow not dim.
　　．　．　．　．　．

"How gay through the glens
　　Of the sweet mountain grass,
　17

> Loud sounding, all free
>   From complaining, they pass.
> Though the snow come, they 'll ask
>   For no roof-tree to bield them;
> The deep Corrie Altrum,
>   His rampart will shield them.
> There the rifts, and the clefts,
>   And deep hollows they 'll be in,
> With their well-sheltered beds
>   Down in lone Aisan-teean."

Again, in an urlar, or slow trochaic strophe, he returns to the same theme —

> " O! sweet to me at rising
>   In early dawn to see,
> All about the mountains,
>   Where they 've right to be,
> Twice a hundred there
>   Of the people without care,
> Starting from their lair,
>   Hale and full of glee;
> Clear-sounding, smooth, and low,
>   From their mouths the murmurs flow,
> And beautiful they go,
>   As they sing their morning song.
> .   .   .   .   .   .
>
> Sweeter to me far,
>   When they begin their croon,
> Than all melodies that are
>   In Erin — song or tune;
> Than pipe or viol clear,
> More I love to hear
> The breath of the son of the deer
> Bellowing on the face
> Of Bendoran."

Our last sample shall be the description of the roe : —

> " Mid budding sprays the doe
>   Ever restless moves —
> Edge of banks and braes,
>   Haunts that most she loves.
> Young leaves, fresh and sheen,
> Tips of heather green —

Dainties fine and clean,
　Are her choice.
Pert, coquettish, gay,
Thoughtless, full of play,
Creature made alway
　To rejoice.
Maiden-like in mien
Mostly she is seen
In the birk-glens green
　Where lush grasses be.
But sometimes Crag-y-vhor,
　Gives her refuge meet,
Sunday and Monday there
　In a still retreat.
There bushes thick and deep
Cluster round her sleep,
Her all safe to keep
　From rude north-winds blowing
In bield of Doire-chro.
Lying down below
The Sron's lofty brow,
　Where fresh shoots are growing:
There well-springs clear and fine,
　With draughts more benign,
Than ale or any wine,
　Always are flowing.
These, as they pour,
　Their streams unfailing,
Keep her evermore
　Fresh and free from ailing.

Yellow hues and red,
Delicately spread,
On her figure shed
　Loveliness complete.
Hardy 'gainst the cold,
Virtues manifold,
More than can be told,
In her nature meet.

" At the hunter's sound
　Sudden whirling round,
　How lightly doth she bound,

O'er rough mountain ground,
    Far and free.
Quicker ear to hear
Danger drawing near,
Fleeter flight from fear,
    In Europe cannot be."

This long hunting pibroch, of which I have given a
few samples, is a prime favorite with all Gaelic-speaking
men, and is to them what such songs as *Gala Water* or
the *Holms of Yarrow* are to the ear of the Lowlander.
Duncan Ban will ever be remembered among his coun-
trymen as the chief minstrel of the deer, the chase, and
the forest. As a deer-stalker he had lived much in
solitude, —

"had been alone
Amid the heart of many thousand mists."

When he was forester on Ben Doran, in Coire Cheat-
haich, and on Buachail Étie, the inspiration found him.
But solitude left no shade of sadness on his spirit; there
is in his song nothing of the Ossianic melancholy. He
was a blithe, hearty companion, fond of good fellow-
ship, and several of his songs are in praise of it. But,
though he enjoyed such things, he never lost himself in
them. When his foresting days were over, he joined
a volunteer regiment called the Breadalbane Fencibles,
in which he served for six years, till it was disbanded
in 1799.

After his discharge from the Fencibles he migrated
from his hills to Edinburgh, where he served for some
time in the City Guard, which Walter Scott has de-
scribed in one of his novels. The third edition of his
poems was published in 1804, and in 1806 he was able
to retire from the City Guard, and to live for the re-
mainder of his days in comparative comfort, on the

return which this third edition brought him. He died in 1812 in Edinburgh, in his eighty-ninth year, and lies buried in Old Gray Friars' churchyard.

Born at Druimliaghart, on the skirts of the Black Mount, at the head of Glenorchy ; laid to rest in Gray Friars' churchyard, Edinburgh ; beloved in life ; honored after death by his countrymen, who have reared a monument to perpetuate his memory on Loch Awe side ; of him it may be said, as truly as of most sons of songs, " he sleeps well."

Once or twice he wandered through the Highlands, to obtain subscriptions for a new edition of his poems. I knew a Highland lady who remembered to have seen him in her childhood on one of these occasions, when he visited her father's house in Mull. He was wandering about with the wife of his youth, fair young Mary, still fair, though no longer young. He then wore, if I remember aright, a tartan kilt, and on his head a cap made of a fox's skin. He was fair of hair and face, with a pleasant countenance, and a happy, attractive manner. An amiable, sweet-blooded man, who never, it is said, attacked any one, unprovoked ; but, when he was assailed, he could repay smartly in that satire which came naturally to most Highland bards.

After he had settled in Edinburgh he paid one last visit to his native Glenorchy in 1802, where he found that those changes had already set in which have since desolated so many glens, and changed the whole character of social life in the Highlands. What he then felt he has recorded in one of his last and most touching poems entitled —

LAST LEAVE-TAKING OF THE MOUNTAINS.

"Yestreen I was on Ben Doran,
    Which I had good right to know,
I saw all the glens beneath me,
    And the Bens loved long ago.
Bright vision it used to be,
    Walking on that mountain ground,
When the sun was in gladness rising,
    And the deer were bellowing round.

"Joyous the frolicsome herd,
    As they moved in their jaunty pride,
While the hinds were at the cold hill-wells,
    With their dappled fawns by their side;
The little doe and the roe buck,
    The black cock and red grouse-bird,
Their voices were filling the morning air —
    Sweeter melody never was heard.

"There I passed the time of my nursing,
    At the shealings well known to me,
With the kind-hearted maidens mingling there
    In games, and daffing, and glee.
'T was not in the course of nature,
    That should last till now the same;
But sad it was to be forced to go,
    When the time for the parting came.

"But now that old age has smote me,
    I have got a hurt that will last;
On my teeth it hath wrought decay,
    On my eyesight blindness cast.

.   .   .   .

"But though now my head is gray,
    And my locks but thinly spread,
I have slipt the deerhound many a day
    On the lads with high antlered head.
Though I love them dearly as ever,
    Were a herd on the hillside in sight,
I could not go to seek them,
    For my breath has failed me quite.

"Yestreen as I walked the mountain,
    O the thoughts that arose in me;

For the people I loved that used to be there
   In the desert, no more could I see.
Ah ! little I dreamed that Ben
   Such change would undergo,
That I should see it covered with sheep,
   And the world would deceive me so !

" When I looked round on every side,
   How could I feel but drear !
For the woods and the heather all were gone,
   And the men were no longer here.
There was not a deer for the hunting,
   Not a bird, nor a single roe;
Of these the few that were not dead
   Hence have vanished long ago.

" My farewell then to the forests,
   And the marvellous mountains there,
Where the green cresses grow, and the clear wells flow,
   Draughts gentle, and kingly, and fair.
Ye pastures beyond all price !
   Wildernesses, wide and free,
On you, since I go to return no more,
   My blessing forever be ! "

In the close of this pathetic farewell Duncan Ban has
touched on what has since become a great social ques-
tion — I mean the clearing of the glens, the depopula-
tion of the Highlands. This great change — revolution
I might call it — began early in this century, and our
bard saw the first fruits of the new system. The old
native Gael who used to live grouped in hamlets in the
glens, each with so many small sheep and goats, and a
little herd of black cattle, which they pastured in com-
mon on the mountains, these were dispossessed of the
holdings they had held for immemorial time, to make
way for Lowland farmers with large capital, who covered
hill and glen with large flocks of bigger sheep. These
flocks a few shepherds, often Lowlanders, tended on

the mountains from which the old race had been swept, till the land indeed became a wilderness. One question only was asked — What shall most speedily return large rents to the lairds ? What shall grow the largest amount of mutton for the Glasgow and Liverpool markets ? Tried by this purely commercial standard, the ancient Gael were found wanting, and, being dispossessed, went to America and elsewhere. Great Britain thus lost thousands of the finest of its people irrecoverably.

Since Culloden, the Highlands have received from the British Government only one piece of wise and kindly legislation. That was, when the elder Pitt gave the chiefs or their sons commissions to raise regiments from among their clansmen. The result was the Highland regiments, who bore themselves, all know how, in the Peninsula and at Waterloo. Their name and the remembrance of their achievements remain to this day a tower of strength to the British army, although in some of the so-called Highland regiments there is now scarcely one genuine Gael. In the glens which formerly sent forth whole regiments, you could not now get a single man to wear her Majesty's uniform.

But to return from these matters, economical and political, to our bard. It is a noteworthy fact that, as he could neither read nor write, he had to carry the whole of his poetry, which amounts to about six thousand lines, in his memory, which was also stored with a large equipment of Ossianic and other current lays. After he had preserved his poems for years, a young minister committed them to writing from Duncan's recital, and in time they were published. Facts like these, and they could easily be multiplied. tend to show how short-

sighted is the view of critics, who refuse to believe in
the preserving power of oral tradition. They also show
how far culture can go, wholly unaided by books. All
who read with open heart the poetry of our bard must
acknowledge that here we havè a man more truly re-
plenished with all that is best in culture than most of
the men who are the products of our modern School
Board system.

MacIntyre has sometimes been called the Burns of
the Highlands. Burns and he lived at the same time,
but MacIntyre's life overlapped that of Burns at both
ends. He was older than Burns by thirty-five years,
and outlived him by sixteen. It is strange, and shows
the great separation there then was between the High-
lands and the rest of the world, that there is no evidence
that either poet knew of the existence of the other.
Yet MacIntyre must have heard of Burns when he
passed his old age in Edinburgh. Though they have
been compared to each other, there is little likeness be-
tween them, except in this : both were natural, spon-
taneous singers ; both sang of human life, as they saw
it with their own eyes ; each is the darling poet of his
own people. Here the likeness ends.

MacIntyre had not the experience of men and soci-
ety, the varied range, of Burns. The problem of the
rich and poor, and many another problem which vexed
Burns, never troubled the bard of Glenorchy. He ac-
cepted his condition, and was content ; had no jealousy
of those above him in rank or wealth. He was happier
than Burns in his own inner man, and had no quarrel
with the world, and the way it was ordered, till they
expelled the deer, and brought in the big long-wooled
sheep. But if MacIntyre knew less of man than Burns,

he knew more of nature in its grand and solitary moods. He took it more to heart; at every turn it more enters into his song and forms its texture.

MacIntyre's poetry eminently disproves — as indeed all Gaelic poetry does — that modern doctrine, that love of nature is necessarily a late growth, the product of refined cultivation. It may be so with the phlegmatic Teuton, not so with the susceptible and impassioned Gael. Their poets, MacIntyre above all, were never inside a schoolroom, never read a book; yet they love their mountains as passionately as Wordsworth loved his, though with a simpler, more primitive love.

Mr. Arnold concluded his lectures delivered on Celtic Literature by pleading for the foundation in Oxford of a Celtic chair. He thought that this might perhaps atone for the errors of Saxon Philistines, and send through the gentle ministrations of science a message of peace to Ireland. Oxford since then has got a Celtic chair, but has not thereby propitiated Ireland.

Another Celtic chair is just about to be founded in Edinburgh University. But the foundation of Celtic chairs will be of small avail, unless the younger generation takes advantage of them. To these let me say that, if they will but master the language of the Gael, and dig in the great quarry of their native song, they will find there, to repay their efforts, much that is weird and wild, as well as sweet and pathetic, thrilling with a piercing tenderness wholly unlike anything in the Saxon tongue. There they may not only delight and reinvigorate their imagination, but they may fetch thence new tones of inspiration for English poetry.

And more than this, they will find there sources of deep human interest. The knowledge of the Gaelic language will be a key to open to them the hearts of a noble people, as nothing else can. England and Lowland Scotland alike owe a real debt to the Scottish Gael, if not so urgent a debt as they owe to Ireland, a debt for the wrongs done last century after Culloden battle — a debt still unrepaid, perhaps now unrepayable. A debt, too, for the world of pleasure which so many strangers annually reap in the Scottish High‑lands. The native Gael are capable of something more than merely to be gillies and keepers to aristocratic or plutocratic sportsmen. Within those dim, smoky sheal‑ings of the west beat hearts warm with feelings which the pushing and prosperous Saxon little dreams of.

That race, last century, sheltered their outlawed Prince at the peril of their own lives. While they themselves and their families were starving, they re‑fused the bribe of thirty thousand pounds which was offered for his head, and cho‑e to be shot down by troopers on their own mountains, rather ᵗhan betray him. Can any nation on earth point to a record of finer loyalty and purer self-devotion? Yet for the race that was capable of these things no better fate has been found than to be driven, unwilling exiles, from the land that reared them.

Perhaps I may fitly close this brief sketch with some lines conveying the feeling with which Duncan Ban's romantic but now desolate birthplace was visited a few years ago : —

> The homes long are gone, but enchantment still lingers
> 　The green knolls around, where thy young life began,
> 　Sweetest and last of the old Celtic singers,
> 　　Bard of the Monadh-dhu, blithe Donach Ban!
>
> 　Never mid scenes of earth fairer or grander
> 　　Poet first lifted his eyelids on light,

Free through these glens, o'er these mountains to wander,
    And make them his own by the true minstrel right.

Around thee the meeting and green interlacing
    Of clear-flowing waters and far-winding glens,
Lovely inlaid in the mighty embracing
    Of sombre pine forests and storm-riven Bens:

Behind thee, the crowding Peaks, region of mystery,
    Fed thy young spirit with broodings sublime,
Gray cairn and green hillock, each breathing some history
    Of the weird under-world or the wild battle-time.

Thine were Ben Starrav, Stop-gyre, Meal-na-ruadh,
    Mantled in storm-gloom, or bathed in sunshine,
Streams from Cor-oran, Glashgower, and Glen-fuadh,
    Made music for thee, where their waters combine.

But more than all others, thy darling Ben Doran
    Held thee entranced with his beautiful form,
With looks ever changing thy young fancy storing,
    Gladness of sunshine, and terror of storm, —

Opened to thee his most secret recesses,
    Taught thee the lore of the red deer and roe,
Showed thee them feed on the green mountain cresses,
    Drink the cold wells above lone Doirè-chro.

There thine eye watched them go up the hill-passes,
    At sunrise rejoicing, a proud jaunty throng,
Learnt the herbs that they love, the small flowers and hill grasses,
    To make these forever bloom green in thy song.

Yet, child of the wilderness! nursling of nature!
    Would the hills e'er have taught thee the true minstrel art,
Had not one visage, more lovely of feature,
    The fountain unsealed of thy tenderer heart?

The maiden that dwelt on the side of Mam-haarie —
    Seen from thy home-door — a vision of joy —
Morning and even, the young fair-haired Mary
    Moving about at her household employ.

High on Bendoa, and stately Benchallader,
  Leaving the dun deer in safety to hide,
Fondly thy doating eye dwelt on her, followed her,
  Tenderly wooed her, and won her thy bride.

O! well for the maiden who found such a lover!
  And well for the Poet; to whom Mary gave
Her fulness of heart, until, life's journey over,
  She lay down beside him to rest in the grave.

From the bards of to-day, and their sad thoughts that darken
  The sunshine with doubt, wring the bosom with pain,
How gladly we fly to the shealings, and hearken
  The clear mountain gladness that sounds through thy strain!

In the uplands with thee is no doubt or misgiving,
  But strength, joy, and freedom Atlantic winds blow,
And kind thoughts are there, and the pure simple living
  Of the warm-hearted Gael in the glens long ago.

The Muse of old Maro hath pathos and splendor,
  The long lines of Homer in majesty roll;
But to me Donach Ban breathes a feeling more tender,
  More akin to the child-heart that sleeps in my soul.

CHAPTER XI.

THE THREE YARROWS.

THE ideal creations of poets generally have their root, whether we can trace it or not, in some personal experience. However remote from actual life the perfected creation may appear, whether it be a *Midsummer Night's Dream* or a presentation of Hamlet, we may well believe that all its finer features were the birth of some chance bright moments, when certain aspects of nature, or expressions of human countenance, or incidents of life, or subtle traits of character, struck on the poet's soul, and impressed themselves indelibly there. But though we may be quite sure of this, yet so subtilely works the transmuting power of imagination, so reticent have poets generally been about their own creations, so little have they been given to analyze themselves, that the cases are few in which we can lay our finger on this and that actual fact, and say, these are the elements out of which the bright creation came. There are, however, some instances among modern poets in which we are allowed to trace the first footprints of their thought. And when we can do so, this, instead of diminishing our admiration of the perfected results, gives them, I believe, an added interest. Lockhart has recorded his belief that there is hardly a scene, incident, or character in all Scott's poems or romances, of which the first suggestion may not be traced to some old verse in the *Border Minstrelsy*, or to some incident or character which he fell in with during those raids, in which he gleaned the materials of that wonderful book from the sequestered places of the green Border hills. It may not be without interest if we turn to a contemporary and friend of Scott's, and trace the actual facts out of which arose three of Wordsworth's most exquisite lyrics, *Yarrow Unvisited, Yarrow Visited,* and *Yarrow Revisited.*

It was in August, 1803, that Wordsworth, though he had been born and reared in sight of Scotland's hills, for the first time set his foot on Scottish ground. He and his sister Dorothy, with Coleridge for their companion, left Keswick, to make a tour through Scotland, mainly on foot. The poet's means, which were then but scanty, his income being not more than £100 a year, would not allow any more costly way of travelling; and well for us that it was so. Out of that " plain living," which circumstances enforced, how much of the " high thinking " came! And certainly, as walking is the least expensive, so it is the best way in which a poet can see a country. Walking alone, or with one congenial friend, he can stop, and gaze, and listen, and saunter, and meditate, at his will, and let all sights and sounds of nature melt into him, as in no other way they can. On foot the three travelled up Nithsdale, by Falls of Clyde, on to Loch Lomond, where Coleridge, with whom the morbid period of his life had set in, having accompanied them thus far, fell foot-sore, got into the dumps, and left them. The other poet, with his hardly less poetic sister, went on alone, and traversed on foot the finest highlands of Argyll and Perthshire. It is needless to trace their route in prose; for the poet has left his imperishable footprints at Ininversnaid in the " Sweet Highland Girl; " on Loch

Awe side and Kilchurn in his address to the "Child
of loud-throated War;" at the Small glen, or head
of Glen Almond, in the poem on *Ossian's Grave;* on
Loch Katrine side in "What? you are stepping west-
ward;" in *Rob Roy's Grave*, which, however, Words-
worth took to be at Glengyle, not, where it really is, in
Balquhidder kirkyard; and at Strathire, in *The Solitary
Reaper.* As they two moved quietly along, the poet's
imagination fell here on some well-known spot, there
on some familiar human incident, and touched them
with a light which will consecrate them forever. It
was, as I have seen on some gray autumnal day among
the mountains, the slanting silver light moving over the
dusky wilderness, and touching into sudden brightness
now a deep-shadowed corrie, now a slip of greensward
by a burn, or flushing a heathery brae, or suddenly
bringing out from the gloom some tremendous precipice,
or striking into momentary glory some far-off mountain
peak. Only that glory was momentary, seen but by a
single eye, and then gone. The light, which the poet
shed on those favored spots, remains a joy for all gen-
erations, if they have but the heart to feel it.

Hardly less beautiful than her brother's poems — in-
deed, sometimes quite equal to them, though far less
known — are the entries which his sister made in her
journal during that memorable tour. Native poets have
done much for Scotland, but nature has done far more,
and all that they have sung is but a poor instalment of
the grandeur and the glory which lies still unuttered.
When Wordsworth, with his fresh eye and strong imagi-
nation, set foot across the border, he saw further and
clearer into the heart of things that met him than any
of the native poets had done, and added a new and
deeper tone to their minstrelsy.

In this first tour, when the poet and his sister had descended from the Highlands, they went to Rosslyn, and then it was, as Lockhart tells us, that Scott first saw Wordsworth. " Their mutual acquaintance, Stoddart, had so often talked of them to each other, that they met as if they had not been strangers, and they parted friends." The 17th of September was the day they first met. Wordsworth and his sister walked in the early morning from Rosslyn down the valley to Lasswade, where Scott was then living, and they arrived before Mr. and Mrs. Scott had risen. " We were received," Wordsworth says, " with that frank cordiality which, under whatever circumstances I afterwards met Scott, always marked his manners. . . . The same lively, entertaining conversation, full of anecdote, and averse from disquisition ; the same unaffected modesty about himself; the same cheerful and benevolent and hopeful view of man and the world." They heard something that day of *The Lay of the Last Minstrel,* of which they were to hear more at Jedburgh. At the close of this day Scott walked with his two friends to Rosslyn, and on parting promised to meet them in two days at Melrose. The tourists passed by Peebles to the Vale of Tweed. There, after looking for a moment at Neidpath Castle, " beggared and outraged " by the loss of its trees, he turned from these

> " Wrongs, which Nature scarcely seems to heed:
> For sheltered places, bosoms, nooks, and bays,
> And the pure mountains, and the gentle Tweed,
> And the green silent pastures, yet remain."

From Peebles, travelling down the Tweed by Traquair, Elibank, Ashestiel, through that vale where as yet rail way was undreamt of, they found it

i 8

"More pensive in sunshine
Than others in moonshine.'

At Clovenford they had reached the spot whence, if at
all, they should have turned aside to Yarrow.   A short
walk to the ridge of the hill behind Yare, and the
whole of Yarrow Vale would have lain at their feet.
They debated about it, and determined to reserve the
pleasure for a future day.   Thence they passed to Mel-
rose, where Walter Scott met them, and became their
guide to the " fair " Abbey.   Being then " Shirra," and
on his official rounds, he took them with him to Jed-
burgh, where the Assize was being held.   The inns
there were so filled with the judges' retinue and the
lawyers that the poet and his sister had difficulty in find-
ing quarters.   As they passed the evening in their lodg-
ing, under the roof of that kind hostess whom Words-
worth celebrated in *The Matron of Jedburgh*, Scott left
his brethren of the bar at their port, and stole away to
spend an hour or two with the water-drinking poet and
his sister.   He then repeated to them a part of *The Lay
of the Last Minstrel*, in which Wordsworth at once
hailed the coming poet, and which he regarded to the
last as the finest of all Scott's poems.   Next day, while
Scott was engaged in court, he left the poet and his sis-
ter to go to Ferneyhurst and the old Jed Forest, with
William Laidlaw for their guide.   Miss Wordsworth in
her journal describes him as " a young man from the
braes of Yarrow, an acquaintance of Mr. Scott's," who,
having been much delighted with some of William's
poems, which he had chanced to see in a newspaper, had
wished to be introduced to him.   He " lives at the most
retired part of the Dale of Yarrow, where he has a farm.
He is fond of reading, and well informed, but at first

meeting as shy as any of our Grasmere lads, and not less rustic in his appearance." This was the author of *Lucy's Flitting*, Laidlaw's one ballad or song, which, for pure natural pathos is unsurpassed, if indeed it is equalled, by any lyric that either of the two great poets ever wrote.

Next day Scott accompanied Wordsworth and his sister for two miles up a bare hill above Hawick. Thence they looked wide " over the moors of Liddesdale, and saw the Cheviot hills. We wished we could have gone with Mr. Scott into some of the remote dales of this country, where in almost every house he can find a home." But the friends were obliged to part, the Wordsworths to take the road by Mosspaul and Ewesdale to Langholm, Scott to return to the duties of his sheriffry. It would have been a curious sight to see how Wordsworth would have comported himself, if he had been ushered into a company of Scott's friends, the Hill Farmers of the Dandy Dinmont stamp, with their big punch-bowls and deep draughts.

When Wordsworth returned to his Grasmere home, he finished the poem *Yarrow Unvisited*, which had been suggested by the incident I have mentioned at Clovenford.

Eleven years passed before Wordsworth again visited Scotland. The visit this time was less memorable. It was not lighted up by that wonderful journal of his sister's, and it called forth from the poet himself only four memorials in verse. Of these, *Yarrow Visited* is the only one in the poet's happiest manner. The road, by which Wordsworth and his travelling companions approached Yarrow, was that leading across the hill from Innerleithen. The night before they passed in the sequestered hamlet of Traquair, perhaps it may have been in Traquair Manse. Next morning the Ettrick Shepherd met the party at Traquair, and became their guide to his own home-land. One can imagine the simple-hearted garrulous vanity with which Hogg would perform the office of guide, and how Wordsworth, who believed himself to be so much the greater of the two, would receive the patronizing attentions.

From Traquair they walked, and so had a full view of Yarrow Vale from the descending road. In Yarrow, they visited in his cottage the father of the Ettrick Shepherd, himself a shepherd, a fine old man, more than eighty years of age. This may have been at one or other of Hogg's two homes on Yarrow, Benger Mount or Altrive Lake. How Wordsworth was solemnized and elevated by this his first look on Yarrow, we shall see when we come to consider the poem *Yarrow Visited*. Their route that day lay up the stream to St. Mary's Loch, which has left its impress on the poem. And from thence they seem to have traversed the whole course of Yarrow, till its union with the Ettrick.

Seventeen more years passed before Wordsworth again crossed the Scottish Border. This time it was on a sad errand, to visit Sir Walter Scott once again before "his last going from Tweedside," in hope of recruiting his shattered health in Italy. " How sadly changed did I find him from the man I had seen so healthy, gay, and hopeful a few years before, when he said at the inn at Patterdale, in my presence, "I mean to live till I am eighty, and shall write as long as I live'!" Wordsworth and his daughter spent the first evening with the family party at Abbotsford, and among them was William Laidlaw, now a very old friend of

Sir Walter's, who had for several years been his aman-
uensis. Next day — it was a Tuesday — they drove to
Newark Castle, accompanied by most of the home
party ; and the two poets, both now stricken with
years, wandered about the woodland walks overhang-
ing that Yarrow, of which each in his prime had sung
so well. They did not, however, penetrate beyond the
wooded banks near the lower part of the river, into the
upper and more pastoral region. It was this day which
Wordsworth commemorated in his *Yarrow Revisited.*
On their return home they came down the north bank
of Tweed, and crossed the river at the ford immediately
under Abbotsford. As the wheels of their carriage
grated upon the pebbles in the bed of the stream,
Wordsworth looked up and saw at that moment a rich
but sad light, purple rather than golden, spread over
Eildon Hills. Thinking that this was, probably, the
very last time that Sir Walter would ever cross the
stream, he was not a little moved, and gave vent to
some of his feelings in the sonnet —

> " A trouble, not of clouds, or weeping rain,
>   Nor of the setting sun's pathetic light
>   Engendered, hangs o'er Eildon's triple height."

Farther on, fain to comfort himself and others, he
breaks out —

> " Lift up your hearts, ye Mourners! for the might
>   Of the whole world's good wishes with him goes ;
>   Blessings and prayers in nobler retinue
>   Than sceptred king or laurelled conqueror knows,
>   Follow this wondrous Potentate. Be true,
>   Ye winds of ocean, and the midland sea,
>   Wafting your Charge to soft Parthenope! "

He appeals to the elements and to the universal heart
of man to come to the help of him, whom elsewhere

he calls " the whole world's darling; " but it will not do.

There were other affecting incidents connected with that visit. It was on the morning of the Thursday, just before Wordsworth left at noon, that Sir Walter wrote in the album of Wordsworth's daughter some imperfectly finished stanzas. As he stood by his desk, and put the book into her hand, he said to her in her father's presence, " I should not have done anything of this kind, but for your father's sake; they are probably the last verses I shall ever write." And they were the last.

One stanza clings to memory. Alluding to the fact that Wordsworth had listened to *The Lay of the Last Minstrel* before it was given to the world, and had hailed it as a true work of genius, Sir Walter says, —

> " And meet it is that he who saw
>   The first faint rays of genius burn
> Should mark their latest light with awe,
>   Low glimmering from their funeral urn."

At parting, Wordsworth expressed to Sir Walter his hope that the mild climate of Italy would restore his health, and the classic remembrances interest him, to which Sir Walter replied in words from *Yarrow Unvisited*, which Wordsworth in his musings in Aquapendente, six years afterwards, thus recalls: —

> " Still, in more than ear-deep seats,
> Survives for me, and cannot but survive,
> The tone of voice which wedded borrowed words
> To sadness not their own, when, with faint smile,
> Forced by intent to take from speech its edge,
> He said, ' When I am there, although 't is fair,
> 'T will be another Yarrow.' Prophecy
> More than fulfilled, as gay Campania's shores
> Soon witnessed, and the city of seven hills,
> Her sparkling fountains and her mouldering tombs;

> And more than all, that Eminence which showed
> Her splendors, seen, not felt, the while he stood,
> A few short steps (painful they were) apart
> From Tasso's Convent-haven and retired grave."

These three visits of Wordsworth to Scotland, and the incidents connected with them, called forth his *Three Yarrows*. The first visit and the last are associated with Sir Walter, the second with the Ettrick Shepherd. And each of the three poets has shed on Yarrow the light of his peculiar genius.

It would be an interesting subject to turn aside and note what a different aspect Yarrow wore, what different feelings it called up in each poet, as seen by his own individual eye. But there is an anterior question which may very naturally occur to any one to ask — What is there peculiar about Yarrow, of all the thousand streams of Scotland, to rivet the affection, and call forth the finest minstrelsy of these three poets? A chance comer passing down its green braes and holms, if told that this dale was consecrated to song, might well exclaim, —

> " What 's Yarrow but a river bare
> That glides the dark hills under?
> There are a thousand such elsewhere
> As worthy of your wonder."

To a casual and hurried glance it might well seem so; but there, too, as elsewhere, it is not to the first rapid look that the truth reveals itself.

What is it, then, that has so consecrated Yarrow to song and poetry, made it dear to the hearts of so many poets, dear too to every heart in which there dwells any tone of melody? The very name is itself a poem, sounding wildly sweet, sad, and musical. And when you see it, the place answers with a strange fitness to the name. It is, as it were, the inner sanctuary of

the whole Scottish Border, of that mountain tract which
sweeps from sea to sea, from St. Abb's Head and the
Lammermuir westward to the hills of Galloway. It
concentrates in itself all that is most characteristic of
that scenery. The soft green rounded hills with their
flowing outlines, overlapping and melting into each other,
— the clear streams winding down between them from
side to side, margined with green slips of holm, — the
steep brae-sides with the splendor of mountain grass,
interlaced here and there with darker ferns, or purple
heather, — the hundred side-burns that feed the main
Dale-river, coming from hidden Hopes where the gray
Peel-tower still moulders, — the pensive aspect of the
whole region so solitary and desolate. Then Yarrow is
the centre of the once famous but now vanished Forest
of Ettrick, with its memories of proud huntings and
chivalry, of glamourie and the land of Faery. Again, it
is the home of some " old unhappy far-off thing," some
immemorial romantic sorrow, so remote that tradition
has forgotten its incidents, yet cannot forget the impres-
sion of its sadness. Ballad after ballad comes down
loaded with a dirge-like wail for some sad event, made
still sadder for that it befell in Yarrow. The oldest
ballad that survives, *The Dowie Dens o' Yarrow*, tells of
a knight, one probably of the clan Scott, treacherously
slain in combat by a kinsman : —

> " She 's kiss'd his cheek, she 's kaim'd his hair,
>   As oft she 's done before, O ;
> She 's belted him wi' his noble brand,
>   And he 's awa' to Yarrow."

To Yarrow too belongs that most pathetic *Lament of
the Border Widow*, sung by his wife Marjory over the
grave of the outlaw Piers Cockburn, when she had
buried him by his tower of Henderland : —

"I sew'd his sheet, making my maen;
    I watch'd the corpse, myself alane;
    I watch'd his body, night and day,
    No living creature cam' that way.

"I took his body on my back,
    And whiles I gaed, and whiles I sate,
    I digg'd a grave, and laid him in,
    And happ'd him with the sod sae green.

"But think na ye my heart was sair,
    When I laid the mool on his yellow hair;
    O think na ye my heart was wae,
    When I turn'd about, away to gae ? "

Below Henderland, a mile down Yarrow, moulders
Dryhope Tower, the birthplace in Queen Mary's time
of the famous Mary Scott, the first Flower of Yarrow,
renowned for her beauty, wooed by all the chieftains of
the Border, and won to be his wife by the famous Wat
of Harden. Another mile down, comes into Yarrow
River the Douglas Burn, which, after it flowed past the
now ruined Blackhouse Tower, home of Lady Margaret
and scene of *The Douglas Tragedy,* had its waters dyed
with the blood of the stricken Lord William.

" O they rade on, and on they rade,
    And a' by the light of the moon,
    Until they came to yon wan water,
    And there they lighted doun.

" They lighted doun to tak a drink
    Of the springs that ran sae clear;
    And down the stream ran his gude heart's blood,
    And sair she 'gan to fear."

And all the way down, not a " Hope" or a burn joins
Yarrow from either side, but had its Peel-tower, the
scene of some tragic or romantic incident, many of
them remembered, more forgotten.

Last century the old popular wail was taken up by

two ladies, each of an ancient Border name, and each
the authoress of a beautiful song, set to the old tune of
the *Flowers of the Forest.* But their strains were but
the echoes of a far older refrain, coeval probably with
Flodden, which Scott sought to recover, but found two
lines only : —

> "I ride single in my saddle,
> For the Flowers of the Forest are a' wede away."

Last century, too, Hamilton of Bangour carried on the
strain, but in a lighter mood, in his well-known bal-
lad —

> " Busk ye, busk ye, my bonny, bonny bride."

And soon after Logan recurred to the older and more
plaintive form of the melody, adding to it another note
of sadness : —

> "They sought him east, they sought him west,
> They sought him all the forest thorough,
> They nothing saw but the coming night,
> They nothing heard but the roar of Yarrow.

> " No longer from thy window look,
> Thou hast no son, thou tender mother,
> No longer walk, thou weeping maid,
> Alas! thou hast no more a brother."

Such was the great background of pathetic feeling
out of which Yarrow came forth to meet the poets of
this century. In the earliest years of it Scott, by gath-
ering together and concentrating all that was oldest and
finest in the ancient songs of "The Forest," had con-
ferred a new and deeper consecration on Yarrow.
When Wordsworth passed down Tweed-dale with his
sister from that first interview at Lasswade, Scott had
already published his *Minstrelsy of the Scottish Border,*
but had not yet made the Last Minstrel

> "Pass where Newark's ruined tower
> Looks forth from Yarrow's birchen bower,"

much less dreamed of *Marmion*, with those so interesting introductions, in one of which he sings of St. Mary's silent lake : —

> "There's nothing left to Fancy's guess,
> You see that all is loneliness;
> Your horse's hoof-tread sounds too rude,
> So stilly is the solitude."

Then Wordsworth came, and as he travelled down the bank of Tweed, and felt that on the other side of the hill, within an hour's walk, lay Yarrow, the very sanctuary of old Border song, doubtless the poetic heart was stirred within him, and he longed to look on the romantic river. But he was constrained — probably enough from some quite prosaic reason — to pass on, and the thoughts and feelings came to him which took shape in *Yarrow Unvisited*. Turn to the poem. It opens in a lighter, more frolicsome vein than was usual with Wordsworth — frolicsome, we may call it, not humorous, for to humor Wordsworth never attained. His sister evidently desires to

> "turn aside,
> And see the braes of Yarrow."

To her wish — it may have been importunity — the poet replies, We have seen so many famous rivers all Scotland over ; so many famous streams lie before us yet to see — Galla Water, Leader Haughs, Dryburgh by the "charming Tweed " —

> "There's pleasant Teviotdale, a land
> Made blithe with plough and harrow :
> Why throw away a needful day
> To go in search of Yarrow ?"

And then he breaks out, —

> "What's Yarrow but a river bare
> That glides the dark hills under ?

> There are a thousand such elsewhere
> As worthy of your wonder."

His sister looks up in his face surprised and pained to hear her brother speak in what seemed scorn of the old romantic river.   To her look the poet replies in a somewhat more serious strain, admits that there must be something worth their seeing in Yarrow — the green holms, the fair flowing river — but these for the present they must pass by, and must allow

> "The swan on still St. Mary's Lake,
> Float double, swan and shadow."

And then the deep undertone of feeling which lay beneath all the lighter chaff and seeming disparagement breaks out in these two immortal stanzas : —

> " Be Yarrow stream unseen, unknown;
>   It must, or we shall rue it:
> We have a vision of our own;
>   Ah! why should we undo it?
>
> ' The treasured dreams of times long past
>   We 'll keep them, winsome Marrow!
> For, when we 're there, although 't is fair,
>   'T will be another Yarrow!"

After this ideal gleam has for a moment broken over it, the light of common day again closes in, and the poem ends with the comforting thought that —

> " Should life be dull, and spirits low,
>   'T will soothe us in our sorrow
> That earth has something yet to show,
>   The bonny holms of Yarrow!"

The whole poem, if it contains only two stanzas pitched in Wordsworth's highest strain, is throughout in his most felicitous diction.   The manner is that of the old ballad, with an infusion of modern reflection, which yet does not spoil its naturalness.   The metre is that in which most of the old Yarrow ballads, from *The Dowie Dens* onward, are cast, with the second and the fourth lines in each stanza ending in double rhymes, to let the refrain fall full on the fine melodious name of Yarrow. It plays with the subject, rises and falls — now light-hearted, now serious, then back to homeliness, with a most graceful movement. It has in it something of that ethereality of thought and manner which belonged to Wordsworth's earlier lyrics — those composed during the last years of the preceding and the first few years of this century. This peculiar ethereality — which is a thing to feel rather than to describe — left him after about 1805, and though replaced in the best of his later poems by increased depth and mellowness of reflection, yet could no more be compensated than the fresh gleam of new-fledged leaves in spring can be made up for by their autumnal glory.

Years pass, and Wordsworth at length, guided by the Ettrick Shepherd, looks on the actual Yarrow, and takes up the strain, where he had left it eleven years before. Then the feeling was —

> " We have a vision of our own;
>   Ah! why should we undo it! "

Now it is —

> " And is this — Yarrow? — This the stream,
>   Of which my fancy cherish'd,
> So faithfully, a waking dream,
>   An image that hath perish'd? "

This famous exclamation, which has long since passed into the mind of the world, had scarcely found vent, when there falls a strange sadness on the poet's heart, and he would that some minstrel were near to dispel it with glad music. Yet why should he be sad? The stream wanders on its way clear and silvery —

> "Nor have these eyes by greener hills
>   Been soothed, in all my wanderings;
>
> "And, through her depths, Saint Mary's Lake
>   Is visibly delighted;
>   For not a feature of those hills
>   Is in the mirror slighted."

And "a blue sky bends o'er Yarrow Vale," save where it is flecked by "pearly whiteness" of a fair September morning. Everything that meets his eye is beautiful and soothing. But the braes, though beautiful, look so solitary and desolate, and the solitariness of the present answers too well to the sadness of the past. Summing up all the sorrows of innumerable songs in one question, he exclaims, —

> "Where was it that the famous Flower
>   Of Yarrow Vale lay bleeding?"

And here, if we might pause on details of fact, we might say that Wordsworth fell into an inaccuracy; for Mary Scott of Dryhope, the real "Flower of Yarrow," never did lie bleeding on Yarrow, but became the wife of Wat of Harden, and the mother of a wide-branching race. Yet Wordsworth speaks of *his* bed, evidently confounding the lady "Flower of Yarrow" with that "slaughtered youth" for whom so many ballads had sung lament. This slight divergence from fact, however, no way mars the truth of feeling, which makes the poet long to pierce into the dumb past, and know something of the pathetic histories that have immortalized these braes. But, though he cannot recall the buried histories of the past, he does not fail to read to the life the present sentiment that pervades Yarrow : —

> "Meek loveliness is round thee spread,
>   A softness still and holy;
>   The grace of forest charms decayed,
>   And pastoral melancholy."

No words in the language penetrate more truly and deeply into the very heart of nature. It was one of Wordsworth's great gifts to be able to concentrate the whole feeling of a wide scene into a few words, simple, strong, penetrating to the very core. Many a time, and for many a varied scene, he has done this, but perhaps he has never put forth this power more happily than in the four lines in which he has summed up for all time the true quality of Yarrow. You look on Yarrow, you repeat those four lines over to yourself, and you feel that the finer, more subtle, essence of nature has never been more perfectly uttered in human words. There it stands complete. No poet coming after Wordsworth need try to do it again, for it has been done once, perfectly and forever.

The verses which follow relapse from that high altitude into a more ordinary level of description. Having traversed the stream from St. Mary's Loch to Newark and Bowhill, he leaves it with the impression that sight has not destroyed imagination — the actual not effaced the ideal : —

> " . . . Not by sight alone,
>   Lov'd Yarrow, have I won thee ;
> A ray of fancy still survives —
>   Her sunshine plays upon thee !

> " . . . I know where'er I go,
>   Thy genuine image, Yarrow !
> Will dwell with me, to heighten joy
>   And cheer my mind in sorrow."

Compared with *Yarrow Unvisited*, *Yarrow Visited* does not go with such a swing from end to end. The second poem has in it more of contemplative pause than the first. There is more irregularity in the quality of its stanzas — some of them rising to an excellence which

Wordsworth has not surpassed, and which has impressed them on the poetic memory as possessions forever, others sinking down to the level of ordinary poetic workmanship. But even in a lyric of a dozen stanzas, if a note is struck here and there of the highest pitch, to maintain the strain at the same level throughout seems hardly given to man. It will be found, I think, on examination, that the lyric stanzas which have taken an undying hold on mankind, are almost always embedded among other stanzas not so perfect. Even the most gifted poets cannot keep on expressing their best thoughts in the best words throughout all the stanzas of a long lyric.

Seventeen more years, and then came the farewell visit to Abbotsford, and that last day on Yarrow, when

"Once more, by Newark's Castle-gate,
    Long left without a warder,
I stood, looked, listened, and with me,
    Great minstrel of the Border!

.   .   .   .

" And through the silent portal arch
    Of mouldering Newark enter'd;

"And clomb the winding stair that once
    Too timidly was mounted
By the ' last Minstrel ' (not the last!)
    Ere he his Tale recounted."

It was a day late in September, and, judging by the natural features touched in *Yarrow Revisited*, the party from Abbotsford did not go to the upper course of Yarrow, where the braes are green and treeless, but lingered among the woods of Bowhill, and about the ruin of Newark. The leaves on these woods were sere, but made redder or more golden as the breezes played, or the autumnal sunshine shot through them.

As they wandered through the wooded banks that overhang Yarrow, they

> " Made a day of happy hours,
>   Their happy days recalling:

> " And if, as Yarrow, through the woods
>   And down the meadow ranging,
> Did meet us with unaltered face,
>   Though we were changed and changing;

> " If *then*, some natural shadows spread
>   Our inward prospect over,
> The soul's deep valley was not slow
>   Its brightness to recover."

No wonder that some shadows overspread their mental prospect that day, for, as regarded Scott,

> " . . . Sickness lingering yet
>   Has o'er his pillow brooded;
> And Care waylays his steps, — a sprite
>   Not easily eluded."

Against these forebodings of decay Wordsworth throughout the poem contends with wonderful buoyancy. But the pressure of fact was too heavy to be put by. It required something more than the soothing influences of nature, or even the faith which Wordsworth so cherished,

> " Naught shall prevail against us, or disturb
>   The cheerful faith that all which we behold
>   Is full of goodness,"

to have enabled Scott or his friends to bear his then condition. From the sight of that inevitable decay Wordsworth turned, and tried to soothe himself and his friends with the hope that, though he was compelled to leave his Tweed and Teviot, " Sorrento's breezy waves " would give him gracious welcome, and Tiber before his eyes " with unimagined beauty shine."

> " For Thou, upon a hundred streams,
> By tales of love and sorrow,
> Of faithful love, undaunted truth,
> Hast shed the power of Yarrow;
>
> " And streams unknown, hills yet unseen,
> Wherever they invite Thee,
> At parent Nature's grateful call,
> With gladness must requite thee."

Alas! how different was the reality! In Lockhart's Life of him may be read, with how dull and unstirred a heart he gazed on all that Italy contains of art or nature, how the only things, which for a moment reanimated him, were the Tombs of the Stuarts in St. Peter's, and the sight of the heather on the Apennines, reminding him of his native land.

After the expression of the hope of what Italy may do to restore Scott, Wordsworth passes on, in four more stanzas, to reflect on the power of " localized Romance " to elevate and beautify existence, how

> " The visions of the past
> Sustain the heart in feeling
> Life as she is, — our changeful Life."

And then the poem, longer than either of the two preceding ones, closes with this farewell benediction on the stream, whose immemorial charm his own three poems have so greatly enhanced : —

> " Flow on forever, Yarrow Stream!
> Fulfil thy pensive duty,
> Well pleased that future Bards should chant,
> For simple hearts thy beauty ; "
>
> " To dream-light dear while yet unseen,
> Dear to the common sunshine,
> And dearer still, as now I feel,
> To memory's shadowy moonshine "

This poem, along with the touching sonnet which condenses much of the same sentiment, and tells Scott that

> " the might
> Of the whole world's good wishes with him goes,"

was sent to him soon afterwards, and reached him before he left London for Italy. No record remains as to how he took these poems, or what pleasure they gave him. Probably the pall of gloom was by this time settling down on his mind too heavily, to be lifted off by any song that mortal poet could sing.

Compared with the two former poems, *Yarrow Revisited* falls short of the ideal tone to which they were set. In the former, the poet's mind was free to follow its natural impulse, and, unencumbered with present fact, to see Yarrow Vale in the visionary light which romance and foregone humanities had combined to shed upon it.

In the last poem the sense of Scott's recent misfortunes and declining health was too painfully present to admit of such treatment. Wordsworth was himself conscious of this, and in the ·retrospect he made this remark : " There is too much pressure of fact for these verses to harmonize, as much as I could wish, with the two preceding poems." This is true. And yet if it wants the idealizing touch, it has qualities of its own, which well compensate for that want. It is one of the latest of Wordsworth's poems, in which his natural power is seen still unabated; and if it falls below the best things he did in his best days, it is only second to these, and displays his later or autumnal manner in its best form. Several of the stanzas above quoted are only a little below the finest verses in the best of the

Lyrical Ballads, written in his poetic prime. But if some may estimate the artistic merit of *Yarrow Revisited* lower than I am inclined to do, they cannot deny its human and historic interest. It is an enduring record of the friendship of two poets, the greatest of their time, and of the last scene in that friendship. Commencing with that first meeting at Lasswade, before either was much known to fame, their friendship lasted, unabated till death parted them.

The two poets had lived apart, and met only by occasional visits, when Wordsworth crossed the Scottish border, or Scott visited the Lakes. On one of these latter occasions they had together ascended Helvellyn, and some have supposed, but, I believe, without reason, that Wordsworth commemorated that ascent in the lines beginning : —

> "Inmate of a mountain dwelling."

But there is no doubt that in one of his latest poems, " Musings in Aquapendente," he reverted to that day on

> " Old Helvellyn's brow,
> Where once together, in his day of strength,
> We stood rejoicing, as if earth were free
> From sorrow, like the sky above our heads."

The characters of Wordsworth and Scott were not less different than were the views and methods on which their poetry was constructed. But they each esteemed and honored the other, throughout their days of active creation, and now they had met for what they well knew, though they did not say it, must be their final interview. It was an affecting and solemn interview, according to the prose account of it which Wordsworth and Lockhart have each given ; not less affecting than this, its poetic record.

Then, again, the poem is a memorial of the very last visit Scott ever paid, not to Yarrow only, but to any scene in that land which he had so loved and glorified. A memorial of that day, struck off on the spot, even by an inferior hand, would have been precious. But when no less a poet than Wordsworth was there to commemorate this, Scott's last day by his native streams, and when into that record he poured so much of the mellow music of his autumnal genius, the whole poem reaches to a quite tragic pathos. As you croon over its solemn cadences, and think of the circumstances out of which it arose, and the sequel that was so soon to follow, you seem to overhear in every line

"The still sad music of humanity."

Wordsworth never revisited those scenes. But once again, on hearing of the death of James Hogg, in November, 1835, in thought he returned to Yarrow, and poured out this *Extempore Effusion*, probably the very last outburst in which his genius flashed forth with its old poetic fervor : —

"When first, descending from the moorlands,
  I saw the Stream of Yarrow glide
Along a bare and open valley,
  The Ettrick Shepherd was my guide.

"When last along its banks I wandered,
  Through groves which had begun to shed
Their golden leaves upon the pathways,
  My steps the Border-minstrel led.

"The mighty minstrel breathes no longer,
  'Mid mouldering ruins low he lies;
And death upon the braes of Yarrow,
  Has closed the Shepherd-poet's eyes.
  .   .   .   .
"Like clouds that rake the mountain summits,
  Or waves that own no curbing hand,

> How fast has brother followed brother,
>   From sunshine to the sunless land!
>
> "Yet, I, whose lids from infant slumber
>   Were earlier raised, remain to hear
> A timid voice, that asks in whispers,
>   'Who next will drop and disappear?'"

These lines are a fitting epilogue to the three poems, "by which," as Lockhart has said, "Wordsworth has connected his name to all time with the most romantic of Scottish streams," and, he might have added, with the greatest of Scottish poets.

CHAPTER XII.

WHAT induced Wordsworth for once to stray into the field of romance, and to choose for his theme this last effort of decaying chivalry — Wordsworth, whose genius we generally associate with incidents which are homely, and subjects which are' reflective? His other poems all turn upon modern persons and experiences. But *The White Doe of Rylstone* goes back to the feudal period of England's history, just before its close. In choosing such a theme, does not Wordsworth seem to have forsaken his proper region, and to have trespassed for once upon the domain of Scott? For is not the story of the "Fall of the Nortons" just such an one as might have inspired one of Scott's metrical romances? So at first sight it might seem. And yet a closer study of this poem will, perhaps, show more than anything else could how wide is the contrast between the genius of the two poets. The whole way in which Wordsworth handles the subject, and the peculiar effect which he brings out of it, are so unlike Scott's manner of treatment, are so entirely true to Wordsworth's special vein of thought and sentiment, that this contrast, even if there were nothing else, would make the poem worthy of close regard.

The incidents on which the *White Doe* is founded belong to the year 1569, the twelfth of Queen Elizabeth.

It is well known that as soon as Queen Mary of Scotland was imprisoned in England, she became the centre around which gathered all the intrigues which were then on foot, not only in England, but throughout Catholic Europe, to dethrone the Protestant Queen Elizabeth. Abroad, the Catholic world was collecting all its strength, to crush the heretical island. The bigot Pope Pius V., with the dark intriguer Philip II. of Spain, and the savage Duke of Alva, were ready to pour their forces on the shores of England.

At home, a secret negotiation for a marriage between Queen Mary and the Duke of Norfolk had received the approval of many of the chief English nobles. The Queen discovered the plot, threw Norfolk and some of his friends into the Tower, and summoned Percy, Earl of Northumberland, and Neville, Earl of Westmoreland, immediately to appear at court. These two earls were known to be holding secret communication with Mary, and longing to see the old faith restored.

On receiving the summons, Northumberland at once withdrew to Brancepeth Castle, a stronghold of the Earl of Westmoreland. Straightway all their vassals rose and gathered round the two great earls. The whole of the North was in arms. A proclamation went forth that they intended to restore the ancient religion, to settle the succession to the crown, and to prevent the destruction of the old nobility. As they marched forward they were joined by all the strength of the Yorkshire dales, and, among others, by a gentleman of ancient name, Richard Norton, accompanied by eight brave sons. He came bearing the common banner, called the Banner of the Five Wounds, because on it was displayed the Cross with the five wounds of our

Lord. The insurgents entered Durham, tore the Bible, caused mass to be said in the cathedral, and then set forward as for York. Changing their purpose on the way, they turned aside to lay siege to Barnard Castle, which was held by Sir George Bowes for the Queen. While they lingered there for eleven days, Sussex marched against them from York, and the earls, losing heart, retired towards the Border, and disbanded their forces, which were left to the vengeance of the enemy, while they themselves sought refuge in Scotland. Northumberland, after a confinement of several years in Loch Leven Castle, was betrayed by the Scots to the English, and put to death. Westmoreland died an exile in Flanders, the last of the ancient house of the Nevilles, earls of Westmoreland. Norton, with his eight sons, fell into the hands of Sussex, and all suffered death at York. It is the fate of this ancient family on which Wordsworth's poem is founded.

Wordsworth was not the first poet who had touched the theme. Some nameless North England minstrel had before composed a not unspirited ballad upon it, which appears in Percy's *Reliques,* under the title of *The Rising in the North.*

Although these incidents might perhaps have contained too little of martial prowess, battle, and adventure to satisfy Scott, yet we can all imagine what he would have made of them; how he would have revelled in the description of the mustering vassals; the hot haste in which they flew from their homes to the standard of the earls; the varieties of armor; the emblazonment of the shields, the caparisoned steeds on which the earls rode; the scene when the army entered Durham and filled the cathedral; the siege of Barnard

Castle by the Tees; the countermarch of Sussex; the dismay spreading from the earls among their followers; the retreat and the final catastrophe. What vigorous portraits we should have had of Northumberland and of Westmoreland; nor less of Bowes and Sussex, each standing out distinct, in his own individual guise and personality!

Of all this pomp and pageantry of war Wordsworth gives little or nothing. In fact, he hardly attempts to " conduct the action," or to bring out the main incidents at all, or to portray the chief personages. So entirely, in the poet's thought, is the action subordinated to the one pervading sentiment he desires to convey, that the narrative portion of the poem seems broken, feeble, and ill-adjusted. For not on the main action at all, but on quite a side incident — not on the obvious, but on a more hidden aspect of the story, has Wordsworth fixed his eye.

Not that the epic faculty was wholly wanting in him. In the song of *Brougham Castle* he had struck a true epic strain : —

> " Armor rusting in his halls
>   On the blood of Clifford calls; —
> ' Quell the Scot,' exclaims the lance —
> ' Bear me to the heart of France,'
>   Is the longing of the shield."

This, if no other of his poems, proves that he was not insensible to the thought that —

> "In our halls is hung
> Armor of the invincible knights of old."

But his delights were not with these. Nowhere does this appear more clearly than in *The White Doe of Rylstone*, where, with such temptation to dwell on one of the latest outbursts of the feudal spirit in England, he turned so persistently aside to contemplate quite another aspect of things.

What that aspect is — what were the incidents in that rising in the North, which arrested Wordsworth's imagination and drew forth from him this poem, we shall see by and by.

It is well, in studying any poet, to note at what period of his life each particular poem was written. It is, I think, of especial importance to do so in the study of Wordsworth. For, as has been often noted, he had at least two distinct periods — each of them marked by its own style, both of sentiment and of diction.

The period of his first and finest inspiration reached from about the year 1795 to 1805, or perhaps 1807. This decade is the period of his restoration to mental health and hopefulness, after the depression and despondency into which the failure of the French Revolution had plunged him. His mind had just come back from chaos to order, and yet retained the full swing of the impulse it had received, by having passed through that great world-agony. To these ten years belong most of the poems to which men now turn with most delight, as containing the essence of that new inspiration which Wordsworth let in upon the world. There is in them the freshness, ethereality, "the innocent brightness," as "of the new-born day." Or, they are like the reawakening that comes upon the moors and mountains, when the first breath of spring is blowing over them. The best poems of his later era have a quality of their own — a deepened thoughtfulness, a pensive solemnity, like the afternoon of an autumnal day.

Now *The White Doe of Rylstone* was composed in 1807, just at the close of his first period, though not published till 1815. It was during the summer of 1807, the poet tells us, that he visited, for the first time, the beautiful scenery that surrounds Bolton Priory ; and the poem of *The White Doe*, founded on a tradition connected with the place, was composed at the close of the same year. That tradition, as preserved by Dr. Whitaker, in his *History of Craven*, runs thus : Not long after the Dissolution of the Monasteries, "a white doe, say the aged people of the neighborhood, long continued to make a weekly pilgrimage from Rylstone over the fells of Bolton, and was constantly found in the Abbey churchyard during the divine service ; after the close of which she returned home as regularly as the rest of the congregation." This is the story which laid hold of Wordsworth's imagination, and to which we owe the poem. The earlier half, he tells us, was composed, at the close of the year 1807, while on a visit to his wife's relatives at Stockton-upon-Tees, and the poem was finished on his return to Grasmere. That year had just seen the publication of the two volumes of *Lyrical Ballads*, which contain perhaps his highest inspirations and, as it were, wind up the productions of his first great creative period.

The White Doe, therefore, marks the beginning of the transition to his second period, the period of *The Excursion*. But in the finest parts of *The White Doe* we still feel the presence of the same ethereal spirit, which animated his earlier day. The introduction to the poem, which bears the date of 1815, is altogether in his later vein.

Without, however, saying more of the circumstances

under which the poem was composed, let me now turn to itself, and note its contents canto by canto.

The First Canto opens with a Sunday forenoon, and the gathering of the people from the moorlands and hills around the Wharf to the church-service in Bolton Abbey. This beautiful ruin of the middle age stands on a level green holm down by the side of the Wharf, surrounded by wooded banks and moorland hills. From these, on the Sunday morn, the people come trooping eagerly, for they are in the first zeal of the Reformation era. The place where they meet for worship is the nave of the old Abbey Church, which at the Dissolution had been preserved, when everything else belonging to the monastic house had gone down before the fury of the spoiler. The throng of country people has passed within the church, the singing of the prelusive hymn has been heard outside. Then silence ensues, for the priest has begun to recite the liturgy, when suddenly a white doe is seen pacing into the churchyard ground.

> " A moment ends the fervent din,
> And all is hushed, without and within;
> For though the priest, more tranquilly,
> Recites the holy liturgy,
> The only voice which you can hear
> Is the river murmuring near.
> — When soft! — the dusky trees between,
> And down the path through the open green,
> Where is no living thing to be seen;
> And through yon gateway where is found,
> Beneath the arch with ivy bound,
> Free entrance to the churchyard ground,
> And right across the verdant sod
> Towards the very house of God;
> — Comes gliding in with lovely gleam,
> Comes gliding in, serene and slow,
> Soft and silent as a dream,
> A solitary doe!

White she is as lily of June,
And beauteous as the silver moon,
When out of sight the clouds are driven,
And she is left alone in heaven;
Or like a ship some gentle day
In sunshine sailing far away,
A glittering ship, that hath the plain
Of ocean for her own domain.
Lie silent in your graves, ye dead!
Lie quiet in your churchyard bed!
Ye living, tend your holy cares;
Ye multitude, pursue your prayers;
And blame not me if my heart and sight
Are occupied with one delight!
'T is a work for Sabbath hours
   If I with this bright creature go:
Whether she be of forest bowers,
   From the bowers of earth below;
Or a spirit, for one day given,
A gift of grace from purest heaven.
What harmonious pensive changes
Wait upon her as she ranges
Round and round this pile of state,
Overthrown and desolate!
Now a step or two her way
Is through space of open day,
Where the enamored sunny light
Brightens her that was so bright;
Now doth a delicate shadow fall,
   Falls upon her like a breath,
From some lofty arch or wall,
   As she passes underneath:
Now some gloomy nook partakes
Of the glory that she makes, —
High-ribbed vault of stone, or cell
With perfect cunning framed as well
Of stone, and ivy, and the spread
Of the elder's bushy head;
Some jealous and forbidding cell,
That doth the living stars repel,
And where no flower hath leave to dwell."

I know not any lines in the octosyllabic metre more

perfect in their rhythm, and with melody more attuned
to the meaning and sentiment they are intended to con-
vey. They might be placed next after the most ex-
quisite parts of *Christabel.* If metre has its origin, as
Coleridge suggests, in the balance produced by the
power of the will striving to hold in check the working
of emotion — if it is the union and interpenetration of
will and emotion, of impulse and purpose, I know not
where this balance can be seen more beautifully ad-
justed. As for the description of the ruined Bolton
Abbey, seen in the light of a Sabbath noon, it may well
be compared with Scott's description of Melrose, seen
while still in its prime, under the light of the moon.

Presently, service over, the congregation pass out,
and then begin many questionings and surmises as to
what mean these visits of the doe, renewed every Sun-
day, to the Abbey churchyard and that solitary grave.
First a mother points her out to her boy, but he shrinks
back in a kind of superstitious awe —

> " ' But is she truly what she seems ? '
> He asks, with insecure delight,
> Asks of himself — and doubts — and still
> The doubt returns against his will."

Then an old man comes, a soldier returned from the
wars, and he has his explanation. It is the spirit of the
lady who, in grief for her son drowned in the Wharf
many centuries ago, founded Bolton Priory, and now
returns in the shape of this beautiful creature, to grieve
over her holy place outraged and overthrown.

Then a dame of haughty air, followed by a page to
carry her book, opines that the doe comes with no good
intent, for often she is seen to gaze down into a vault,
" where the bodies are buried upright."

> " There, face by face, and hand by hand,
>   The Claphams and Mauleverers stand.''

There too is buried the savage John de Clapham, who, in the Wars of the Roses,

> " Dragged Earl Pembroke from Banbury Church,
>   And smote off his head on the stones of the porch.''

This high dame has the blood of the Pembrokes in her veins, and believes the doe has something to do with the Earl's murderer.

> " The scholar pale
> From Oxford come to his native vale,''

he has a conceit of his own ; he believes the doe to be none other than the gracious fairy or ministrant spirit, who in old time waited on the Shepherd-Lord Clifford, when in the neighboring tower of Barden he gave himself to the study of the stars, and alchemy, and other such glamourie, with the monks of Bolton for companions of his researches.

At last, after the people have gazed and questioned to their hearts' content, they disperse, and the doe also disappears.

Left alone, the poet turns to give the true version, and to chant —

> " A tale of tears, a mortal story.''

In Canto II. he passes at once from the doe to her, whose companion, years before, she had been, the only daughter of the House of Norton. He glances back to the days just before the rising in the North, when there stood in the hall of Rylstone that banner, embroidered with the cross and the five wounds, which Emily had wrought with her own hands, but against her will, in obedience to her father.

"That banner, waiting for the call,
Stood quietly in Rylstone Hall."

At length the call came, and at the summons Norton
and his sons go forth to join the two Earls, who were
in arms for the Catholic cause. With eight sons he
went; but one, Francis, the eldest, would not go. He
and his only sister, who had received the Reformed
faith long ago from their mother ere she died, now look
with sorrow and foreboding on the rash enterprise, in
which their father and brothers are going forth. Fran-
cis makes one effort to avert their fate; he throws him-
self at his father's feet, and though he knew he would
be scorned as a recreant, entreats him to hold his hand,
and not to join the rising, urging many reasons, — most
of all, would he thus forsake his only daughter? In
vain — the old man goes forth from the hall, and is re-
ceived with shouts by the assembled tenantry, and all
together, squire and vassals, march off to Brancepeth
Castle, the trysting-place.

Here was a passage of which Scott would have made
much; the gathering around the old hall of the yeomen
of Rylstone, their marching forth, and their reception
by their confederates at Brancepeth. Of this there is
scarce a hint in Wordsworth. He turns aside, wholly
occupied with the brother and sister left behind.

When these two are left alone, Francis tells his sis-
ter of his last interview with their father, and of seeing
him and his eight brothers march forth. For himself,
though he cannot be one with them, he is determined to
follow them, and be at hand to render what service he
may, when misfortune comes, as come it must. For he
does not try to hide or extenuate the certainty of the
doom that was overtaking their house. He himself was

20

going to share it, and his sister must brace her heart to bear what was impending.   Possessed, as by a spirit of mournful divination, he tells her —

> "Farewell all wishes, all debate,
> All prayers for this cause, or for that!
> Weep, if that aid thee; but depend
> Upon no help of outward friend.
> Espouse thy doom at once, and cleave
> To Fortitude without reprieve.
> For we must fall, both we and ours, —
> This mansion, and these pleasant bowers,
> The blast will sweep us all away,
> One desolation, one decay!"

Then, pointing to the White Doe which was feeding by, he continued —

> " Even she will to her peaceful woods
> Return, and to her murmuring floods,
> And be in heart and soul the same
> She was, before she hither came,
> Ere she had learned to love us all,
> Herself beloved in Rylstone Hall."

He bids his sister prepare for the doom that awaits them, to look for no consolation from earthly sources, but to seek it in that purer faith which they had learned together.   These are his words to her : —

> " But thou, my sister, doomed to be
> The last leaf which by Heaven's decree
> Must hang upon a blasted tree ;
> If not in vain we breathed the breath
> Together of a purer faith —
> If on one thought our minds have fed,
> And we have in one meaning read —
> If we like combatants have fared,
> And for this issue been prepared —
> If thou art beautiful, and youth
> And thought endue thee with all truth —
> Be strong; — be worthy of the grace
> Of God, and fill thy destined place:
> A soul by force of sorrows high,

> Uplifted to the purest sky
> Of undisturbed humanity."

When he had by this solemn adjuration, as it were, consecrated his sister to fulfil her destiny, and to become a soul beatified by sorrow, they part, and he follows his armed kinsmen. This consecration, and the sanctifying effect of sorrow on the heroine, is, as Wordsworth himself has said, "the point on which henceforth the whole moral interest of the poem hinges."

The Third Canto describes the mustering of the host at Brancepeth Castle, which was the Earl of Westmoreland's stronghold on the Were, the meeting of Norton and his eight sons with the two Earls, and his high-spirited address to these —

> "Brave earls, to whose heroic veins
> Our noblest blood is given in trust,"

urging them to rise for their outraged faith and the old and holy Church.

Then follows the unfurling of the banner which Norton's child had wrought, to be the standard of the whole army, the march to Durham, where, after they

> "In Saint Cuthbert's ancient see
> Sang mass — and tore the Book of Prayer —
> And trod the Bible beneath their feet,"

the whole host musters on Clifford Moor,

> "Full sixteen thousand fair to see."

Among them all the finest figure is the aged Squire of Rylstone : —

> "No shape of man in all the array
> So graced the sunshine of the day;
> The monumental pomp of age
> Was with this goodly Personage;
> A stature, undepressed in size,
> Unbent, which rather seemed to rise

> In open victory o'er the weight
> Of seventy years, to higher height;
> Magnific limbs of withered state,
> A face to fear and venerate,
> Eyes dark and strong, and on his head
> Bright locks of silver hair, thick spread,
> Which a bright morion half concealed,
> Light as a hunter's of the field."

The stirring incidents of this Canto afford much scope for pictorial painting; but this is perhaps the one passage in which Wordsworth has attempted it. There are several speeches, which, though not without a certain quaint homely expressiveness, have nothing of the poetic oratory which Scott would have imparted to them.

The intention was to march direct on London; but news reaches them on the way that Dudley had set out against them, and was nearing York with a large and well-appointed force. Westmoreland's heart fails him; a retreat is ordered; Norton remonstrates in vain. A disorderly march is begun backward toward the Tees, there to wait till Dacre from Naworth, and Howard, Duke of Norfolk, come to reinforce them. Francis Norton, who had followed unarmed, and

> " Had watched the banner from afar,
> As shepherds watch a lonely star,"

once more throws himself in the way of his father, and beseeches him to retire from these craven-hearted leaders, who, by their incompetence and cowardliness, were leading so many brave men to sure destruction. He had done his part by them, and was now by their misconduct freed from farther obligation. The old man spurns aside his son, who retires to wait another opportunity. In this narrative part of the poem, though there are many lines of quaint and rugged strength, there is none of the clear, direct, forward-flowing march of Scott's best narrative poetry. Wordsworth is encumbered, as it were, by reflectiveness of manner ; the thought, instead of a rapid onward flow, keeps ever eddying round itself.

Canto IV.   A clear full moon looks down upon the insurgents beleaguering Barnard Castle on the River Tees.   The same moon shines on Rylstone Hall, with its terraces, parterres, and the wild chase around it, all untenanted, save by Emily and her White Doe.   Here is the description of it : —

> " And southward far, with moors between,
> Hill-tops, and floods, and forests green,
> The bright moon sees that valley small,
> Where Rylstone's old sequestered Hall
> A venerable image yields
> Of quiet to the neighboring fields;
> While from one pillared chimney breathes
> The smoke, and mounts in silver wreaths,
> — The courts are hushed ; — for timely sleep
> The grey-hounds to their kennel creep;
> The peacock to the broad ash-tree
> Aloft is roosted for the night,
> He who in proud prosperity
> Of colors manifold and bright
> Walked round, affronting the daylight;
> And higher still, above the bower
> Where he is perched, from yon lone tower
> The Hall-clock in the clear moonshine
> With glittering finger points at nine."

The gleam of natural loveliness here let in wonderfully relieves the pressure of the human sadness.   Indeed, the whole passage from which these lines come gives so truthfully, yet ideally, the image of an old family mansion seen at such an hour, that I cannot recall any moonlight picture which equals it.

Wandering in the moonlight around her old home, Emily enters by chance a woodbine bower, where in her childhood she had often sat with her mother. The woodbine fragrance recalls, as scents only can, those long-vanished hours, and —

> " An image faint,
> And yet not faint — a presence bright
> Returns to her, — 't is that blest saint,
> Who with mild looks and language mild
> Instructed here her darling child,
> While yet a prattler on the knee,
> To worship in simplicity
> The Invisible God, and take for guide
> The faith reformed and purified."

By that vision she is soothed, and strengthened to check her strong longing to follow her father and her brothers, and to disobey the injunction to passive endurance laid on her by Francis.

That same moon, as it shines on the Tees, sees another sight — the insurgent host, wildly assaulting Barnard Castle, Norton and his eight sons, as they dash recklessly into a breach in the wall, made prisoners, and the whole rash levy scattered to the winds.

In Canto V. an old retainer, whom Emily Norton had sent to gain tidings of her father, returning, finds her by a watch-tower or summer house, that stood high among the wastes of Rylstone Fell, and tells her the tragic end of her father and brothers. They had been led in chains to York, and were condemned to die. Francis had followed them, got access to their prison, and received the last commands of his father with his blessing,

The banner was, by the cruel order of Sussex, to be carried before them in mockery to the place of execution. But Francis, claiming it as his own by right, takes it from the hands of the soldier to whom it was entrusted, and bears it off through the unresisting crowd. Richard Norton and his eight sons go forth, and calmly and reverently meet their doom.

Emily returns to Rylstone Hall to await the coming of her now only brother. But he comes not. As he was leaving York, there fell on his ear the sound of the minster bell, tolling the knell of his father and his brothers. Bearing the banner, though not without misgivings as to his own consistency in doing so, he held west over the great plain of York, up Wharfdale, and on the second day reaches a summit whence he can descry the far-off towers of Bolton. On that spot he is overtaken by a band of horsemen sent by Sussex, under command of Sir George Bowes, is accused of being a coward and traitor, who had held aloof from the rising only to save his father's land, and is overpowered and slain. Two days his body lay unheeded; on the third it was found in that lonely place by one of the Norton tenantry, who, along with other yeomen, bears it to Bolton Priory, and there, with the aid of the priest, they lay it in a grave apart from the other graves, because this was not the family burial-place. While they are so engaged, his sister, who was wandering towards Bolton, overhears the dirge they are singing,

> "And, darting like a wounded bird,
> She reached the grave, and with her breast
> Upon the ground received the rest,
> The consummation, the whole ruth
> And sorrow of this final truth."

But it is in the Seventh and last Canto, when all incident and action are over, and suffering, and the beauty rising out of suffering, alone remain, that the full power

of the poet comes out.   Just as in the First Canto the
calm contemplation of the ruined abbey, the sabbath
quiet, and the apparition of the doe, had prompted his
finest tones, so here, the sight of the only sister, sole
survivor of her ruined house, left alone with her sorrow,
awakens a strain of calm, deep melody, which is a meet
close for such a beginning.

Now that Emily Norton knows to the full her fami-
ly's doom, the poet turns and asks, —

> " Whither has she fled ?
> What mighty forest in its gloom
> Enfolds her ?   Is a rifted tomb
> Within the wilderness her seat ?
> Some island which the wild waves beat,
> Is that the sufferer's last retreat ?
> Or some aspiring rock, that shrouds
> Its perilous front in mists and clouds ?
> High climbing rock — low sunless dale —
> Sea — desert — what do these avail ?
> Oh, take her anguish and her fears
> Into a deep recess of years ! "

And years do pass ere we see her again.   Neglect and
desolation have swept over Rylstone, and in their an-
cient home the name of Norton is unknown.   Many a
weary foot she has wandered, far from her home, which
from the day of Francis' burial she has not looked
upon.   At length, after many years, she returns to the
neighborhood, and is seen on a bank once covered with
oaks, but now bare, seated under one sole surviving
mouldering tree.

> " Behold her, like a virgin queen,
> Neglecting in imperial state
> These outward images of fate,
> And carrying inward a serene
> And perfect sway, through many a thought
> Of chance and change, that hath been brought

> To the subjection of a holy,
> Though stern and rigorous, melancholy !
> The like authority, with grace
> Of awfulness, is in her face —
> There hath she fixed it ; yet it seems
> To overshadow, by no native right,
> That face, which cannot lose the gleams,
> Lose utterly the tender gleams,
> Of gentleness and meek delight,
> And loving-kindness ever bright :
> Such is her sovereign mien : — her dress
> (A vest, with woolen cincture tied ;
> A hood of mountain-wool undyed)
> Is homely — fashioned to express
> A wandering Pilgrim's humbleness."

That is the nearest approach the poem contains to a visible picture of this daughter of the house of Norton. Yet how little of a picture it is ! — her features, her hair, her eyes, not one of these is mentioned. She is painted almost entirely from within. Yet so powerfully is the soul portrayed, that no adequate painter would find any difficulty in adding the form and face, which would be the outward image of such a character.

There, while she sits, a herd of deer sweeps by. But one out of the herd pauses and draws near. It is her own White Doe, which had run wild again for years. Now it comes to her feet, lays its head upon her knee, looks up into her face, —

> " A look of pure benignity,
> And fond unclouded memory."

Her mistress melted into tears,

> " A flood of tears that flowed apace
> Upon the happy creature's face."

The doe restored came like a spirit of healing and consolation to Emily Norton. Thenceforth, go where she will, the creature is by her side. First to one cottage in the neighborhood, then to another, where old tenants of the family lived, she went and sojourned, and the White Doe with her. At length she finds courage to revisit her old haunts about Rylstone — Norton Tower, — that summer-house, where the messenger of the sad tidings had found her — near which, years before, her youngest brother had found the doe, when a fawn, and carried it in his arms home to Rylstone Hall. The prophecy of Francis, she thinks, has been fulfilled almost to the letter — in one detail only had it been falsified — all else was taken, but the White Doe remained to her, her last living friend. With this companion, she dared to visit Bolton Abbey and the single grave there.

So, through all the overthrow and the suffering, there had come at last healing and calm, and with it

> "A reascent in sanctity
> From fair to fairer; day by day
> A more divine and loftier way!
> Even such this blessed Pilgrim trod,
> By sorrow lifted toward her God;
> Uplifted to the purest sky
> Of undisturbed mortality."

At length, after she had returned and sojourned among the Wharfdale peasants, and joined in their Sabbath worships, she died, and was laid in Rylstone church by her mother's side.

The White Doe long survived her, and continued to haunt the spots which her mistress had longed to visit. But the close, which rounds off the whole with perfect beauty, must be given in the poet's own words: —

> "Most glorious sunset! and a ray
> Survives — the twilight of this day —
> In that fair creature whom the fields
> Support, and whom the forest shields;

Who, having filled a holy place,
Partakes, in her degree, Heaven's grace ;
And bears a memory and a mind
Raised far above the law of kind;
Haunting the spots with lonely cheer
Which her dear mistress once held dear:
Loves most what Emily loved most —
The enclosure of this churchyard ground;
Here wanders like a gliding ghost,
And every Sabbath here is found;
Comes with the people when the bells
Are heard among the moorland dells,
Finds entrance through yon arch, where way
Lies open on the Sabbath-day;
Here walks amid the mournful waste
Of prostrate altars, shrines defaced,
And floors encumbered with rich show
Of fret-work imagery laid low;
Paces slowly or makes halt
By fractured cell, or tomb, or vault,
By plate of monumental brass
Dim-gleaming among weeds and grass,
And sculptured forms of warriors brave;
But chiefly by that single grave,
That one sequestered hillock green,
The pensive visitant is seen.
Thus doth the gentle creature lie
With these adversities unmoved;
Calm spectacle, by earth and sky
In their benignity approved!
And aye, methinks, this hoary pile,
Subdued by outrage and decay,
Looks down upon her with a smile,
A gracious smile that seems to say,
'Thou, thou art not a child of time,
But daughter of the Eternal Prime.' "

The main aim of the whole poem is to set forth the
purification and elevation of the heroine's character by
the baptism of sorrow through which she was doomed
to pass. Let us hear Wordsworth's own account of it.
In one of those reminiscences which he dictated in his

later years, after noting that the *White Doe* had been compared with Scott's poems, because, like them, the scene was laid in feudal times, —

"The comparison," he says, "is inconsiderate. Sir Walter pursued the customary and very natural course of conducting an action, presenting various turns of fortune, to some outstanding point, as a termination or catastrophe. The course I attempted to pursue is entirely different. Everything that is attempted by the chief personages in the *White Doe* fails, so far as its object is external and substantial; so far as it is moral and spiritual it succeeds. The heroine knows that her duty is not to interfere with the current of events, either to forward or delay them ; but

> "To abide
> The shock, and finally secure
> O'er pain and grief a triumph pure."

The anticipated beatification, if I may say so, of her mind, and the apotheosis of the companion of her solitude, are the points at which the poem aims, and constitute its legitimate catastrophe — far too spiritual a one for instant and widespread sympathy, but not therefore the less fitted to make a deep and permanent impression upon those minds who think and feel more independently, than the many do, of the surfaces of things, and of interests transitory, because belonging more to the outward and social forms of life than to its internal spirit."

Such is Wordsworth's account of his aim, given late in life, to the friend who wrote down his reminiscences of his own poems.

Writing to a friend at the time of its publication, he says : —

"The *White Doe* will be acceptable to the intelligent, for whom alone it is written. It starts from a high point of imagination, and comes round, through various wanderings of that faculty, to a still higher — nothing less than the apotheosis of the animal who gives the title to the poem. And as the poem begins and ends with fine and lofty imagination, every motive and impetus that actuates the persons introduced is from the same source; a kindred spirit pervades and is intended to harmonize the whole. Throughout, objects (the banner, for instance) derive their influence, not from properties inherent in them, not from what they actually are in themselves, but from such qualities as are bestowed on them by the minds of those who are conversant with or affected by those objects. Thus the poetry, if there be any in the work, proceeds, as it ought to do, from the soul of man, communicating its creative energies to the images of the external world."

Such accounts in sober prose of what he aimed at in poetry, are valuable as coming from the poet himself; especially so in the case of Wordsworth, who, though he composed, as all poets must do, under the power of emotion and creative impulse, was yet able afterwards to reflect on the emotion that possessed him, and lay his finger on the aim that actuated him, as few poets have been able to do. Some have adduced this as a proof that it was not the highest kind of inspiration by which Wordsworth was impelled, for such, they say, is unconscious, and can give little or no account of itself. Without going into this question, there is no doubt that Wordsworth had reflected on the workings of imagination more, and could describe them better, than most poets. To the later editions of the poem he has further prefixed some lines in blank verse, which are his own comment on the supreme aim of the poem — namely, the total subordination in it of action to endurance : —

> "Action is transitory — a step, a blow,
> The motion of a muscle — this way or that —

> 'T is done, and in the after-vacancy of thought
> We wonder at ourselves as men betrayed.
> Suffering is permanent, obscure and dark,
> And has the nature of infinity.
> Yet through that darkness, infinite though it seem
> And irremovable, gracious openings lie,
> By which the soul — with patient steps of thought,
> Now toiling, wafted now on wings of prayer —
> May pass in hope, and, though from mortal bonds
> Yet undelivered, rise with sure ascent
> Even to the fountain-head of peace divine."

It is an obvious remark that the purifying and hallowing effect of suffering, which is here so prominently brought out, does not belong to suffering merely in itself. There are many cases where suffering only hardens and degrades. If it elevates, it does so, not by its own inherent nature, but by virtue of the primal moral bias — the faith which receives and transmutes it. Though Wordsworth does not dwell on this, he everywhere implies it. And yet here, as elsewhere in his works, notably in the book of the *Excursion*, entitled *Despondency Corrected*, Wordsworth is, perhaps, disposed to attribute a greater sanative power to the influences of outward nature, and to the recuperative forces inherent in the individual soul, than experience warrants, not to speak of revelation. It is not that he anywhere denies the need of direct assistance from above — indeed, he often implies it. But the error, if error there be, lies in not observing the due proportions of things — in giving to nature, and the soul's inherent resources, too great a prominence in the work of restoration; and in marking, with too faint emphasis, the need of a help which is immediately divine. Late in life, when this characteristic of his writings was alluded to, Wordsworth said that he had been slow to deal directly with Christian truths, partly from feeling their sacredness, partly from a sense of his inability to do justice to them, and to interweave them with sufficient ease, and with becoming reverence, into his poetic structures. And in one or two passages of his poem, where the defect above noticed was most apparent, he afterwards altered the passages, and, while he increased their Christian sentiment, did not, perhaps, improve their poetic beauty.

But to return to the poem. What is it that gives to it its chief power and charm? Is it not the imaginative use which the poet has made of the White Doe? With her appearance the poem opens, with her reappearance it closes. And the passages in which she is introduced are radiant with the purest light of poetry. A mere floating tradition she was, which the historian of Craven had preserved. How much does the poet bring out of how little! It was a high stroke of genius to seize on this slight traditionary incident, and make it the organ of so much. What were the objects which he had to describe and blend into one harmonious whole? They were these:

1. The last expiring gleam of feudal chivalry, ending in the ruin of an ancient race, and the desolation of an ancestral home.

2. The sole survivor, purified and exalted by the sufferings she had to undergo.

3. The pathos of the decaying sanctities of Bolton, after wrong and outrage, abandoned to the healing of nature and time.

4. Lastly, the beautiful scenery of pastoral Wharfdale, and of the fells around Bolton, which blends so well with these affecting memories.

All these were before him — they had melted into his imagination, and waited to be woven into one harmonious creation. He takes the White Doe, and makes her the exponent, the symbol, the embodiment of them all. The one central aim — to represent the beatification of the heroine — how was this to be attained? Had it been a drama, the poet would have made the heroine give forth in speeches her hidden mind and character. But this was a romantic narrative. Was the poet to make her soliloquize, analyze her own feelings, lay bare her heart in metaphysical monologue? This might have been done by some modern poets, but it was not Wordsworth's way of exhibiting character, reflective though he was. When he analyzes feelings they are generally his own, not those of his characters. To shadow forth that which is invisible, the sanctity of Emily's chastened soul, he lays hold of this sensible image — a creature, the purest, most innocent, most beautiful in the whole realm of nature — and makes her the vehicle in which he embodies the saintliness, which is a thing invisible. It is the hardest of all tasks to make spiritual things sensuous, without degrading them. I know not where this difficulty has been more happily met; for we are made to feel that, before the poem closes, the doe has ceased to be a mere animal, or a physical creature at all, but in the light of the poet's imagination has been transfigured into a heavenly apparition — a type of all that is pure, and affecting, and saintly. And not only the chastened soul of her mistress, but the beautiful Priory of Bolton, the whole vale of Wharf, and all the surrounding scenery, are illumined by the glory which she makes; her presence irradiates them all with a beauty and an interest more than the eye discovers. Seen through her as an imaginative transparency, they become spiritualized ; in fact, she and they alike become the symbols and expression of the sentiment which pervades the poem — a sentiment broad and deep as the world. And yet, any one who visits these scenes in a mellow autumnal day, will feel that she is no alien or adventitious image, imported by the caprice of the poet, but one altogether native to the place, one which gathers up and concentrates all the undefined spirit and sentiment which lie spread around it. She both glorifies the scenery by her presence, and herself seems to be a natural growth of the scenery, so that it finds in her its most appropriate utterance. This power of imagination to divine and project the very corporeal image, which suits and expresses the spirit of a scene, Wordsworth has many times shown. Notably, for instance, do those ghostly shapes, which might meet at noontide under the dark dome of the fraternal yews of Borrowdale, embody the feeling awakened when one stands there. But never perhaps has he shown this embodying power of imagination more felicitously than when he made the White Doe the ideal exponent of the scenery, the memories, and the sympathies which cluster around Bolton Priory.

One more thing I would notice. While change, destruction, and death overtake everything else in the poem, they do not touch this sylvan creature. So entirely has the poet's imagination transfigured her, that she is no longer a mere thing of flesh, but has become an image of the mind, and taken to herself the permanence of an ideal existence. This is expressed in the concluding lines.

And so the poem has no definite end, but passes off, as it were, into the illimitable. It rises out of the perturbations of time and transitory things, and, passing upward itself, takes our thoughts with it, to calm places and eternal sunshine.

CHAPTER XIII.

THE HOMERIC SPIRIT IN WALTER SCOTT.

THE poetry of Scott is so familiar to all men from their childhood, the drift of it is so obvious, the meaning seems to lie so entirely on the surface, that it may appear as if nothing more could be said about it, nothing which every one did not already know. In the memory of most men it almost blends with their nursery rhymes; their childhood listened to it, their boyhood revelled in it; but when they came to manhood they desired, perhaps, to put aside such simple things, and to pass on to something more subtle and reflective. Yet if we consider the time at which this poetry appeared, the conditions of the age which produced it, the great background of history out of which it grew, and to which it gave new meaning and interest — if we further compare it with poetry of a like nature belonging to other nations and ages, and see its likeness to, and its difference from, their minstrelsies, we shall perhaps perceive that it has another import and a higher value than we suspected. As sometimes happens with persons who have been born and have always lived amid beautiful scenery, that they know not how beautiful their native district is till they have travelled abroad, and found few other regions that may compare with it, so I think it is with the poetry of Scott. We have been so long familiar with it, that we hardly know how unique it is, how truly great.

A wide knowledge of the poetry of all ages and na-
tions, so far from depreciating the value of Scott's min-
strelsy, will only enhance it in our eyes. When we
come to know that many nations which possess an abun-
dant literature have nothing answering to the poetry of
Scott, that all the national literatures, ancient and mod-
ern, which the world has produced, can only show a
very few specimens of poetry of this order, and these
separated from each other by intervals of centuries,
we shall then perhaps learn to prize, more truly and in-
telligently, the great national inheritance which Scott
has bequeathed to us in his poetic romances.

It might be too great a shock to the nerves of critics
to assert that Scott is distinctively and peculiarly a
great epic poet. But even the strictest criticism must
allow that, whatever other elements of interest his
poems possess, they contain more of the Homeric or
epic element than any other poems in the English lan-
guage. If, to a reader who could read no other lan-
guage than his own, I wished to convey an impression
of what Homer was like, I should say let him read the
more heroic parts of Scott's poems, and from these he
would gather some insight into the Homeric spirit; in-
adequate, no doubt, meagre, some might perhaps say,
yet true it would be, as far as it goes.

First, then, let us ask what is meant by an epic
poem. Aristotle has answered this question in the
Poetics, and the definition he there gives holds good to
this day. Its substance has been thus condensed by
Mr. Thomas Arnold in his interesting *Manual of Eng-
lish Literature:* " The subject of the epic poem must be
some one, great, complex action. The principal per-
sonages must belong to the high places of the world,

and must be grand and elevated in their ideas and in their bearing. The measure must be of a sonorous dignity, befitting the subject. The action is carried on by a mixture of narrative, dialogue, and soliloquy. Briefly to express its main requisites, the epic poem treats of one great, complex action, in a grand style and with fulness of detail."

Few European nations possess more than one real epic — some great nations possess none. The *Iliad*, the *Æneid*, the *Niebelungen Lied*, the *Jerusalem Delivered*, and *Paradise Lost*, these are the recognized great epics of the world. It was the fashion in the last century to institute elaborate comparisons between some of them, as though they were all poems of exactly the same order. So much was this the case that Addison in the *Spectator* wrote a series of papers, in which he compares the *Iliad*, the *Æneid*, and *Paradise Lost*, first, with respect to the choice of subject, secondly, to the mode of treatment; and in both respects he gives the palm to Milton. And so little was the essential difference between Homer and Milton perceived up to the very end of last century, that so genuine a poet as Cowper, when he set himself to translate Homer, chose as his vehicle the blank verse of Milton. Grand, impressive, but elaborate, involved, full of "inversion and pregnant conciseness," as Milton's verse is, nothing in the world could be a more unfit medium for conveying to the English reader the general effect produced by the direct, rapid, easy-flowing yet dignified narrative of Homer. As Mr. Matthew Arnold has said, "Homer is not only rapid in movement, simple in style, plain in language, natural in thought; he is also, and above all, noble." Between the popular epic and the literary epic there is a deep and essential difference, a difference which, though Addison and Cowper failed to discern it, we cannot too much lay to heart, if we would really understand and appreciate the spirit of epic poetry. The first critic, as far as I know, who pointed out this distinction was the famous German scholar Wolf, who in his Prolegomena or introductory essays to Homer, published in 1795, insisted on it with much earnestness. He says, " That view of things has not yet been entirely exploded, which makes men read in the same spirit Homer and Callimachus and Virgil and Milton, and take no pains to weigh and observe how different are the productions to which the age of each of these gives birth." This distinction, first noted by Wolf, Professor Blackie, in his *Homeric Dissertations* prefixed to his translation of the *Iliad*, has enforced and illustrated in his own lively way. The following, he shows, are the chief notes of the popular epic : —

1. It is the product of an early and primitive age, before a written literature has come into existence, while the songs or ballads of the people were still preserved in memory — repeated orally, and not yet committed to writing.

2. It is founded on some great national event which has impressed itself deeply on the national imagination, and it portrays, celebrates, glorifies, some great national hero.

3. The popular epic tells its story in a plain, easy-flowing, direct, and ample style. There is no daintiness either as to the things the poet describes, or the language in which he describes them ; no object is too homely to be noticed, or too simple to furnish an apt simile.

4. Closely connected with this is the naturalness, the simplicity, the *naïveté* of the whole. Many things are told and mentioned in the most unconscious way, which a later, more conscious age could not notice without either coarseness or studied imitation.

Finally, the minstrel himself lives amidst the natural healthy life which he describes; he is himself a part of it.

These characteristics of the popular epic are, I need hardly say, generalized from the Homeric poems. For these afford the highest, most perfect specimen the world has seen, or ever will see, of the popular epic — of a nation's minstrelsy. Without going here into the vexed question of their authorship, whether there was one Homer or more, I may say that the fact of such poems presupposes a whole world of ballad poetry or minstrelsy previously existing, from which the great minstrel king, when he arises, takes his traditions, his materials, his manner — perhaps many of his verses. Such a poem as the *Iliad* could not rise up, full-fledged and perfect, without many shorter and lesser poems going before it. A whole atmosphere of antecedent song is the very condition of a great popular epic being born. But, while saying that Homer's poetry grew out of a ballad literature, we must not forget how different it is in style from the ballads as we conceive of them. To the naturalness, the ease, the rapid flow of the ballad, the Homeric genius, using as its vehicle the majestic hexameter measure, has added a nobleness, a grandeur, which even the best of our ballads have never reached.

Homer probably lived on the latest verge of the heroic age, while its traditions and feelings were still fresh in memory, but were ready to vanish away before a new age of manners and society. There is in his poems a tone of admiring regret, as he looks back on the great champions whom he celebrates. He feelingly complains that there are no such men as those nowadays.

In the *Iliad* the popular epic is seen in its highest, most perfect form. And though the world can show but one *Iliad*, yet the primitive ages of other countries can show poems which, though vastly inferior to the *Iliad*, are yet in their character and spirit of the same order of poetry. The Teutonic race had its *Niebelungen Lied;* the Celtic its Fingalian battle-songs; the middle age its poems of the Arthurian cycle; Spain the heroic ballads that cluster round the Cid; and England, though it does not possess a national epic, according to the form, yet has inherited the substance of it in the grand succession of Shakespeare's historical plays, especially in *Richard II.*, in *Henry V.*, and in *Richard III.*

From these specimens of the popular epic, turn to the literary epics, the *Æneid*, the *Jerusalem Delivered*, the *Paradise Lost*, and see how entirely different they are in origin, in character, in style, and in the spirit which animates them. These last are elaborate works of art, produced in a later age, by literary men, working consciously according to recognized rules, and imitating, more or less, ancient models of the primitive time, not singing unconsciously and spontaneously as native passion dictated. The first lesson the critic has to learn is to feel the entire difference of the *Iliad* and the *Æneid*, — to see how wide a world of thought and feeling separates the popular or national from the learned or literary epic. For, however they may seem to agree somewhat in form — and even in form they are distinct — in the age which creates each, in the sentiment which animates them, and in the impression they leave on the reader, they stand almost as wide apart as any two kinds of poetry can do.

This somewhat long digression into the nature of Epic Poetry will not be in vain, if it enables us to see how nearly the poetry of Scott approaches the province of the popular epic, how true it is that he, more than any poet in the English language, — I might say than any poet of modern Europe, — has revived the Homeric inspiration, and exhibited, even in this late day, something of the primitive spirit of Homer.

How can this be? perhaps you say. Scott, born in literary Edinburgh, within the last thirty years of the eighteenth century, where Hume had expounded his sceptical philosophy a generation before, where Robertson and Hugh Blair were shedding their literary light during his childhood, and Dugald Stewart expounded his polished metaphysics over his unregarding boyhood — how could it be that he should be in any other than an imitative sense a real rhapsodist, a genuine minstrel of the olden stamp? It is a natural question, but one to which a little thought will supply an answer. It is characteristic of modern Europe, as compared with ancient Greece or Rome, that its society is much more complex, contains more numerous and diverse elements existing side by side, that its cable is composed of many different strands twisted into one. Yet even in Greece did not Herodotus, with his childlike simplicity, live on into the age of the sophists? Was he not contemporary with the reflective Thucydides, father of philosophic history? Still more, in modern nations we find stages of society the most diverse, and apparently the most opposed, the most primitive simplicity and the most ar-

tificial culture, coexisting in the same age, side by side.
So it was with the Scotland into which Scott was born.
His native town had, in the sixty years that followed
the Union, made a wonderful start in elegant literature.
It contained a coterie of literary men, which rivalled
Paris for polish and scepticism, London for shrewdness
and criticism. Yet in Edinburgh, such men were but
a handful — one cannot be sure that they are to be taken
as samples of the mental condition even of educated
Scots of the day. But if we turn to the country places,
especially to the remoter districts, we find a wholly
different condition of society. Over large tracts of
Scotland, both south and north, though men were
plying busily their farming or pastoral industries, the
traditions of former times still prevailed, and formed
the intellectual atmosphere which they breathed. In
some places where the Covenant had struck deep root,
and on which Claverhouse had come down most heavily,
tales of slaughtered sons of the Covenant, and of the
cruel persecution, still fed the flame of religious fervor.
In other places, where the Covenant and its spirit had
less penetrated, traditions of English invasion and of
Border feuds and battles were still rife, though a cent-
ury and a half had passed since the reality had ceased.
And through all the wilder Highlands, and in a great
part of the Lowlands, the romantic adventures of the
Fifteen and the Forty-five, with the stern sufferings
which followed, were still preserved by the people in
affectionate though mournful remembrance.

It was in an atmosphere filled with these elements
that Scott first began to breathe. He himself tells us
that it was at Sandyknowe, in the home of his paternal
grandfather, that he had the first consciousness of exist-

ence. Edinburgh was his physical, but Sandyknowe his mental birthplace — Sandyknowe, the old farmhouse on the southern slope of Smailholme Crags, crowned with the grim old Peel-tower, commanding so brave an outlook over all the storied Border-land. Every one will remember Lockhart's description of the scene, and yet so graphic it is, it cannot be here omitted : — .

" On the summit of the crags which overhang the farmhouse stands the ruined tower of Smailholme, the scene of *The Eve of St. John;* and the view from thence takes in a wide expanse of the district in which, as has been truly said, every field has it battle, and every rivulet its song.

> 'The lady looked in mounful mood,
>   Looked over hill and vale,
>   O'er Mertoun's wood, and Tweed's fair flood,
>   And all down Teviotdale.'

Mertoun, the principal seat of the Harden family, with its noble groves; nearly in front of it, across the Tweed, Lessudden, the comparatively small but still venerable and stately abode of the Lairds of Raeburn; and the hoary Abbey of Dryburgh, surrounded with yew-trees ancient as itself, seem to lie almost below the feet of the spectator. Opposite him rise the purple peaks of Eildon, the traditional scene of Thomas the Rhymer's interview with the Queen of Faerie; behind are the blasted Peel which the seer of Erceldoun himself inhabited, ' the Broom of the Cowden-knowes,' the pastoral valley of the Leader, and the bleak wilderness of Lammermoor. To the eastward the desolate grandeur of Hume Castle breaks the horizon as the eye travels towards the range of the Cheviot. A few miles westward Melrose, ' like some tall rock with lichens gray,' appears clasped amidst the windings of the Tweed; and the distance presents the serrated mountains of the Gala, the Ettrick, and the Yarrow, all famous in song. Such were the objects that had painted the earliest images on the eye of the last and greatest of the Border minstrels."

To this beautiful description there is but one drawback. " Serrated " is the last epithet which should have been chosen to describe the rounded, soft and flowing outlines of the hills that cradle Ettrick and Yarrow.

His human teachers were his grandmother by her parlor fire, with her old gudeman seated on the armchair opposite, while she told to the grave three-years' child at her feet many a tale of Watt of Harden, Wight Willie of Aikwood, Jamie Telfer of the fair Dodhead, and other heroes, whose wild Border forays were still fresh in memory; his aunt, Miss Janet Scott, who taught him old ballads before he could read — among others, that of Hardiknute, "the first poem I ever learnt, the last I shall ever forget; " "Auld Sandy Ormistoun," the shepherd, or "cow-bailie," who used to carry him on his shoulder up the Smailholme Crags, and leave him on the grass all day long to play with the sheep and lambs, till the child and they became friends. Could there be more fitting nursery for a poet-child? The infant on the green ledges of Smailholme Crags, rolling among the lambs, while his eye wandered lovingly over that delightful land! Or forgotten among the knolls, when the thunder-storm came on, and found by his affrighted aunt lying on his back, clapping his hands at the lightning, and crying out, "Bonny, bonny!" at every flash, brave child that he was! The old shepherd poured into his ear his own wealth of stories and legends, and no doubt pointed, as he spoke, to many a spot where the scenes were transacted, lying at their feet; and when summer was past, and the child could no longer roll on the grass out of doors, the long winter nights by the fireside were beguiled by the telling of the same tales, the recitation of the same or of still fresh store of ballads. Thus eye and ear alike were steeped in the most warlike traditions of the Border and of Scotland, — the human teachers pouring them daily into the ear of the child, while the far sweep of storied Tweeddale and Teviotdale appealed no less powerfully to his eye. Add to this, that never was child born more susceptible of such impressions — that between these and the soul of Scott there was a preëstablished harmony — and have we not, even in the midst of the eighteenth century, the very materials out of which is fashioned a true epic minstrel ?

Then, when he passed from childhood to boyhood, and read at random every book he could lay hands on, there was one book which struck deeper than all the rest, and kindled to new life those treasures of legend and ballad which had lain embedded in his mind since infancy. Every one will remember his own description — how he lay through the long summer afternoon beneath a huge platanus-tree in the garden, overhanging the Tweed, and read for the first time Percy's *Reliques of Ancient Poetry:* and with him, when anything arrested his imagination, to read and to remember were one.

The publication of Percy's *Reliques* marked the first turning of the tide of literary taste back to a land whence it had long receded. It was, as has been said, the earliest symptom in England of "a fonder, more earnest looking back to the past, which began about that time to manifest itself in all nations." Percy and others, who then began those backward looks, had to gaze at the old time across an interval of perhaps two centuries. In the case of Scott, the past had come down to him in an unbroken succession of traditions and personages. First were the inmates of Sandy-knowe, among whom he spent his childhood. Then came his intercourse with Stewart of Invernahyle, when as a boy he first penetrated the Highlands to share the hospitality of that laird, who had himself fought a broadsword duel with Rob Roy, and had served in the Fifteen under Mar, and in the Forty-five under Prince Charles Edward. Lastly, in early manhood he traversed Ettrick Forest, and made those raids, during seven successive years, into Liddesdale and many another Border dale, whence he returned laden with that spoil of the old riding ballads, which now live secured to all time in his *Border Minstrelsy*. In those and in other ways Scott came face to face with the feudal and heroic past — a past which was then on the eve of disappearing, and which, had he been born thirty years later, might have disappeared forever, and no one to record it. With that past, before it was wholly past, he came in contact, as did countless others of his generation ; but the contact would have been as little to him as it was to his contemporaries, had he not been gifted with the eye to see, and the soul to feel it. Scott had born in him the heroic soul, the epic inspiration ; and the circumstances in which his childhood and youth were cast supplied the fuel to feed the flame. The fuel and the flame were long pent up together, long smouldered within, before they blazed out to the world. Scott was past thirty when he published the *Minstrelsy*, and at the close of the work he gave original ballads of his own, which were the first notes of the fuller song that was to follow. Eminent among these ballads is

The Eve of St. John, in which Scott repeoples the tower of Smailholme, and consecrates forever the haunt of his infancy. In this he gave a sample of the genius that was in him, and, as an expression of old Border heroism daunted before conscience and the unseen world, he himself has never surpassed, and none other has equalled it. But it is not only the original ballads which he contributed to the *Minstrelsy*, excellent as these are, which show what was the deepest bias of his poetic nature. At the time when the book first appeared, one of its critics prophetically said that it contained " the elements of a hundred historical romances ; " and Lockhart has noted that no one who has not gone over the *Minstrelsy* for the purpose of comparing its contents with his subsequent works can conceive to what an extent it has been the quarry out of which he has dug the materials of all his after creations. Of many of the incidents and images which are elaborated in these latter works, the first hints may be found either in those old primitive ballads, or in the historical and legendary notices which accompany them.

We thus have in Walter Scott a spirit in itself naturally of the heroic or epic order, waking up to its first consciousness in a secluded district, which was still redolent of traditions of the old feudal and fighting times — meeting in his boyhood with the first turn of that tide which, setting towards the neglected past, he himself was destined to carry to full flood ; spending all the leisure of his youth and early manhood in gathering from the Southern dales every ballad, Border song, or romantic legend that was still lingering there ; — now and then trying with some stave of his own to match

those wild native chants that had charmed his ear and
imagination; and living and finding his delight in this
enchanted world till past the mature age of thirty.   Is
there not here, if anywhere for the last three hundred
years, the nurture and training of the genuine rhapso-
dist?   When, after such long and loving abode in that
dreamland, his mind addressed itself to original crea-
tion, it was not with any mere literary or simulated fer-
vor, but out of the fulness of an overflowing heart, that
he poured forth his first immortal *Lay*.   In that poem
the treasured dreams of years first found a voice, the
stream that had been so long pent up at last flowed full
and free.   Arnold used to say — and the late Dean Stan-
ley, in the inimitable outburst with which he thrilled his
hearers at the Scott Centenary, repeated the saying —
that the world has seen nothing so truly Homeric, since
the days of Homer, as those opening lines of the *Lay*,
in which Scott describes the custom of Branksome
Hall,

> " Nine-and-twenty knights of fame."

If anywhere the ballad metre has risen to the true epic
pitch, it is in the concentrated fire and measured tread
of those noble stanzas.   Nor less in the true heroic
style is the description of Deloraine's nightly ride from
Branksome to Melrose.   In those lines, especially, as
indeed throughout all that poem, Scott at last found a
fit poetic setting for all those dear localities, over which
his eye had dreamed, as he lay an infant on Smailholme
crags, which he had traversed on foot and horseback in
his boyish wanderings, or in those raids of early man-
hood, in which he bore back from Liddesdale and Esk-
dale his booty of ancient ballads, with as much zest as
ever moss-trooper drove a prey from the English Border.

In his descriptions of the feudal and battle time, the usages of chivalry and the rites of the mediæval Church are everywhere introduced ; for these are the true modern representatives of the Homeric rites and priests, and blazing hecatombs. Not otherwise except in this their native garb could the heroic times of modern Europe be truly rendered into poetry. Chivalry, romance, and mediæval beliefs were the real accompaniments of our heroic times, and if these were discarded for what are thought to be more classical garniture, you might have a modern imitation of the ancient Homeric poem; but no genuine heroic poetry, standing to our age in something of the same relation as Homer's poetry stood to later Grecian life.

If Scott had been asked, when he was writing his poem, to what class or style of poetry his belonged, likely enough he would have smiled, and said that he never troubled himself with such questions, but sang as he listed, and let the form take care of itself. In fact, in the advertisement to *Marmion* he actually disavows any attempt on his part to write an epic poem. But it is the very spontaneity, the absence of all artistic consciousness, which forms one of his greatest poetic charms, compensating for much that might, on merely artistic and literary grounds, be lightly esteemed. And it is this spontaneity, this naturalness of treatment, this absence of effort, which marks out Scott's poetry as belonging essentially to the popular, and having little in common with the literary epic. This welling forth of an overflowing heart characterizes the *Lay* more than any of his subsequent poems, and imparts to it a charm all its own. Hence it is that lovers of Scott revert, I think, to the *Lay* with a greater fondness than to any of his other productions, though in some of these they acknowledge that there are merits which the *Lay* has not. Of course, little as Scott may have troubled himself about it, his poetry had a very decided form of its own, as all poetry must have. It was formed, as his mind had been, on the old Border ballad, with some intermixture of the mediæval romance ; and the earlier cantos of the *Lay* were touched by some remembrance of *Christabel*, which, however, died away before the end of the poem, and did not reappear in any subsequent one.

But though the *Lay* here and there rises into a truly epic strain, it is in *Marmion* that whatever was epic in Scott found fullest vent. In that, his second poetic work, he had chosen a national and truly heroic action, as the centre or climax of the whole poem — the battle of Flodden — an event second only to that still greater battle which he essayed to sing at a later day, and in a feebler tone. Flodden had been the most grievous blow that Scotland ever received. It had cost her the lives of her chivalrous king, and of the flower of all the Scottish nobility, gentry, and men-at-arms. It had pierced the national heart with an overpowering sorrow, so pervading and so deep that no other event, not even Culloden, ever equalled it. It had lived on in remembrance down to Scott's boyhood as a source of the most pathetic refrains that ever blended with the people's songs. When, therefore, he addressed himself to it he had a subject which, though old, was still fresh in remembrance, and full of all that epic and tragic interest which a great poem requires. He was aware of the greatness of the theme, and he tells us that he set to it, resolved to bestow on it more labor than he had yet done on his productions, and that particular passages of the poem were elaborated with a good deal of care by one by whom much care was seldom bestowed. Throughout, the poem has more of epic stateliness, if it wants some other graces of the *Lay*. From beginning to end, it rises now into the epic pitch, then recedes from it into the romantic, sometimes falls into the prosaic, then rises into the epic again, up to the grand close. The passages in which the heroic gleams out most clearly are such as these: — the well-known opening stanzas describing Marmion's approach to Norham at sunset; the muster of the Scottish army on the Borough muir before marching to Flodden; and, above all, the whole last canto, in which the battle itself is depicted. It is on this last that Scott put out all his strength, and by this canto, if by anything in his poetry, it is that his claim to the epic laurel should be judged. Before reaching this last culmination, the poem had wound on, now high, now low, spirited or tame, in stately or in homely strain. But from the moment that the poet gets in sight of Flodden, and sees the English army defiling through the deep ravine of Till, while the Scots from the ridge above gaze idly on — from that moment to the close, he soars steadily on the full pinion of epic poetry.

It was a fine thought to describe the great battle, not from the thick of the *mêlée*, but as seen by Clara and the two pages from a vantage-ground apart. This does not diminish one whit the animation of the scene, yet greatly enhances the totality and perfection of the picture. It is needless to quote lines which every one who cares for such things knows by heart. But the passage beginning with —

> "At length the freshening western blast
>   Aside the shroud of battle cast;"

and the one following, which thus opens: —

> "Far on the left, unseen the while,
>   Stanley broke Lennox and Argyle;"

ending with that so powerful incident —

> "When, fast as shaft can fly,
>   Bloodshot his eyes, his nostrils spread,
>   The loose rein dangling from his head,
>   Housing and saddle bloody red,
>   Lord Marmion's steed rushed by;"

and last of all, the picture of the desperate ring that
fought and died, but did not yield, around their gallant
king. To find any battle scenes that can match with
these we must go back to those of the *Iliad*. As far as
I know, the poetry of no land, in the interval between
Homer and Scott, can show anything that can be placed
by their side.

Perhaps we may find the best counterpart to these
passages of Scott in the sixteenth book of the *Iliad*,
where Patroclus does on the armor of Achilles and
comes to the rescue of the Achaian host.

Take that passage where Hector and Patroclus close
in mortal conflict over the dead body of Cebriones,
charioteer of Hector: —

> "Upon Cebriones Patroclus sprang,
>   Down from his car too Hector leaped to earth,
>   So over Cebriones opposed they stood;
>   As on the mountain, o'er a slaughtered stag,
>   Both hunger-pinched, two lions fiercely fight,
>   So o'er Cebriones two mighty chiefs,
>   Menoetius' son and noble Hector, strove,
>   Each in the other bent to plunge his spear.
>   The head, with grasp unyielding, Hector held;
>   Patroclus seized the foot; and, crowding round,
>   Trojans and Greeks in stubborn conflict closed.

As when encountering in some mountain glen,
Eurus and Notus shake the forest deep,
Of oak, or ash, or slender cornel-tree,
Whose tapering branches are together thrown
With fearful din and crash of broken boughs;
So, mixed confusedly, Greeks and Trojans fought,
No thought of flight by either entertained.
Thick o'er Cebriones the javelins flew,
And feathered arrows bounding from the string,
And ponderous stones that on the bucklers rang,
As round the dead they fought; amid the dust
That eddying rose, his art forgotten all,
A mighty warrior, mightily he lay."

Those only who have read the original know how much it loses both in vividness of edge and in swinging power, when dulled down into the blank verse of the translation. To the English reader, Lord Derby's verse sounds flat and tame compared with the rapid and ringing octosyllabics of Scott, when he is at his best, as in his description of Flodden. And yet Scott's best eight-syllable lines may not compare with

" The long resounding march and energy divine "

of the Homeric hexameters.

It will be said, I am aware, that in Scott's romantic poems, though heroic subjects are handled, yet "neither the subject nor the form rises to the true dignity of the epic." That they are regular epics, as these are defined by the canons of the critics, no one would contend. But that they abound in the epic element, as no other English poems abound, cannot be gainsaid. In subject, neither *Marmion* nor *The Lord of the Isles* falls below the epic pitch, unless it be that the whole history of Scotland is inadequate to furnish material for an epic. And as to form, if the large admixture of romantic incident and treatment be held to mar the epic dignity, this does not hinder that these poems rise to the true epic height, in such passages as the battle of Flodden, and the priest's benediction of the Bruce.

It would be a pleasant task to go through the other poems of Scott, laying one's finger on the scenes and passages in which the epic fire most clearly breaks out ; and showing how epically conceived many of his heroes are, with what entire sympathy he thew himself into the heroic character. But this task cannot be attempted now. Suffice it that in *The Lady of the Lake*, though its tone is throughout more romantic than epic, yet there are true gleams of heroic fire, as in the Gathering ; still stronger in the combat between Roderick and Fitz James, and again in that battle-stave which the bard sings to the dying Roderick, in which occur these two lines, breathing the very spirit of Homer himself : —

> "'T were worth ten years of peaceful life,
> One glance at their array ! '"

In his last long poem Scott essayed a subject more fitted for a national epic than any other which the history of either Scotland or England supplies — the wanderings of Bruce and his ultimate victory at Bannockburn. Delightful as *The Lord of the Isles* in many of its parts is, I cannot agree with Lockhart's estimate of it, when he says, that " the Battle of Bannockburn, now that we can compare these works from something like the same point of view, does not appear to me in the slightest particular inferior to the Flodden of *Marmion*." This will hardly be the verdict of posterity. It was not to be expected that the same poet should describe in full two such battles with equal vigor and effect. There is a fire and a swing about the former, a heroic spirit in the short octosyllabics describing Flod-

den, which we look for in vain in the careful and almost
too historic accuracy of the earlier battle. Flodden, the
less likely of the two themes to kindle a Scottish poet's
enthusiasm, in order of poetic composition, came first.
Scott was then in the prime of his poetic ardor. When
he touched Bruce and Bannockburn that noon was past;
he was tired of the trammels of metre, and was hasten-
ing on to his period of prose creation. Had he, on the
contrary, begun with Bruce, and given him the full force
of his earlier inspiration, he would no doubt have made
out of the adventures of the great national hero the
great epic poem of Scotland, which *The Lord of the Isles*
can hardly claim to be. There is no subject in all his-
tory more fitted for epic treatment; it requires no fiction
to adorn it. The character of Bruce, the events of his
wanderings, as described by Barbour, in the mountain
wilds, through which the outlawed king passed, where
tradition still preserves the track of his footsteps, —
these in themselves are enough. They need no added
fiction, but only the true singer to come in the prime of
inspiration, and render them as they deserve. What-
ever similarity may exist between Homer and Scott
must have come from intrinsic likeness of genius, not
from conscious imitation. For Scott is said to have
been so innocent of any knowledge of Greek, that the
light of Homer could only have reached him, dimly re-
flected, from the horn lanterns of Pope's or Cowper's
translations. The similarity is not confined only to the
spirit by which the two poets are animated. It comes
out not less strikingly in small details of mannner — in
the constant epithets, for instance, by which Scott de-
scribes his heroes, " the doughty Douglas," " the bold
Buccleuch," " William of Deloraine, good at need." It

is seen, too, in the plain yet picturesque epithets with which Scott hits off the distinctive character of places. Who that has sailed among the Hebrides but must at once feel the graphic force of such expressions as " lonely Colonsay," " the sandy Coll," " Ronin's mountains dark " ?

Space has not allowed me to touch, much less exhaust, the many phases of Scott's poems, in which the heroic element appears. The Homeric spirit which breathes through his novels I have not even alluded to. But I would suggest it as a pleasant and instructive task to any one who cares for such things, to read once again the Waverley novels, noting, as he passes, the places where the Homeric vein most distinctly crops out. In such a survey we should take the Homeric vein in its widest range, as it appears in the romantic adventures and beautiful home-pictures of the *Odyssey*, not less than in the battle scenes of the *Iliad*.

Scott's earliest novel supplies much that recalls *Odyssey* and *Iliad* alike. In the Charge of Preston-pans, " ' Down with your plaids,' cries Fergus MacIvor, throwing his own. ' We 'll win silks for our tartans, before the sun is above the sea.' . . . The vapors rose like a curtain, and showed the two armies in the act of closing." Again, in a story so near our own day as that of *The Antiquary*, with what grand relief comes in the old background of the heroic time, behind the more modern characters and incidents, when the aged croon Elspeth is overheard in her cottage chanting her old-world snatches about the Earl of Glenallan and the red Harlaw, where Celt and Saxon fought out their controversy, from morn till evening, a whole summer's day!

" Now haud your tongue, baith wife and carle,
    And listen, great and sma',
  And I will sing of Glenallan's Earl,
    That fought on the red Harlaw.

" The coronach 's cried on Bennachie,
    And doun the Don and a'
  And Hieland and Lawland may mornfu' be
    For the sair field of Harlaw !"

Or I might point to another of the more modern
novels, to *Redgauntlet,* and Wandering Willie's Tale.
Every one should remember — yet perhaps some forget
— auld Steenie's visit to the nether world, and the
sight he got of that set of ghastly revellers sitting round
the table there. " My gude sire kend mony that had
long before gane to their place, for often had he piped
to the most part in the hall of Redgauntlet. There was
. . . And there was Claverhouse, as beautiful as when he
lived, with his long, dark, curled locks, streaming down
over his laced buff-coat, and his left hand always on his
right spule-blade, to hide the wound that the silver bullet
had made. He sat apart from them all, and looked at
them with a melancholy, haughty countenance ; while
the rest hallooed, and sung, and laughed, that the room
rang." Turn to the novel, and read the whole scene.
There is nothing in the Odyssean Tartarus to equal it.
If Scott is not Homeric here, he is something more.
There is in that weird ghastly vision a touch of sublime
horror, to match which we must go beyond Homer, to
Dante, or to Shakespeare.

Moralists before now have asked, What has Scott
done by all this singing about battles, and knights, and
chivalry, but merely amuse his fellow-men ? Has he
in any way really elevated and improved them ? It
might be enough to answer this question by saying,

that of all writers in verse or prose, he has done most to make us understand history, to let in light and sympathy upon a wide range of ages, which had become dumb and meaningless to men, and which but for him might have continued so still.

But I shall not answer it only in this indirect way. It has been too pertinaciously and pointedly asked to be put thus aside.

Wordsworth is reported to have said in conversation that, as a poet, Scott cannot live, for he has never written anything addressed to the immortal part of man. This he said of his poetry, while speaking more highly of his prose writings. Carlyle, on the other hand, has included both Scott's prose and his poetry under the same condemnation. He has said that our highest literary man had no message whatever to deliver to the world ; wished not the world to elevate itself, to amend itself, to do this or that, except simply to give him, for the books he kept writing, payment, which he might button into his breeches pocket. All this moralizing bears somewhat hard upon Scott. Is it true ? Is it the whole truth ? Is there nothing to be set over against it ? On Scott's side, may it not be said, that it is no small thing to have been the writer who, above all others, has delighted childhood and boyhood, delighted them and affected them in a way that the self-conscious moralizing school of writers never could do ? There must be something high or noble in that, which can so take unsophisticated hearts. In his later days Scott is reported to have asked Laidlaw what he thought the moral influence of his writings had been. Laidlaw well replied that his works were the delight of the young, and that to have so reached their hearts was surely a good work to have done. Scott was affected almost to tears, as well he might be. Again, not the young only but of the old, those who have kept themselves most childlike, who have carried the boy's heart with them farthest into life, — they have loved Scott's poetry, even to the end. Something of this, no doubt, may be attributed to the pleasure of reverting in age to the things that have delighted our boyhood. But would the best and purest men have cared to do this, if the things which delighted their boyhood had not been worthy? It is the great virtue of Scott's poetry, and of his novels also, that, quite forgetting self, they describe man and outward nature broadly, truly, genially, as they are. All contemporary poetry, indeed all contemporary literature, goes to work in the exactly opposite direction, shaping men and things after patterns self-originated from within, describing and probing human feelings and motives with an analysis so searching, that all manly impulse withers before it, and single-hearted straightforwardness becomes a thing impossible. Against this whole tendency of modern poetry and fiction, so weakening, so morbidly self-conscious, so unhealthily introspective, what more effective antidote than the bracing atmosphere of Homer, and Shakespeare, and Scott?

Lastly, it may be said, the feelings to which Scott's poetry appeals, the ideals which it sets before the imagination, if not themselves the highest types of character, are those out of which the highest characters are formed. Cardinal Newman has said, " What is Christian high-mindedness, generous self-denial, contempt of wealth, endurance of suffering, and earnest striving after perfection, but an improvement and transformation, under the influence of the Holy Spirit, of that natural character of mind which we call romantic?" To have awakened and kept alive in an artificial and too money-loving age "that character of mind which we call romantic," which, by transformation, can become something so much beyond itself, is, even from the severest moral point of view, no mean merit. To higher than this few poets can lay claim. But let the critics praise him, or let them blame. It matters not. His reputation will not wane, but will grow with time. Therefore we do well to make much of Walter Scott. He is the only Homer who has been vouchsafed to Scotland — I might almost say to modern Europe. He came at the latest hour when it was possible for a great epic minstrel to be born. And the altered conditions of the world will not admit of another.

CHAPTER XIV.

PROSE POETS: THOMAS CARLYLE.

PROSE, Coleridge used to say, is the opposite, not of poetry, but of verse or metre — a doctrine which, however contrary to common parlance, commends itself at once to all who think about it.

If, as I have been accustomed in these lectures to say, "poetry is the expression, in beautiful form and melodious language, of the best thoughts and the noblest emotions, which the spectacle of life awakens in the finest souls," it is clear that this may be effected by prose as truly as by verse, if only the language be rhythmical and beautiful.

I was pleased to find the same view taken by my friend Mr. Shadworth Hodgson, in an essay which he has lately published on English Verse, an essay which, for its suggestiveness and subtlety of thought, may be commended to all who are curious in these matters. In that essay he says, "Metre is not necessary to poetry, while poetry is necessary to metre." Again, "Prose, when it rises into poetry, becomes as nearly musical as language without metre can be; it becomes rhythmical."

But I need not enlarge on this view, or quote authorities in favor of it. Every one must remember sentences in his favorite prose-writers, which, for their beauty, dwell upon the memory, like the immortal lines of the great poets, or passages of the finest music.

Who does not recall words of Plato, such as the description of the scenery in the opening of the *Phaedrus*, or in the same dialogue the vision of the procession of the Twelve Immortals, or the closing scene in the *Phaedo*, or a passage here and there in the *Republic*, or in the *Theaetetus*, which haunt him with the same feeling of melody as that with which famous lines in Homer or in Shakespeare haunt us?

Again, Tacitus is generally set down as a rhetorician, and no doubt he had caught much of his manner from the schools of the rhetoricians. But there is in him something more, something peculiarly his own, which is of the true essence of poetry — his few condensed clauses, hinting all the sadness and hopelessness of his time, or the vivid scenes he paints so full of human pathos. Such is the description of Vitellius as he walked forth from his palace to meet his doom. The " nec quisquam adeo rerum humanarum immemor, quem non commoveret illa facies " lingers in the mind in the same way as Virgil's

" Sunt lacrimae rerum, et mentem mortalia tangunt."

In French literature you find a truer poetry both of thought and language in some of the best prose-writers, than in any of the so-called French poets. Such passages, so beautiful in thought, so sweet in expression, occur in Pascal of the elder writers, in Maurice de Guérin of the moderns.

Among our own elder prose-writers, two may be named, who break out, every here and there, into as real poetry, both in substance, and in form, as any of the metrical poets of their time ; Bishop Jeremy Taylor, and Sir Thomas Browne, author of the *Religio Medici*.

There is a passage in the late Mr. Keble's *Praelec-*

tiones Academicae, in which he compares one of those poetical prose passages from Jeremy Taylor's writings, with a well-known passage from Burke's *Reflections on the French Revolution,* describing Marie Antoinette as she appeared for the first time in Paris, and for the last. The purpose with which Keble compares the two passages is to show the difference between a thought which is only eloquently expressed and one which is truly poetical.

What is the distinction between the highest eloquence and true poetry is an interesting question, but not one to detain us now. Perhaps, in passing, one may say that in eloquence, whatever imagination is allowed to enter is kept consciously and carefully subordinate to an ulterior object, either to convince the hearers of some truth, or to persuade them to some course of action. On the other hand, when in prose composition the whole or any part of it is felt to be poetical, the thoughts which are poetical appear to be dwelt upon for the pure imaginative delight they yield, for their inherent truth, or beauty, or interest, without reference to anything beyond. If the writer is more intent on the effect he wishes to produce than on the imaginative delight of the thought he utters, it then ceases to be true poetry.

It is characteristic of our modern literature that at no former period have so many men, richly endowed with the poetic gift, expressed themselves through the medium of prose. Why it should be so may well be asked; but the answer to the question given by Carlyle, that the metrical form is an anachronism, — that verse as the vehicle of true thought, and feeling is a thing of the past, — cannot, I think, be accepted. It is one of the many strong, one-sided statements, in which Carlyle was wont to indulge, from judging all things by his own idiosyncrasy. He himself was but a poor performer in verse, as may be seen from his few attempts at metrical rendering of German lyrics. But this defect in him cannot change the fact that there are shades of thought and tones of feeling for which metre will always continue to be the most natural vehicle, to those at least who have the gift of using it.

Great poets who have expressed themselves in verse are, as we have often seen, possessed by some great truth, inspired, as we say, by some master-vision, which fills their whole soul. To see such a vision is the poet's nature, to utter it is his office. If this be the case with metrical poets, it is not less, but rather more true of those whom we call prose poets. Some aspect of things they have been permitted to see, some truths have come home to them with peculiar power, till their hearts are all aglow, and they long to utter them. In truth, the prose poet must be more fully possessed, more intensely inspired by the truth which he sees, than the metrical poet need be, in order to fuse and mould his more intractable material of prose language into that rhythmical, melodious cadence, which we feel to be poetry. It will be our duty in the sequel to note some of those great primal truths by which prose poets have been possessed, in order that we may see how essentially poetical has been the way in which they expressed them.

In dwelling upon Carlyle as such a prose poet, those of us who are old enough cannot but look back — so strange it seems — to the time when his light first dawned on the literary world, a wonder and a bewilderment. Not that his first appearance was hailed with any noise or loud acclaim. Unobserved, almost silent, his first reception was recognized only by one or two here and there, who had some special means of knowing about him. I can remember his *French Revolution* being, for the first time, put into my hands when a boy, in a country house, by one who knew something of him. " Here is a strange book, written by a strange man, who is a friend of some of our family." I opened it, and read some chapter styled " Symbolic," which, if at the time wholly unintelligible, still left behind it a sting of curiosity.

Again, the young Glasgow Professor of Greek, newly come from the first place in the Cambridge Classical Tripos, and fresh from the society of the Cambridge Apostles, told how he had lately heard Carlyle lecture upon Heroes, more like a man inspired than any one he had ever listened to. Then early in the 1840's, when the *Miscellanies* appeared, and became known to undergraduates here in Oxford, I remember how they reached the more active-minded, one by one, and thrilled them as no printed book ever before had thrilled them. The very spot one can recall, where certain passages first flashed upon the mind, and stamped themselves indelibly on the memory. Indeed, it used to be said, and I believe with truth, that, with but few exceptions, none of the abler young men of that date escaped being, for a time at least, Carlyle-bitten. What exactly he taught us, what new doctrine he brought, or whether he brought any new doctrine at all, we perhaps did not care to ask. Only this we knew, that he had a way of looking at things which was altogether new, that his words penetrated and stirred us, as no other words did.

23

What there was of true or false, of one-sided or exaggerated, in his teaching, what of good or of evil, we could not measure then — perhaps it would not be easy to measure now. But to him we owed exaltations of spirit more high, depressions more profound, than we had ever known before, — wild gleams of unearthly light, alternating with baleful glooms. "He has given most of us a bad half-hour," one has lately said; more than half-hours he gave to many. In what directions he affected young minds, how his burning thoughts mingled with the tenor of their thoughts, it were hard to say; only somehow they did; and these men held on their way, most of them modified, but not revolutionized, not wholly driven from their path, by having passed through the tempestuous fire-atmosphere, in which Carlyle had for a time enveloped them.

One or two there were, the noblest of their generation, who took Carlyle not only for a prophet, as others did, but for *the* prophet, the only prophet then alive. To them he seemed the man of all men living who had truly read the secret of the world, who had spoken the deepest word about human life, and the universe which encompasses it. Feeling intensely the truth and the power of his teaching in certain directions in which he was well at home, they took him to be equally wise, because his words were equally strong, in other directions in which he was not at all at home, in which, to say truth, he had little insight. And giving over to his guidance their noble and too confiding natures, they broke with all traditions and beliefs of the past, burst away from their natural surroundings, and followed him out into the wilderness, to find there no haven of rest, but only the vagueness of his so-called " immensities," and '' eternities," and abysses fathomless.

It is hard to think of these things, and not to feel some indignation, that such noble spirits should have trusted him so unreservedly. They would not have done so, had they lived longer, and been permitted to see the whole man, as his self-revelations have lately forced. us to see him. Comments more than enough have been made, and will yet be made on these, and I refrain from adding to them. But as we have from his other works long known his strength, in these last we see his weakness; if we have hitherto owned his unique powers, these bring home his no less marked limitations. They make us feel that a prophet universal he could not be, that he could not see life and the world steadily and see them whole, who, from his peculiar constitution and temperament, looked at them through such a dismal and distorting atmosphere, whose habitual element was so deep a gloom. Some imagined that he had come to be the revealer of a new morality, higher and nobler than Christianity. It is now plain that, as to his theory, the best truths he taught so powerfully are essential parts of Christianity, lie at the base of it, and of all spiritual religion ; while in actual practice, so far from having exhausted its teaching, and passed beyond it, he, like most of his neighbors, fell far enough short of the full Christian stature. We now see plainly enough that Carlyle's teaching, so far from discrediting, serves only to exalt the Christian ideal by the contrast which it suggests.

But though it is true that Carlyle's whole view of things no reasonable man can adopt; though his one-sided idiosyncrasy shut him out from all possibility of being accepted as a universal teacher, it did not hinder, rather it helped, his seeing the truths and things which he did

see, with an intense insight which few men possess,
and uttering them with a force which still fewer are
capable of. As he looked out from his own solitary
soul upon the universe, it seemed to him all one great
black element encompassing him, lit only, here and
there, with central spots of exceeding brightness. On
these he fixed his gaze, and these he made other men
see and feel, with something of that vividness with
which they shone for himself. As a sample of his
power to render poetically a human countenance, take
this description of Dante, —

"To me it is a most touching face ; perhaps of all faces
that I know, the most so. Blank there, painted on vacancy,
with the simple laurel wound round it ; the deathless sorrow
and pain, the known victory which is also deathless ; sig-
nificant of the whole history of Dante ! I think it is the
mournfullest face that ever was painted from reality ; an
altogether tragic, heart-affecting face. There is in it, as
foundation of it, the softness, tenderness, gentle affection as
of a child ; but all this is as if congealed into sharp contra-
diction, into abnegation, isolation, proud hopeless pain. A
soft ethereal soul looking out so stern, implacable, grim-
trenchant, as from imprisonment of thick-ribbed ice !
Withal it is a silent pain too, a silent scornful one : the lip
is curled in a kind of godlike disdain of the thing that is
eating out his heart, — as if it were withal a mean insig-
nificant thing, as if he whom it had power to torture and
strangle were greater than it. The face of one wholly in
protest, and life-long unsurrendering battle, against the
world, affection all converted into indignation : an impla-
cable indignation ; slow, equable, implacable, silent, like that
of a god ! The eye, too, it looks out as in a kind of sur-
prise, a kind of inquiry, Why the world was of such a sort?
This is Dante : so he looks, this 'voice of ten silent centu-
ries,' and sings us 'his mystic unfathomable song.'"

But the critics, I observe, have been repeating, one after another, that Carlyle was not great as a thinker, but only as a word-painter. If by a thinker they mean one who can table a well-adjusted theory of the universe, in which he can locate every given fact or phenomenon, such a formula as Mr. Herbert Spencer has favored the world with, Carlyle was not such a thinker; no one would have more scornfully rejected the claim to be so. But if he is a thinker, who has seen some great truths more penetratingly, and has felt them more profoundly than other men have done, then in this sense a thinker Carlyle certainly was. Isolated truths these may have been, but isolated truths were all he cared or hoped to see: he felt too keenly the mystery of things ever to fancy that he or any other man could see them all in well-rounded harmony. It was just because he saw and felt some truths so keenly, that he was enabled to paint them in words so vividly. It was the insight that was in him which made him a word-painter; without that insight, word-painting becomes a mere trick of words.

The presence of personality, we are told, is that which distinguishes literature from science, which is wholly impersonal. It is this which gives to the finest literature its chief charm, that it is illuminated by the presence of an elevated personality, — personality observe, not egotism, which is a wholly different and inferior thing. Great literature, we may say, is the emanation of a noble, or at least of an interesting personality.

In Carlyle this element of a marked, altogether peculiar personality was eminently present, and shot itself through every word he wrote.

An Annandale peasant, sprung from a robust and

rugged peasant stock, reared in a home in which the Bible, especially the Old Testament, was the only book; taught in the parish school, and in such lore as it afforded; passing thence to Edinburgh University, gathering such learning as was current then and there, but holding his Professors in but little honor, — " hidebound pedants," he somewhere calls them; an omnivorous devourer of books, almost exhausting the college library; bursting afterwards into the then almost unknown sea of German literature and philosophy, and coming back thence to be, after Coleridge, its next interpreter to his countrymen; — such was the intellectual outfit with which he had to face the world. To a Scottish rustic, with brains, but no funds, who had received a college training, there were at that time only two outlets possible — the Church or teaching. From the former partly Carlyle's own questioning and not too docile nature, partly his newly-acquired German lights, wholly excluded him. The latter, or the gerund-grinding business, as he called it, he tried but hated, and spurned from him as contemptuously as if he had been the haughtiest of born aristocrats.

Then followed some years of idleness, ill-health, and apparent aimlessness; during which, however, he was waging grim conflict with manifold doubts, with darkness as of the nether pit. The final issue of the long and desperate struggle is recorded symbolically in *Sartor Resartus;* and the climax or ultimate turning-point of the whole is that strange incident in the Rue St. Thomas de l'Enfer, which happened to himself, he tells us, quite literally in Leith Walk. That he then and there wrestled down once and for all " the Everlasting No," he verily believed. Yet " the Everlasting Yea," which he thought he found on the farther side, whatever it may have been, never seems to have brought assured peace to his spirit, never to have fully convinced him that he was in a world ruled by One who has " good will towards men." Peace indeed was not one of those things which he deemed attainable, or even much to be desired, except by craven spirits.

But meanwhile, whatever else remained unsettled, that which Coleridge calls the Bread and Butter question could not be put by, but imperiously demanded an answer. The only way of solving it that now remained open to him was literature. But even here the path for him was hemmed in by high and narrow walls. To write supply for demand, to say the thing that would please the multitude and command sale, to batter his brains into bannocks, — against this his whole nature rebelled. Something, he felt, was burning down at the bottom of his heart, and this was the only thing he cared to utter. How to utter it was he long in finding, and whether, when uttered, it would be listened to, was all uncertain. At last, after years of solitary struggle, hag-ridden, as he says, by dyspepsia, which made his waking thoughts one long nightmare, " without hope," as he tells, or at best with a desperate " hope, shrouded in continual gloom and grimness," he did get himself uttered, and his *Sartor Resartus*, his *Miscellaneous Essays*, and his *French Revolution* are the outcome. Thus, by slow degrees, he won the world's ear, and by 1840 or thereabouts, it began to be recognized that in Carlyle a new light had arisen in England's literature.

No doubt the narrow though bracing atmosphere of his youth, the grinding poverty, the depressing ill-health, the fierce struggle, the want of all appreciation, which beset his early years, working on his naturally proud and violent temper, made him the rugged, stern, ungenial man he seemed to be. But had he missed this stern discipline, and been reared in soft and pleasant places, how different would he, how different would his teachng, have been! Would it have burnt itself into the world's heart, as his best words have done?

However this may be, the strong, isolated, self-reliant man, when he settled at Chelsea, and began to meet face to face London celebrities, literary, social, and political, — it is strange to see with what a haughty self-assertion he eyed and measured them. Full of genius as he was, strong in imagination, keen in sympathy for great historic characters, yet on the men he met in society he looked with a proud peasant's narrowness and bigotry of contempt. Whatever was strange to him, or uncongenial, he would seem to have regarded with an unsympathizing eye, and judged by narrow standards. Something of the same kind of too conscious self-assertion there was in him which we see in Burns. Determined not to cringe to men socially their superiors, whom they thought to be intellectually their inferiors, neither of them escaped some rudeness in their manners, some harshness in their judgments. Unlike as they were in temperament — Burns the jovial Epicurean, Carlyle the abstinent Stoic — in this they were alike, that neither moved at ease through the new social circumstances to which their genius introduced them. But who can wonder if both failed to solve quite successfully that hardest of social problems, — when a man rises in society by force of his ability, to bear himself with becoming self-respect and dignity, and at the same time to show due consideration for others, — at once to be true to his own past, and in no way turn his back upon it, and at the same time genially and gracefully to adapt himself to new situations?

Whether it was owing to continual ill-health, or to the dire struggle he had to wage with poverty and untoward circumstances, it cannot be said that Carlyle looked genially on the world of his fellow men. Dowered with a deep capacity for love, nor less with strong power of scorn — the love he reserved for a few chosen ones of his own family and his immediate circle; the scorn he dealt out lavishly and promiscuously on the outer world, whether of chance acquaintances or of celebrities of the hour. Yet from behind all this scorn — or seeming scorn — there would break out strange gleams of reverence and tenderness, where you would least look for them; and the reverence and the tenderness, we fain believe, lay deeper than the scorn.

What then were some of those truths which Carlyle laid to heart, and preached with that emphatic power, which formed his poetic inspiration? He was a prophet of the soul in man. Deeply sensible, as he himself expressed it, that " the clay that is about man is always sufficiently ready to assert itself; that the danger is always the other way, that the spiritual part of man will become overlaid with his bodily part," he asserted with all the strength that was in him, and in every variety of form, the reality of man's spiritual nature in opposition to all the materialisms that threatened to crush it. More alive than most men to the mysteriousness of our present being, often weighed down under a sad sense of the surrounding darkness, having done long battle with all the doubts that issue out of it, he yet planted his foot firmly on deep ineradicable convictions as to the soul's divine origin and destiny, which he found at the roots of his being. These primal instincts were to him "the fountain light of all his seeing;" and on these, not on any nostrums of so-called analytical philosophies, taking his stand, he set his face towards this world and the next. Against the mud-philosophies, which, with their protoplasms, their natural selections, their hereditities, would have robbed him of these cherished convictions, all his works are one long indignant protest — a protest conducted not by argument mainly, but by vehement assertion of what he found in his own personal consciousness — assertion illuminated with high lights of imagination, grotesque with droll humor, and grim with scornful raillery.

In this he was akin to all the prophets, one of their brotherhood, — that he maintained the spiritual and dynamic forces in man as against the mechanical. While so many, listening to the host of materializing teachers, are always succumbing to the visible, and selling their birthright for the mess of pottage which this world offers, Carlyle's voice appealed from these to a higher tribunal, and found a response in those deeper recesses which lie beyond the reach of argument and analysis. This he did with all his powers, and by doing so rendered a great service to his generation, whether they have listened to him or not.

This sense, that the spirit in man is the substance, the I the reality, and that the bodily senses are the tools we use for a little time, then lay aside ; that we are "spirits in a prison, able only to make signals to each other, but with a world of things to think and say which our signals cannot describe at all," has been expressed many times by Carlyle, but never more powerfully than in words which Mr. Justice Stephen has called "perhaps the most memorable utterance of our greatest poet."

"It is mysterious, it is awful to consider, that we not only carry each a future ghost within him, but are in very deed ghosts. These limbs, whence had we them? this stormy force, this life-blood with its burning passion? They are dust and shadow; a shadow-system gathered round our Me, wherein through some moments or years the Divine Essence is to be revealed in the flesh. That warrior on his strong war-horse, fire flashes through his eyes, force dwells in his arms and heart; but warrior and war-horse are a vision, a revealed force, nothing more. Stately they tread the earth, as if it were a firm substance. Fools! the earth is but a film; it cracks in twain, and warrior and war-horse sink beyond plummet's sounding. Plummet's? Fantasy herself will not follow them. A little while ago they were not; a little while and they are not, their very ashes are not.

"So has it been from the beginning, so will it be to the end. Generation after generation takes to itself the form of a body; and forth issuing from Cimmerian night on heaven's mission *appears*. What force and fire is in each, he expends. One grinding in the mill of industry, one hunter-like climbing the giddy Alpine heights of science, one madly dashed in pieces on the rocks of strife in war with his fellows, and then the heaven-sent is recalled, his earthly vesture falls away, and soon even to sense becomes a vanished shadow. Thus, like some wild flaming, wild thundering train of Heaven's artillery, does this mysterious mankind thunder and flame in long-drawn quick-succeeding grandeur through the unknown deep. Thus, like a god-created, fire-breathing spirit-host, we emerge from the inane, haste stormfully across the astonished earth, then plunge again into the inane. Earth's mountains are levelled, and her seas filled up in our passage. Can the earth, which is dead, and a vision, resist spirits which have reality and are alive? On the hardest adamant some footprint of us is stamped in The last rear of the host will read traces of the earliest van. But whence? Oh, Heaven! whither? Sense knows not, faith knows not, only that it is through mystery to mystery, from God and to God.

> ' We are such stuff
> As dreams are made of, and our little life
> Is rounded with a sleep.' "

Closely connected with the thought thus powerfully expressed was his sense of the mysteriousness of Time as the vestibule of Eternity, and of our life here as a narrow isthmus between two eternities. This deep conviction, instilled into him by his early Biblical training, and confirmed, though changed in form, by German transcendentalism, is ever present to his imagination. "Remember," he says to the young man entering on life, " Remember now and always that life is no idle dream, but a solemn reality, based upon Eternity and encompassed by Eternity." Again, he speaks of the priceless " gift of life, which a man can have but once, for he waited a whole eternity to be born, and now has a whole eternity waiting to see what he will do when born."

This is a very old truth —- a primeval truth, one may say. But into Carlyle it had sunk so profoundly, and he has uttered it so impressively, that it comes from his lips as if heard for the first time. It is the undertone of many of his truest and most poetic utterances, this thought of Time, with its birth and its decay, its tumult and unceasing change, hiding the Eternity that lies close behind it. The wonder with which the spectacle filled him, as he stood on the shore of Time, and looked out on the Infinite beyond, he has in many ways expressed. Here is one of his most touching and melodious expressions of it : —

" He has witnessed overhead the infinite Deep, with greater and lesser lights, bright-rolling, silent-beaming, hurled forth by the hand of God ; around him, and under his feet, the wonderfullest Earth, with her winter snow-storms and her summer spice-airs, and (unaccountablest of all) himself standing here. He stood in the lapse of Time ; he saw Eternity behind him, and before him. The all-encircling mysterious tide of Force, thousandfold (for from force of thought to force of gravitation what an interval !) billowed shoreless on ; bore him along, — he too was part of it. From its bosom rose and vanished in perpetual change the lordliest Real-Phantasmagory (which was Being) ; and ever anew rose and vanished ; and ever that lordliest many-colored scene was full, another yet the same. Oak-trees fell, young acorns sprang : men too, new-sent from the Unknown, he met, of tiniest size, who waxed into stature, into strength of sinew, passionate fire and light : in other men the light was growing dim, the sinews all feeble ; they sank, motionless, into ashes, into invisibility ; returned back to the Unknown, beckoning him their mute farewell. He wanders still by the parting spot ; cannot hear *them;* they are far, how far ! It was sight for angels and archangels ; for, indeed, God Himself had made it wholly.''

With all this deep sense of the Eternal brooding over him, yet if one were asked how he conceived of the nature of this Eternal, with what powers he peopled it, the answer would not be easy ; for of this he has nowhere spoken plainly, often spoken contradictorily. He had, no one can doubt, a real belief in " the Everlasting Mind behind nature and history." But what was the character of this Mind, what its attitude towards men, this was a question he would probably have put aside with some impatience. To formulate it, either in speech or in thought, he would have held to be an impertinence.

To him it was the Unnamable, the Inconceivable; man's only becoming attitude towards it was not speech, nor conception, nor sentiment, — but silence, absolute silence. When he did allow himself any definite thought about this unnamable centre of Things, he conceived that it was Power, Force, that there lay the fountain of law and order, and that to this law and order belonged a kind of stern unbending justice, which had power, and would use it to vindicate itself and execute its inexorable decrees. To these man has to bow, not to question or investigate them. As to attributing mercy, forgiveness in any sense, not to speak of love, to this inexorable power, this peremptory fate, that, as he thought, could only be done by weakness or self-deception.

Sir Henry Taylor is reported to have said of Carlyle that he was "a Puritan who had lost his creed." But though the superstructure of Puritanism had disappeared, the original substratum remained — the stern stoical Calvinism of his nature was the foundation on which all his views were built. Nor is this to be wondered at. The religion in which he had been reared was of a rigid, unelastic kind. Like cast-iron it would break under pressure, but would not bend. Either the whole of the Westminster Confession or none of it; of that larger, more expansive Christianity, which can assimilate and absorb the best elements of modern culture, he knew nothing, and would have rejected it as a delusion. His religious faith, if we may venture to trace it, would seem to be the result of three things, his own strong stern nature, his early Calvinistic training, and these two transformed by the after influx of German transcendentalism tempered by Goethism.

That such an idealist should have become a historian and achieved so much on the field of history may seem surprising. Yet this idealism, which might have gone to dreaminess, was counterbalanced and held in check by inherent tendencies that went in the opposite direction, and kept him close to actual reality. He had strong love of concrete facts, keen insight into the picturesque and expressive traits of human character, indefatigable industry in getting at the facts that interested him, and a wonderful eye to read their inner meaning. His glowing imagination not only bodied forth the past, but made its characters live before us down to the minutest detail, — their looks, the peculiarity of their gait, their very dress. He throws himself into the part of his heroes, and represents it, as an actor would. No historian before him, it has been well said, was ever such a dramatist. As you read him, you see his hero not only in action, and outward appearance, but you hear him utter, in side hints, in soliloquy, or otherwise, the inner secrets of his heart. This made him a quite un-rivalled interpreter of characters and epochs for which he had sympathy, lighting up with wonderful power some of the foremost men and some of the most thrill-ing crises in the world's history. He did this because of his intense sympathy with those men and those crises. But where his sympathy failed, his insight also failed. A glowing poet, a vivid painter, as few have ever been, or can be, he was ; but a historian, impartial, calm-judging, judicial-minded, this it was not in him to be. To a large portion of what makes up history, the growth of institutions, the checks and counterchecks of constitutional government (indeed constitutionalism was always a bugbear to him), the necessity of compromise, the power of traditional usage, the value of habit and routine, — to all these things he was utterly blind; or if for a moment made aware of their exist- ence, he dismissed them scornfully as red-tapeism, effete formulas. But great men and great crises, when per- sonal emotion and popular passions are at the white heat, when iron will struggles with popular fury and overmasters it, — these were the subjects that exactly suited his peculiar temperament and turn of imagina- tion. This it was which made the French Revolution so fascinating a theme for him. All history, ancient or modern, did not furnish such another for one who had power to grapple with it: in De Quincey's words, " Not Nineveh nor Babylon with the enemy in all their gates, not Memphis nor Jerusalem in their latest ago- nies."

Carlyle's book on the French Revolution has been called the great modern epic, and so it is — an epic as true and germane to this age, as Homer's was to his. Chaos come again, and overwhelming all extant order, — the wild volcano of mad democracy bursting and consuming the accumulated rubbish and corruption of centuries, — all the paradoxes of human nature face to face, blind popular passion and starving multitudes con- fronting court imbecility, conventionality, nostrums of political doctrinaires and effete diplomacy, — panic and trembling uncertainty controlled by clear-seeing deter- mined will, and all these by great inscrutable forces to- gether driven on to their doom. In the midst of all the tumults and confusion, some Mirabeau appearing as the cloud-compeller — the one man who, had he lived, might have guided the tremendous forces to some cer- tain end. " Honor to the strong man in these ages who has shaken himself loose of shams, and is something. There lay verily in him sincerity, a great free earnestness ; nay, call it Honesty." This is a word we have heard almost to weariness. This, though said of Mirabeau, is the refrain in all his works — the admiration of clear-seeing penetrating intelligence, backed by adamantine will. So these be present, we shall not much inquire what may be their moral purpose, or whether they have a moral purpose at all. The strong intellect and the strong will are an emanation from the central force of the universe, and as such have a right to rule.

The two elements we have noted in Carlyle's way of thinking, the fundamental idealism, and the strong grasp of realism, his firm hold on actual facts, combined with his deep sense of the mysteriousness of life, — these two tendencies, seemingly contradictory, yet each enhancing the other, are everywhere visible in his treatment of history. In all affairs of men, no one was so aware of the little known, the vast unknown. You see it equally in his portraits of men, and in his accounts of great movements. A recent writer in the *Spectator* has well pointed out how much of Carlyle's power is due to the way he has apprehended and brought out these two elements. These conflicting tendencies, so powerfully operating in all great tumults, Carlyle takes full account of, interweaves the one with the other, and by doing so wonderfully heightens not only the truthfulness, but also the effectiveness of his pictures. In this how unlike Macaulay, and other historians of his kind! with whom the most complex characters are explained down to the ground, the greatest and most confused movements and revolutions accounted for by definite causes, tabulated one, two, three. With such writers,

24

when they have said their say, there remains no more behind — they think they can lay their finger on the most secret springs of Providence. Their very definiteness and too great knowingness is their condemnation.

Here is the description of Marie Antoinette, taken from one of Carlyle's Essays, which seems a sort of prelude to his *French Revolution :* —

" Beautiful Highborn, that wert so foully hurled low! For, if thy Being came to thee out of old Hapsburg Dynasties, came it not also (like my own) out of Heaven? . . . Oh, is there a man's heart that thinks, without pity, of those long months and years of slow-wasting ignominy; — of thy Birth, soft cradled in imperial Schönbrunn, the winds of heaven not to visit thy face too roughly, thy foot to light on softness, thy eye on splendor; and then of thy Death, or hundred deaths, to which the guillotine and Fouquier-Tinville's judgment-bar was but the merciful end? Look *there,* O man born of woman! The bloom of that fair face is wasted, the hair is gray with care; the brightness of those eyes is quenched, their lids hang drooping; the face is stony, pale, as of one living in death. Mean weeds (which her own hand has mended) attire the Queen of the World. The death hurdle, where thou sittest, pale, motionless, which only curses environ, must stop : a people, drunk with vengeance, will drink it again in full draught: far as eye reaches, a multitudinous sea of maniac heads; the air deaf with their triumph-yell! The Living-dead must shudder with yet one other pang : her startled blood yet again suffuses with the hue of agony that pale face, which she hides with her hands. There is, then, no heart to say, God pity thee? "

Open his *French Revolution* itself almost anywhere, and you will find examples of the unique power I have spoken of. Here is one from the second volume of the book : —

" As for the King, he as usual will go wavering chame-
leon-like ; changing color and purpose with the color of his
environment ; — good for no kingly use.   On one royal per-
son, on the Queen only, can Mirabeau perhaps place depend
ence.   It is possible, the greatness of this man, not unskilled
too in blandishments, courtiership, and graceful adroitness,
might, with most legitimate sorcery, fascinate the volatile
Queen, and fix her to him.   She has courage for all noble
daring; an eye and a heart, the soul of Theresa's daugh-
ter. . . . ' She is the only man,' as Mirabeau observes,
' whom his Majesty has about him.'   Of one other man
Mirabeau is still surer — of himself. . . . Din of battles,
wars more than civil, confusion from above and from below:
in such environment the eye of prophecy sees Comte de
Mirabeau, like some Cardinal de Retz, stormfully maintain
himself; with head all-devising, heart all-daring, if not vic-
torious, yet still unvanquished, while life is left him.   The
specialities and issues of it, no eye of prophecy can guess
at : it is clouds, we repeat, and tempestuous night ; and in
the middle of it, now visible, far-darting, now laboring in
eclipse, is Mirabeau indomitably struggling to be cloud-com-
peller !   One can say that, had Mirabeau lived, the history
of France and of the world had been different. . . . Had
Mirabeau lived another year ! . . . But Mirabeau could
not live another year, any more than he could live another
thousand years. . . .

" The fierce wear and tear of such an existence has wast-
ed out the giant oaken strength of Mirabeau.   A fret and
fever that keeps heart and brain on fire. . . . On Saturday,
the second day of April, Mirabeau feels that the last of the
days has risen for him; that on this day he has to depart
and be no more.   His death is Titanic, as his life has been!
Lit up, for the last time, in the glare of coming dissolution,
the mind of the man is all glowing and burning ; utters
itself in sayings, such as men long remember.   He longs to
live, yet acquiesces in death, argues not with the inexorable.
His speech is wild and wondrous ; unearthly phantasms

dancing now their torch-dance round his soul; the soul look-ing out, fire-radiant, motionless, girt together for that great hour! At times comes a beam of light from him on the world he is quitting. ' I carry in my heart the death-dirge of the French monarchy; the dead remains of it will now be the spoil of the factions.' . . . While some friend is sup-porting him: ' Yes, support that head; would I could be-queath it thee ! ' For the man dies as he has lived; self-conscious, conscious of a world looking on. He gazes forth on the young Spring, which for him will never be Summer. The sun has risen ; he says, ' Si ce n'est pas le Dieu, c'est du moins son cousin germain.' . . . So dies a gigantic Heathen and Titan, stumbling blindly, undismayed, down to his rest. At half-past eight in the morning, Doctor Petit, standing at the foot of the bed, says, ' Il ne souffre plus.' His suffering and his working are now ended.''

Of all Carlyle's works, his *French Revolution* is, no doubt, the greatest, that by which he will probably be longest remembered. It is a thoroughly artistic book, artistically conceived and artistically executed. On it he expended his full strength, and he himself felt that he had done so.

His *Cromwell* and his *Frederick*, with all their power, are comparatively amorphous productions, as he would have called them. There is in them far less of the shaping power that he put forth on the *French Revolu-tion*. For Carlyle, rugged and gnarled though he was, none the less was a great artist, not of the mellifluous, but of the strong and vehement order, delighting in the Titanic, yet intermingling it, ever and anon, with soft bursts of pathos ; as you see some rough granite mount-ain, with here and there well-springs of clearest water, and streaks of greenest verdure. Had time served I could have cited from the two latter histories passages in which his pictorial and poetic power shine forth conspicuously. Such is the description of the battle of Dunbar, in *Cromwell.* In this passage his graphic power of rendering a landscape is seen, the same power that appears in another way in the description he gives of the Border hills and dales in the Reminiscences of Edward Irving.

I have said that Carlyle was essentially a great artist, both in the way in which he conceived things, and in the way in which he expressed his conception of them. An artist, not of the Raphael or Leonardo order, but of the Rembrandt, or even of the Michael Angelo type, — forceful, rugged, gnarled, lurid, Titanic.

Being an artist, he wrought out for himself a style of his own, highly artificial, no doubt intensely self-conscious, but yet one which reflected with wonderful power and exactness his whole mental attitude, — the way in which he habitually looked out from his dark soul on men and things. He was weary of glib words, and fluent periods, which impose on reader and writer alike, which film over the chasms of their ignorance, and make them think they know what they do not know. As to style, he himself gives this rule in his *Reminiscences :* " Learn, so far as possible, to be intelligible and transparent — no notice taken of your style, but solely of what you express by it : this is your clear rule, and if you have anything which is not quite trivial to express to your contemporaries, you will find such rule a great deal more difficult to follow than many people think."

Excellent precept ; but, alas for performance ! none ever broke the rule more habitually than Carlyle himself. The idiom which he ultimately forged for himself

was a new and strange form of English — rugged, dis-
jointed, often uncouth ; in his own phrase, "vast, fitful,
decidedly fuliginous," but yet bringing out with marvel-
lous vividness the thoughts that possessed him, the few
truths which he saw clearly, and was sure of — while it
suggested not less powerfully the dark background of
ignorance against which those truths shone out.   In all
this he was a great and original artist, using words, his
tools, to bring out forcibly the effects most present
to his own mind, and to convey them to the minds of
others.   To achieve this, he cared not how much he
violated all the decorums, and shocked the proprieties
of literature.   He set at naught what are usually
called the models of English composition — he laid un-
der contribution the most diverse and outlandish sources
of speech, borrowing now something from his native
Annandale idiom and vocabulary, largely from German
sources (Jean Paul Richter is especially named), im-
porting not only words and phrases, but whole turns of
language, hitherto unheard in English, while, to express
the droll humors and grim fancies that possessed him,
he dashed in grotesque side-lights, copious nicknames,
that seem to have been native to him, or a trick inher-
ited from his shrewd, caustic old father.

Read page after page, such a style soon wearies.
One gets to feel as if driven over a rough stony road,
in a cart without springs.   But in short descriptions
and pictures, it is stimulative and impressive, as few
other styles are.   What effect, if any, it has had on our
language, may be a question.   One thing only is certain.
Carlyle must be left alone with his own style.   When
taken up by imitators, it becomes simply unendurable.

I shall close with a few words from the lament he

breathed over Edward Irving, written as long ago as 1835. They give a glimpse of the nobleness that was in Carlyle's heart beneath all his moroseness, as well of the height of poetry to which, on fitting occasions, he could rise.

"Edward Irving's warfare has closed; if not in victory, yet in invincibility, and faithful endurance to the end. . . . The voice of our ' son of thunder,' with its deep tone of wisdom, has gone silent so soon. . . . The large heart, with its large bounty, where wretchedness found solacement, and they that were wandering in darkness, the light as of a home, has paused. The strong man can no more : beaten on from without, undermined from within, he must sink overwearied, as at nightfall, when it was yet but the mid-season of the day. Scotland sent him forth a Herculean man; our mad Babylon wore him and wasted him, with all her engines; and it took her twelve years. He sleeps with his fathers, in that loved birth-land : Babylon, with its deafening inanity, rages on ; to him henceforth innocuous, unheeded — forever.

"One who knew him well, and may with good cause love him, has said : ' But for Irving, I had never known what the communion of man with man means. His was the freest, brotherliest, bravest human soul mine ever came in contact with : I call him, on the whole, the best man I have ever (after trial enough) found in this world, or now hope to find.'

"The first time I saw Irving was six and twenty years ago, in his native town, Annan. He was fresh from Edinburgh, with college prizes, high character, and promise. . . . We heard of famed professors of high matters classical, mathematical, a whole Wonderland of knowledge : nothing but joy, health, hopefulness without end, looked out from the blooming young man.

"The last time I saw him was three months ago, in London. Friendliness still beamed from his eyes, but now from amid unquiet fire; his face was flaccid, wasted, unsound; hoary as with extreme age: he was trembling on the brink of the grave. Adieu, thou first Friend; adieu, while this confused twilight of existence lasts! Might we meet where Twilight has become Day!"

CHAPTER XV.

PROSE POETS : CARDINAL NEWMAN.

DURING the first fifty years of this century, there were living in England three men, three teachers of men, each of whom appealed to what is highest in man, to the moral and spiritual side of human nature, and by that appeal told most powerfully on his generation. These men were William Wordsworth, Thomas Carlyle, and John Henry Newman. Each gathered round himself in time, whether consciously or not, a group of disciples, whom he influenced, and who became conductors of his influence to the minds of his countrymen. All three were idealists, believers in the mental and spiritual forces, as higher than the material, and as ruling them — but idealists each after his own fashion. The strength of each lay in a large measure in his imagination, and in the power with which he stirred his fellow-men, by bearing home to their imaginations his own views of truth. But here any likeness between them begins and ends.

No three men of power, living in the same epoch, lived more aloof from each other, borrowed less from each other, were more independent of each other's influence, were less appreciative of each other's gift.

What Carlyle thought of Wordsworth we know too well, from the brief notice in the *Reminiscences*, in which Carlyle speaks out his "intelligent contempt" for the great poet — a contempt which does not prove his own superiority. And Wordsworth, if he did not return the contempt, was, we have reason to believe, in no way an admirer of Carlyle, or of any of his works; and, when they met, turned but a cold side towards him.

There is no reason to think that Carlyle and Cardinal Newman knew much or anything of each other's works; certainly they never met. For High Church doctrine Carlyle expresses nothing but scorn, whenever he alludes to it, and cannot preserve either equanimity or good manners in presence of anything that looked like sacerdotalism.

Had they ever met, we can well imagine the refined Cardinal Newman turning toward the rough Scot that reticence and reserve which none knew better how to maintain, in presence of the uncongenial. Then, as to Wordsworth and Cardinal Newman, while the old poet knew and appreciated *The Christian Year*, and used to comment on it, there is nowhere any evidence that Cardinal Newman's works had ever reached, or any way affected him. And as for the younger of these two, it was only this time last year that he told one in Oxford, that he was quite innocent of any familiarity with Wordsworth. "No! I was never soaked in Wordsworth, as some of my contemporaries were."

Strange, is it not? that three such teachers, who have each at different times influenced so powerfully men younger than themselves, should have lived so apart, as little appreciating each other, as if they had been inhabitants of different countries, or even of different planets.

Of these three teachers, the two elder are no longer here. The third still remains among us, in beautiful and revered old age. It is of him that I have now to speak.

We saw how that which lay at the centre of Carlyle's great literary power was the force of a vigorous personality, a unique character, an indomitable will. Not less marked and strong is the personality of Cardinal Newman, but the two personalities passed through very different experiences. In the one the rough ore was presented to the world, just as it had come direct from mother earth, with all the clay and mud about it. The other underwent in youth the most searching processes, intellectual and social ; met, in rivalry or in friendship, many men of the highest order, his own equals, and came forth from the ordeal seven times refined. But this training no way impaired his native strength or damped his ardor. Only it taught him to know what is due to the feelings and convictions of others, as well as what became his own self-respect. He did not consider it any part of veracity to speak out, at all hazards, every impulse and prejudice, every like and dislike which he felt. That a thing is true was, in his view, " no reason why it should be said, but why it should be done, acted on, made our own inwardly." And as the firm fibre of his nature remained the same, all the training and refining it went through made it only more sure in aim, and more effective in operation. The difference of the two men is that between the furious strength of Roderick Dhu, and the trained power and graceful skill of James Fitz-James.

There are many sides from which the literary work of Cardinal Newman might be viewed ; but there is only one aspect in which, speaking in this place, it would be pertinent to regard it. To dwell on his work as a theologian, or as a controversialist, or even as he is a preacher or a religious teacher, would be unbecoming

here.   It is mainly as he is a poet that I feel warranted
to advert to his writings now.

When I speak of him as one of the great prose poets
of our time, this is not because, as in the case of Carlyle,
he had not the gift of expressing himself in verse, or
did not at times practise it.   That he could do so ef-
fectively, readers of the *Lyra Apostolica* do not need to
be informed.   They remember his few impressive lines
on *The Call of David*, rendering in a brief page of verse
the whole outline of that wonderful life ; his lines too
on *David and Jonathan*, and those on *The Greek Fa-
thers*, and those entitled *Separation*, upon a friend lately
lost.

Here are some lines entitled *Rest of Saints Departed:*

> " They are at rest:
> We may not stir the heaven of their repose
> By rude invoking voice, or prayer addrest
>   In waywardness, to those
> Who in the mountain grots of Eden lie,
> And hear the fourfold river as it murmurs by.
>
>   " They hear it sweep
> In distance down the dark and savage vale;
> But they at rocky bed, or current deep,
>   Shall never more grow pale ;
> They hear, and meekly muse, as fain to know,
> How long untired, unspent, that giant stream shall flow."

Or the next poem of the book, called *Knowledge*, which
means the knowledge which saints departed have of
what goes on on earth : —

> " A sea before
> The Throne is spread; its pure, still glass
> Pictures all earth-scenes as they pass.
>   We, on its shore,
> Share, in the bosom of our rest,
> God's knowledge, and are blest."

Just one more, the condensed severity of the lines entitled *Deeds not Words*.

> " Prune thou thy words, the thoughts control,
>   That o 'er thee swell and throng ;
> They will condense within thy soul,
>   And change to purpose strong.
>
> " But he, who lets his feelings run
>   In soft luxurious flow,
> Shrinks when hard service must be done,
>   And faints at every woe.
>
> " Faith's meanest deed more favor bears,
>   Where hearts and wills are weighed,
> Than brightest transports, choicest prayers,
>   Which bloom their hour and fade."

Such short poems as these showed, long before *The Dream of Gerontius* appeared, that Cardinal Newman possessed the true poet's gift, and could speak the poet's language, had he cared to cultivate it. But he was called to another duty, and passed on. To an age which was set, as this age is, on material prosperity, easy living, and all that gratifies the flesh, he felt called to speak a language long unheard ; to insist on the reality of the things of faith, and the necessity of obedience ; to urge on men the necessity to crush self, and obey ; to press home a severer, more girt-up way of living ; to throw himself into strenuous conflict with the darling prejudices of his countrymen. It was in his *Parochial Sermons*, beyond all his other works, that he spoke out the truths which were within him — spoke them with all the fervor of a prophet and the severe beauty of a poet. Modern English literature has nowhere any language to compare with the style of these Sermons, so simple and transparent, yet so subtle withal ; so strong yet so tender; the grasp of a strong man's hand, combined with the trembling tenderness of a woman's heart, expressing in a few monosyllables truth which would have cost other men a page of philosophic verbiage, laying the most gentle yet penetrating finger on the very core of things, reading to men their own most secret thoughts better than they knew them themselves.

Carlyle's style is like the full untutored swing of the giant's arm ; Cardinal Newman's is the assured self-possession, the quiet gracefulness, of the finished athlete. The one, when he means to be effective, seizes the most vehement feelings and the strongest words within his reach, and hurls them impetuously at the object. The other, with disciplined moderation, and delicate self-restraint, shrinks instinctively from overstatement, but penetrates more directly to the core by words of sober truth and " vivid exactness."

One often hears a lament that the mellow cadence and perfect rhythm of the Collects and the Liturgy are a lost art — a grace that is gone from the English language. It is not so. There are hundreds of passages in Cardinal Newman's writings which, for graceful rhythm and perfect melody, may be placed side by side with the most soothing harmonies of the Prayer Book.

In his mode of thought the first characteristic I would notice is his innate and intense idealism. Somewhere in his *Apologia* he says that there had been times in his life when the whole material world seemed to him unreal, unsubstantial as a dream. And all through life it would seem that the sense of his own soul, of his spiritual nature, and of the existence of God, was more present to him than the material world which surrounded him.

It is a thought of his, always deeply felt, and many times repeated, that this visible world is but the outward shell of an invisible kingdom, a screen which hides from our view things far greater and more wonderful than any which we see, and that the unseen world is close to us, and ever ready as it were to break through the shell, and manifest itself.

" To those who live by faith," he says, "everything they see speaks of that future world; the very glories of nature, the sun, moon, and stars, and the richness and the beauty of the earth, are as types and figures, witnessing and teaching the invisible things of God. All that we see is destined one day to burst forth into a heavenly bloom, and to be transfigured into immortal glory. Heaven at present is out of sight, but in due time, as snow melts and discovers what it lay upon, so will this visible creation fade away before those greater splendors which are behind it, and on which at present it depends. In that day shadows will retire, and the substance show itself. The sun will grow pale and be lost in the sky, but it will be before the radiance of Him whom it does but image, the Sun of Righteousness. . . . Our own mortal bodies will then be found in like manner to contain within them an inner man, which will then receive its due proportions, as the soul's harmonious organ, instead of the gross mass of flesh and blood which sight and touch are sensible of."

In this, and in many another place, he expresses the feeling that here he is walking about "in a world of shadows," and that there is behind it "that kingdom where all his real." To his eye the very movements of nature, and the appearances of the sky, suggest the presence of spiritual beings in them. In his Sermon, on the Feast of St. Michael and all Angels, this thought occurs : —

" Whenever we look abroad, we are reminded of those most gracious and holy Beings, the servants of the Holiest, who deign to minister to the heirs of salvation. Every breath of air and ray of light and heat, every beautiful prospect, is, as it were, the skirts of their garments, the waving of the robes of those, whose faces see God in heaven."

In the same strain he says : —

" Bright as is the sun, and the sky, and the clouds ; green as are the leaves and the fields; sweet as is the singing of the birds; we know that they are not all, and we will not take up with a part for the whole. They proceed from a centre of love and goodness, which is God Himself; but they are not His fulness; they speak of heaven, but they are not heaven; they are but as stray beams and dim reflections of His Image; they are but crumbs from the table. We are looking for the day of God, when all this outward world, fair though it be, shall perish. . . . We can bear the loss, for we know it will be but the removing of a veil. We know that to remove the world which is seen will be the manifestation of the world which is not seen. We know that what we see is as a screen hiding from us God and Christ, and His Saints and Angels. And we earnestly desire and pray for the dissolution of all we see, from our longing after that which we do not see."

This is, no doubt, not a common state of mind, but it is one which is in some way shared by all great spiritual teachers. We saw how, taking the form of transcendentalism, it lay at the base of Carlyle's whole way of looking at things. But the passage I have just read, if compared with a like passage which I quoted from Carlyle, shows how very differently the two writers apprehended the same truth. To Carlyle the eternal world, which he felt to be so near and so all-absorbing, appeared in a stern, often in a lurid light. To Cardinal Newman it appears in its calmness and its majesty, invested with a light which, if pensive — even awful — is still calm and serene. The eternity which Carlyle conceived was filled only with that which his own grim imagination pictured, stern, over-ruling Force at the centre, whence proceeded adamantine law. To Cardinal Newman it is peopled with all the soul-subduing, yet soothing objects which Christianity reveals.

Again, there is another powerful conviction which we noted in Carlyle, which also, though in a very different way, is ever present to Cardinal Newman. It is the sense of the mysteriousness of our present being — that we even now belong to two worlds; and that the invisible world, and that part of ourselves which we cannot see, are far more important than the part which we do see.

" All this being so, and the vastness and mystery of the world being borne in upon us, we begin to think that there is nothing here below, but, for what we know, has a connection with everything else; the most distant events may yet be united, and meanest and highest may be parts of one; and God may be teaching us, and offering knowledge of His ways if we will but open our eyes, in all the ordinary matters of the day."

One way in which he shows this sense of mystery is the feeling of wonder with which he looks upon the brute creation : —

" Can anything," he asks, " be more marvellous or startling, unless we were used to it, than that we should have a race of beings about us whom we do but see, and as little know their state, or can describe their interests, or their destiny, as we can tell of the inhabitants of the sun and

25

moon? It is indeed a very overpowering thought, when we get to fix our minds on it, that we familiarly use, I may say hold intercourse with, creatures who are as much strangers to us, as mysterious, as if they were fabulous, unearthly beings, more powerful than man, and yet his slaves, which Eastern superstitions have invented. They have apparently passions, habits, and a certain accountableness, but all is mystery about them. We do not know whether they can sin or not, whether they are under punishment, whether they are to live after this life. . . . Is it not plain to our senses that there is a world inferior to us in the scale of be- ings, with which we are connected without understanding what it is? And is it difficult to faith to admit the word of Scripture concerning our connection with a world superior to us?"

And to thoughtful minds that world of brute animals is as mysterious still, nor is the veil of mystery removed by talk about evolution, and the impudent knowingness it often engenders.

Again, Cardinal Newman's mind dwelt much in the remote past; but the objects it there held converse with were of a different order from those which at- tracted the gaze of Carlyle. Not the rise and fall of mighty kingdoms and dynasties; not

"The giant forms of empires on their way
To ruin;"

not heroes, and conquerors, the "massive iron hammers" of the whole earth; not the great men and the famous in the world's affairs. With these he could deal, as his Lectures on the Turks prove. But the one object which attracted his eye in all the past was the stone hewn out of the side of the mountain, which should crush to pieces all the kingdoms of the earth. The kingdom of Christ " coming to us from the very time of the apostles, spreading out into all lands, triumphing over a thousand revolutions, exhibiting an awful unity, glorying in a mysterious vitality, so majestic, so imperturbable, so bold, so saintly, so sublime, so beautiful." This was the one object which filled his heart and imagination. This was the vision which he had ever in his eye, and these are the feelings with which it inspired him : —

" What shall keep us calm and peaceful within ? What but the vision of all Saints of all ages, whose steps we follow. . . . The early times of purity and truth have not passed away ! they are present still ! We are not solitary, though we seem so. Few now alive may understand or sanction us; but those multitudes in the primitive time, who believed, and taught, and worshipped as we do, still live unto God, and in their past deeds and present voices cry from the Altar. They animate us by their example; they cheer us by their company; they are on our right hand and our left, Martyrs, Confessors, and the like, high and low, who used the same creeds, and celebrated the same mysteries, and preached the same gospel as we do. And to them were joined, as ages went on, even in fallen times, nay, even now in times of division, fresh and fresh witnesses from the Church below. In the world of spirits there is no difference of parties. . . . The truth is at length simply discerned by the spirits of the just; human additions, human institutions, human enactments, enter not with them into the unseen state. They are put off with the flesh. Greece and Rome, England and France, give no color to those souls which have been cleansed in the One Baptism, nourished by the One Body, and moulded upon the One Faith. Adversaries agree together directly they are dead, if they have lived and walked in the Holy Ghost. The harmonies combine and fill the temple, while discords and imperfections die away."

This was to him no sentimental dream, cherished in the closet, but unfit to face the world. It was a reality

which moulded his own character and his destiny, and
determined the work he set himself to do on earth. He
saw, as he believed, a religion prevalent all around,
which was secular and mundane, soft, and self-indulgent,
taking in that part of the gospel which pleases the flesh,
but shrinking from its sterner discipline and higher
aspirations. He made it the aim of his life to intro-
duce some iron into its blood, to import into the relig-
ion of his day something of the zeal and devotion and
self-denying sanctity which were the notes of the early
Faith. The vision which he beheld in the primitive ages
he labored to bring home and make practical in these
modern times. It will be said, I know, that Cardinal
Newman is an Ascetic, and teaches Asceticism. And
there are many who think that, when they have once
labelled any view with this name, they have as good as
disproved it. Do such persons deny that Asceticism, in
some sense, is an essential part of Christianity, that to
deny self, to endure hardness, is one of its most charac-
teristic precepts? Those who most fully acknowledge
this precept know that it is one thing to acknowledge,
quite another to obey it. But the world is so set on the
genial, not to say the jovial, it so loves the padding of
material civilization in which it enwraps itself, that it
resents any crossing of the natural man, and will always
listen greedily to those teachers — and they are many —
who persuade it that the flesh ought to have its own
way. A teacher so to its mind the world has not found
in Cardinal Newman.

It is not, however, our part here to estimate the need
or the value of the work he has done. But it is easy
to see how well his rare and peculiar genius fitted him
for doing it. If, on the one side, he had the imagina-

tive devotion which clung to a past ideal, he had, on the other side, that penetrating insight into human nature, which made him well understand his own age, and its tendencies. He was intimately acquainted with his own heart, and he so read the hearts of his fellow-men, that he seemed to know their inmost secrets. In his own words he could tell them what they knew about themselves, and what they did not know, till they were startled by the truth of his revelations. His knowledge of human nature, underived from books and philosophy, was intuitive, first-hand, practical. In this region he belonged to the pre-scientific era. He took what he found within him, as the first of all knowledge, as the thing he was most absolutely certain of. The feelings, desires, aspirations, needs, which he felt in his own heart, the intimations of conscience, sense of sin, longing for deliverance, these were his closest knowledge, to accept, not to explain away, or to analyze into nothing. They were his original outfit, they fixed his standard of judgment; they furnished the key by which he was to read the riddle of life, and to interpret the world; they were the " something within him, which was to harmonize and adjust " all that was obscure and discordant without him. The nostrums by which these primal truths are attempted to be explained away nowadays, heredity, antecedent conditions, these had not come much into vogue in his youth. But we know well enough how he would have dealt with them. What I feel and know intimately at first hand, that I must accept and use as the condition of all other knowledge; I am not to explain this away by uncertain theories or doubtful analyses ; I cannot unclothe myself of myself, at the bidding of any philosophical theory, however plausible. This is what he would have said.

The sermons are full of such heart-knowledge, such reading to men of their own hidden half-realized selves.

But it is not my purpose here to go into this, but to exhibit those places in Dr. Newman's teaching which break almost involuntarily into poetry, and become poetical, not in feeling and conception only, but in expression also. Who has so truly and beautifully touched those more subtle and evanescent experiences, by which tender and imaginative natures are visited?

This is the way he describes our feelings in looking back on much of our life that is past: —

" When enjoyment is past, reflection comes in. Such is the sweetness and softness with which days long past fall upon the memory, and strike us. The most ordinary years, when we seemed to be living for nothing, these shine forth to us in their very regularity and orderly course. What was sameness at the time is now stability; what was dullness is now a soothing calm; what seemed unprofitable has now its treasure in itself; what was but monotony is now harmony; all is pleasing and comfortable, and we regard it all with affection. Nay, even sorrowful times (which at first sight is wonderful) are thus softened and illuminated afterwards."

Thus too he describes the remembrance of our childhood: —

" Such are the feelings with which men look back on their childhood, when any accident brings it vividly before them. Some relic or token of that early time, some spot, or some book, or a word, or a scent, or a sound, brings them back in memory to the first years of their discipleship, and they then see, what they could not know at the time, that God's presence went up with them and gave them rest. Nay, even now, perhaps, they are unable to discern fully what it was which made them so bright and glorious. They are full of tender, affectionate thoughts towards those first years, but they do not know why. They think it is those very years which they yearn after, whereas it is the presence of God which, as they now see, was then over them, which attracts them. They think that they regret the past, when they are but longing after the future. It is not that they would be children again, but that they would be Angels and would see God; they would be immortal beings, crowned with amaranth, and with palms in their hands, before His Throne."

There is one thing which makes a difficulty in quoting the passages in Dr. Newman's writings which are most touching and most truly poetical. They do not come in at all as " purpurei panni " — as pieces of ornamental patchwork in the midst of his religious teaching, introduced for rhetorical effect. They are interwoven with his religious thought, are indeed essential parts of it, so that you cannot isolate without destroying them. And to quote here for the purpose of literary illustration, what were meant for a more earnest purpose, would seem to be out of place, if not irreverent. But there are touching passages of another kind, which are characteristic of Dr. Newman's writings and give them a peculiar charm. They are those which yield momentary glimpses of a very tender heart that has a burden of its own, unrevealed to man. Nothing could be more alien to Dr. Newman's whole nature than to withdraw the veil, and indulge in those public exhibitions of himself which are nowadays so common and so offensive. It is but a mere indirect hint he gives — a few indirect words, dropped as it were unawares, which many might read without notice, but which, rightly understood, seem breathed from some very inward experience. It is, as I have heard it described, as though he suddenly opened a book, and gave you a glimpse for a moment of wonderful secrets, and then as quickly closed it. But the glance you have had, the words you have caught, haunt you ever after with an interest in him who uttered them, which is indescribable. The words, though in prose, become, what all high poetry is said to be, at once a revelation and a veil.

Such a glimpse into hidden things seems given in a passage in the sermon on " a Particular Providence."

" How gracious is the revelation of God's particular providence . . . to those who have discovered that this world is but vanity, and who are solitary and isolated in themselves, whatever shadows of power and happiness surround them. The multitude, indeed, go on without these thoughts, either from insensibility, as not understanding their own wants, or changing from one idol to another, as each successively fails. But men of keener hearts would be overpowered by despondency, and would even loathe existence, did they suppose themselves under the mere operation of fixed laws, powerless to excite the pity or the attention of Him who has appointed them. What should they do especially, who are cast among persons unable to enter into their feelings, and thus strangers to them, though by long custom ever so much friends! or have perplexities of mind they cannot explain to themselves, much less remove them, and no one to help them, — or have affections and aspirations pen up within them, because they have not met with objects to which to devote them, — or are misunderstood by those around them, and find they have no words to set themselves right with them, or no principles in common by way of appeal, — or seem to themselves to be without place or purpose in the world, or to be in the way of others, — or have to follow their own sense of duty without advisers or supporters, nay, to resist the wishes and solicitations of superiors or relatives, — or have the burden of some painful secret, or of some incommunicable solitary grief!"

And then follows a passage showing with wonderful tenderness what this particular providence really is to each individual soul, how close, how sympathizing, how consoling! but it is almost too sacred to quote here.

I have heard a very thoughtful man say that he knew many passages of these sermons off by heart, and that he found himself repeating them to himself, for comfort and strengthening, more often than any poetry he knew. Just such a passage is the sequel to that which I have last quoted.

I am, as I have said, unwilling to intrude here upon what is distinctly religious in Dr. Newman's teaching. But I feel it necessary to do so, in some measure, to show the intimacy of his heart-knowledge, the inwardness, which is the special character of his thought. Unless this is seen, we do not understand him. Therefore I venture to give these words of his: —

" We do not know, perhaps, what or where our pain is; we are so used to it that we do not call it pain. Still, so it is; we need a relief to our hearts, that they may be dark and sullen no longer, or that they may not go on feeding upon themselves; we need to escape from ourselves to something beyond ; and much as we may wish it otherwise, and may try to make idols to ourselves, nothing short of God's presence is our true refuge. Everything else is either a mockery, or but an expedient useful for its season and in its measure. . . . Created natures cannot open us, or elicit the ten thousand mental senses which belong to us, and through which we really live. . . . The contemplation of God, and nothing but it, is able fully to open and relieve the mind, to unlock, occupy, and fix our affections. . . . Life passes, riches fly away, popularity is fickle, the senses

decay, the world changes, friends die. One alone is con-
stant; One alone is true to us ; One alone can be true ; One
alone can be all things to us ; One alone can supply our
needs; One alone can train us up to our full perfection;
One alone can give a meaning to our complex and intricate
nature; One alone can give us tune and harmony; One
alone can form and possess us. Are we allowed to put our-
selves under His guidance? this surely is the only question."

Let me quote but one passage more of a like nature
to the foregoing one. It is from the sermon " Warfare
the Condition of Victory." The writer has been show-
ing that, in some way or other, trial, suffering, is the
path to peace ; that this has been the experience com-
mon to all Christians, and that the law remains un-
altered.

" The whole Church," he says, " all elect souls, each in
its turn is called to this necessary work. Once it was the
turn of others, and now it is our turn. Once it was the
Apostles' turn. It was St. Paul's turn once. . . . And
after him, the excellent of the earth, the white-robed army
of Martyrs, and the cheerful company of Confessors, each in
his turn, each in his day, likewise played the man. And so
down to our time, when faith has well-nigh failed, first one
and then another have been called out to exhibit before the
great King. It is as though all of us were allowed to stand
around His Throne at once, and He called on first this man,
and then that, to take up the chant by himself, each in his
turn having to repeat the melody which his brethren have
before gone through. Or as if we held a solemn dance to
His honor in the courts of heaven, and each had by him-
self to perform some one and the same solemn and graceful
movement, at a signal given. Or as if it were some trial
of strength, or of agility, and, while the ring of bystanders
beheld, and applauded, we in succession, one by one, were
actors in the pageant. Such is our state ; — Angels are

looking on, Christ has gone before, — Christ has given us an example, that we may follow His steps. Now it is our turn; and all ministering spirits keep silence and look on. O let not your foot slip, or your eye be false, or your ear dull, or your attention flagging! Be not dispirited ; be not afraid; keep a good heart; be bold ; draw not back ; — you will be carried through."

Observe here one very rare gift which Cardinal Newman has; he can in the midst of his most solemn and sacred thoughts introduce the homeliest illustrations, the most familiar images, and they produce no jar ; you feel that all is in keeping. Who but he, speaking of man's earthly trial, could, without offence, have described it as a solemn dance held in the courts of heaven, in which each has in his turn to perform some difficult and graceful movement at a signal given? But here it is done with so delicate a touch, that you feel it to be quite appropriate.

In the same way, when speaking of St. John as having outlived all his friends, and having had to "experience the dreariness of being solitary," he says : —

" He had to live in his own thoughts, without familiar friend, with those only about him who belonged to a younger generation. Of him were demanded by his gracious Lord, as pledge of his faith, all his eye loved and his heart held converse with. He was as a man moving his goods into a far country, who at intervals and by portions sends them before him, till his present abode is well-nigh unfurnished."

He compares St. John in his old age to a man who is " flitting " from his house, and has sent his furniture by instalments before him. Imagine how such a comparison would have fared in the hands of any ordinary writer — of any one, in short, not possessed of most consummate taste.

I might go on for a day quoting from the *Parochial Sermons* alone passages in which the poet as well as the preacher speaks. I shall, however, give but one more. It is where he speaks of what is to be the Christian life's ultimate issue.

" All God's providences, all God's dealings with us, all His judgments, mercies, warnings, deliverances, tend to peace and repose as their ultimate issue. All our troubles and pleasures here, all our anxieties, fears, doubts, difficulties, hopes, encouragements, afflictions, losses, attainments, tend this one way. After Christmas, Easter, and Whitsuntide, comes Trinity Sunday and the weeks that follow; and in like manner, after our soul's anxious travail; after the birth of the Spirit ; after trial and temptation ; after sorrow and pain ; after daily dyings to the world ; after daily risings unto holiness ; at length comes that 'rest which remaineth unto the people of God.' After the fever of life ; after wearinesses and sicknesses ; fightings and despondings ; languor and fretfulness ; struggling and failing, struggling and succeeding ; after all the changes and chances of this troubled and unhealthy state, at length comes death, at length the White Throne of God, at length the Beatific Vision. After restlessness comes rest, peace, joy ; our eternal portion, if we be worthy."

I know not how this and other passages I have quoted may strike those to whom they have not been long familiar. To me it seems, they have a sweetness, an inner melody, which few other words have. They fall upon the heart like dew, and soothe it, as only the most exquisite music can. It may be that to the few who can still recall the tones of the voice which first uttered them, remembrance lends them a charm, which those cannot feel who only read them. These sermons were the first utterance of new thoughts in a new language, which have long since passed into the deeper heart of England. The presence and personality of the speaker, and the clear pathetic tones of his voice, can only live in the memory of those who heard him in St. Mary's, forty years ago. But the thoughts, and the style in which they are conveyed, are so perfect that they preserve for future generations more of the man who spoke them than most discourses can. It is hardly too much to say that they have elevated the thought and purified the style of every able Oxford man who has written since, even of those who had least sympathy with the sentiments they express. But they, whose good fortune it was to hear them when they were first delivered, know that nothing they have heard in the long interval can compare with the pensive grace, the thrilling pathos of the sounds, as they then fell fresh from the lips of the great teacher.

I have on purpose confined myself to the *Parochial Sermons*, though from many other parts of Cardinal Newman's works I might have adduced samples of the poetry that lies embedded in his prose. And the reason is this: the sermons seem more than any of his other writings to be full of his individuality, and to utter his inner feelings in the best language.

From his more recent discourses, preached to mixed congregations, one might have taken many samples, in which he paints with a broader brush, and lets himself loose in more sweeping periods, than he generally used in Oxford. But these, though high eloquence, do not seem to contain such true poetry as the earlier sermons. Yet there is one passage in the *University Sermons*, well known probably to many here, which I cannot close without referring to. He is speaking of music as an outward and earthly economy, under which great wonders unknown are typified.

"There are seven notes in the scale," he says ; " make them fourteen ; yet what a slender outfit for so vast an enterprise ! What science brings so much out of so little? Out of what poor elements does some great Master in it create his new world ! Shall we say that all this exuberant inventiveness is a mere ingenuity or trick of art, like some game or fashion of the day, without reality, without meaning ? We may do so ; and then, perhaps, we shall account the science of theology to be a matter of words; yet, as there is a divinity in the theology of the Church, which those who feel cannot communicate, so is there also in the wonderful creation of sublimity and beauty of which I am speaking. To many men the very names which the science employs are utterly incomprehensible. To speak of an idea or a subject seems to be fanciful or trifling, to speak of the views it opens upon us to be childish extravagance ; yet is it possible that that inexhaustible evolution and disposition of notes, so rich yet so simple, so intricate yet so regulated, so various yet so majestic, should be a mere sound, which is gone and perishes? Can it be that those mysterious stirrings of heart, and keen emotions, and strange yearnings after we know not what, and awful impressions from we know not whence, should be wrought in us by what is unsubstantial, and comes and goes, and begins and ends in itself? It is not so, it cannot be. No ; they have escaped from some higher sphere ; they are the outpouring of eternal harmony in the medium of created sound ; they are echoes from our ·Home, they are the voice of angels, or the Magnificat of saints, or the living laws of Divine Governance, or the Divine Attributes ; something are they besides themselves, which we cannot compass, which we cannot utter; — though mortal man, and he perhaps not otherwise distinguished above his fellows, has the gift of eliciting them."

These extracts may, perhaps, be fittingly closed with that passionate yet tender lament in which, in the autumn of 1843, he bade farewell to Oxford and to the Church of England : —

" O mother of saints ! O school of the wise ! O nurse of the heroic ! of whom went forth, in whom have dwelt, memorable names of old, to spread the truth abroad, or to cherish and illustrate it at home ! O thou, from whom surrounding nations lit their lamps ! O virgin of Israel ! wherefore dost thou now sit on the ground and keep silence, like one of the foolish women, who were without oil on the coming of the Bridegroom? . . . How is it, O once holy place, that 'the land mourneth, for the corn is wasted, the new wine is dried up, the oil languisheth, because joy is withered away from the sons of men '? . . . O my mother, whence is this unto thee, that thou hast good things poured upon thee and canst not keep them, and bearest children, yet darest not own them? Why hast thou not the skill to use their services, nor the heart to rejoice in their love ? How is it that whatever is generous in purpose, and tender or deep in devotion, thy flower and thy promise, falls from thy bosom and finds no home within thine arms? Who hath put this note upon thee, to have 'a miscarrying womb and dry breasts,' to be strange to thine own flesh, and thine eye cruel towards thy little ones? Thine own offspring, the fruit of thy womb, who love thee and would fain toil for thee, thou dost gaze upon with fear, as though a portent, or thou dost loath as an offence ; — at best thou dost but endure, as if they had no claim but on thy patience, self-possession, and vigilance, to be rid of them as easily as thou mayest. Thou makest them ' stand all the day idle,' as the very condition of thy bearing with them ; or thou biddest them to be gone, where they will be more welcome; or thou sellest them for nought to the stranger that passes by. And what wilt thou do in the end thereof? "

One thing must have struck most persons, — always the pensiveness, often the sadness of tone which pervades these extracts ; and this impression would not be lessened by a perusal of the sermons in full. It is so. The view of life taken by Dr. Newman is more than grave, it is a sad, sometimes almost a heart-broken one.

Canon Liddon has somewhere asked, " How is a man likely to look upon his existence ?   Is existence a happiness or a misery, a blessing or a curse ? "   And he replies, " This question will, probably, be answered in accordance with deep-rooted tendencies of individua-temperament ; but these tendencies, when prolonged and emphasized, become systems of doctrine — as we call them, philosophies.   And so it is that there are two main ways of looking at human life and its surrounding liabilities, which are called optimism and pessimism." There is a whole order of minds, and these sometimes the most thoughtful and deep, on whom the sad side of things, the dark enigmas of existence, weigh so heavily, that the brighter side seems as though it were not. Those especially who enter on life with a high ideal, whether a merely æsthetic, or a moral and spiritual ideal, get it sorely tried by their intercourse with the world.   All they see and meet with in actual experience so contradicts the high vision they once had.   And with the increase of their experience, they are often tempted to despair.   One thing only can save them from this temptation — the entrance into their hearts of the consoling light that comes from above.   In Carlyle this tendency to despair of the world was strongly present from the first, and being in his case unrelieved by the light of Christianity, his view of life darkened more and more as years went on.   The view which Dr. Newman

CARDINAL NEWMAN.   401

takes of the natural condition and destiny of man,
though modified by his gentler disposition, is hardly at
all more hopeful. Those who remember the words in
which he gives his impression of this world and the
children of it, towards the close of his *Apologia*, will
acknowledge this. Nothing can exceed the hopeless-
ness of the picture he there draws. One cannot but
hope that it is too dark and desponding a picture. But
between the two men there is this great difference:
however dark and despondent may be Dr. Newman's
view of man when left to himself, he is supported and
cheered by the faith that he has not been left to him-
self, that there has entered into human nature a new
and divine power, to counterwork its downward tend-
ency, and reinvigorate its decayed energies. Amid the
deepest despair of nature, he is still animated by this
heavenward hope. Beneath all the discords and dis-
tractions of this perplexing world, he overhears a divine
undertone, and hearing it, he can wait and be at peace.

26

THE END.